Group
Process and

Productivity

Group
Process and

Productivity

editors

Stephen Worchel
Wendy Wood
Jeffry A. Simpson

SAGE PUBLICATIONS
The International Professional Publishers
Newbury Park London New Delhi

For information address:

SAGE Publications, Inc.
2455 Teller Road
Newbury Park, California 91320

SAGE Publications Ltd.
6 Bonhill Street
London EC2A 4PU
United Kingdom

SAGE Publications India Pvt. Ltd.
M-32 Market
Greater Kailash I
New Delhi 110 048 India

Printed in the United States of America

Library of Congress Cataloging-in-Publication Data

Main entry under title:

Group process and productivity / edited by Stephen Worchel, Wendy
   Wood, Jeffry A. Simpson.
        p.   cm.
   Includes bibliographical references and index.
   ISBN 0-8039-4225-7. — ISBN 0-8039-4226-5 (pbk.)
   1. Work groups.   2. Labor productivity.   3. Decision-making,
Group.   4. Small groups.   I. Worchel, Stephen.   II. Wood, Wendy,
1954-   .   III. Simpson, Jeffry A.
HD66.G75   1991
658.4'036—dc20
                                                            91-6591
                                                            CIP

FIRST PRINTING, 1992

Sage Production Editor: Astrid Virding

Contents

Acknowledgments

We would like to extend special thanks to those individuals who made the Texas A&M Groups Conference from which this book originated possible. We thank Daniel Fallon, Dean of the College of Liberal Arts at Texas A&M University, for providing us with funds to support the production of both the conference and this book. We thank Vicky Corrington for the countless hours she devoted to planning, organizing, and overseeing a superb conference. Finally, we thank the following graduate students at Texas A&M for their unwavering assistance in hosting the conference: Robert Agans, Michael Biek, Tami Blackstone, Craig Bowden, Dawna Coutant-Sassic, Michele Grossman, Kathy Hannula, Betty Harris, Steve Jenner, Lauri Jensen, Sharon Lundgren, Nancy Rhodes, Susan Shackelford, Frankie Wong, and Brian Young.

—Jeff Simpson
Texas A&M University

Preface

As areas within disciplines become increasingly narrow and clearly defined, it becomes a challenge to find common topics that can link investigators from different fields. One such topic is group dynamics. Not only does research on groups have a rich history in many fields, but a current interest in group dynamics unites fields that seemingly have little else in common. Although the methodology and approach may vary, research on group issues can be found in social psychology, industrial/organizational psychology, clinical psychology, developmental psychology, political science, sociology, business, and education. And there seems to be a resurgence in the interest in group research as we recognize that we cannot truly understand or predict human behavior without understanding the social context in which that behavior occurs.

The Psychology Department at Texas A&M University chose to build a symposium series around the group dynamics topic in an effort to bring together scholars from different areas and perspectives. Each year an area of group dynamics would become the focus of a conference; the area would need to be of central importance to group theory and research and of broad appeal to investigators in a variety of disciplines and fields. Leading scholars from throughout the world would be invited to present their views, and an active audience of teachers and researchers from different disciplines would be encouraged to contribute to Sage Publications discussions. Then a Texas touch would be added to the production as the invited presenters would be sequestered in a hill country ranch and given the opportunity to exchange ideas, discuss future trends in research and theory, and develop joint projects.

The present volume grows out of the first conference held in this format. The issue of "Group Process and Productivity" was chosen because it has deep roots in psychology, business, and sociology, it is currently a major focus of new research and theory in these areas, and the issue is important in today's economic climate. Our aim was to develop a volume that both presents a picture of work that has been done and identifies possible future trends. We hoped to blend theory, research, and application, showing the close relationship between each of these in the groups area. And our goal was to cast a wide enough net to ensnare the interest of researchers and practitioners in psychology, sociology, business, and education.

—Stephen Worchel
Texas A&M University

Introduction
Where Is the Group in Social Psychology?
An Historical Overview

Jeffry A. Simpson
Wendy Wood

Most of our waking hours are spent in, and the bulk of our work-related productivity occurs within, settings consisting of two or more persons (Campbell, Converse, & Rodgers, 1976). Given the importance of groups in society, social scientists have long been interested in how group members interact with each other and with members of other groups to produce various commodities and/or decisions (see Zander, 1979). Group research is a major area of study in the social and behavioral sciences, particularly in the fields of anthropology, sociology, and various branches of psychology.

Despite the widely recognized importance of groups, basic social processes underlying group dynamics have received scant and intermittent attention. This has been particularly true within social psychology. At first glance, this state of affairs seems paradoxical; one would expect that a field devoted to understanding and explaining "how the thought, feeling, and behavior of individuals are influenced by the actual, imagined, or implied presence of others" (Allport, 1985, pp. 3) would allot a primary—perhaps *the* primary—portion of its theoretical and empirical attention to the study of groups. In spite of the dictates of its avowed mission, social psychology has remained fairly ambivalent about the study of groups and group processes per se (see Jones, 1985).

In what follows, we briefly attempt to place the current status of small group research in social psychology in the historical context from which it emanated. More specifically, we discuss some of the reasons why laboratory-based group research waned during the late 1950s in spite of the boost it had received from Lewin's Field Theory two decades earlier. We then note several recent advances and changes in the field which, we believe, should promote the proliferation of group research in the future. We conclude that, although group research may never become a truly mainstream research area within social psychology, a complete understanding of social processes underlying group dynamics is unlikely to occur without substantive contributions from social psychology.

A Brief Historical Overview

Two relatively independent lines of research on groups evolved within social psychology during the first three decades of this century. The earliest of these, which was instigated by Triplett (1898), examined the effects of the presence of other persons on facilitating the performance of individuals across a variety of different tasks. This work later resulted in research on social facilitation/impairment (Zajonc, 1965) and has been continued in work on social loafing (Harkins & Szymanski, 1987). The second line, which became prominent in the late 1920s and 1930s, compared the performance of individuals versus groups on problem-solving and decision-making tasks (see Davis, 1969, for a review). The remnants of this tradition can be seen in work on jury decision making (e.g., Kerr et al., 1976), minority influence in groups (e.g., Moscovici, 1985), conformity (Asch, 1951), and group polarization (e.g., Myers, 1978). Both of these traditions share one fundamental element in common; they both focused primarily on the *outcomes* produced by the group rather than the *processes* internal to the group that led to the outcomes. Relatively little attention was paid to the basic processes that transpired as groups tried to achieve their goals (Jones, 1985; Steiner, 1974).

In the 1930s and 1940s, research on groups was popularized and further legitimized by the pioneering work of Kurt Lewin, who maintained that the behavior of individuals should be understood in terms of the nature of the groups to which they belong (Lewin, 1943, 1948). Borrowing terms and concepts from force-field physics, Lewin suggested that individuals locomote through different regions of their life-space, being either impelled by forces or drawn by valences that exist along power vectors. According to Lewin, some of the strongest forces and valences an individual experiences stem from groups or from the persons who represent them (cf. Lewin, 1943). Field Theory (Lewin, 1951), therefore, viewed the group as an important unit to be studied in its own right, and as a result, a great deal of Lewin's research in the late 1930s and early 1940s was devoted to examining group functioning (e.g., Lewin, 1943, 1948).

During the early 1950s, group research flourished in a variety of different research programs. Studies by Bales (1950, 1953) and his colleagues (Bales & Slater, 1955) on small discussion groups generated critical insight into the patterning of group members' responses and the nature of their roles within the group. Bavelas (1948) and Leavitt (1951) examined information exchange by imposing network structures on decision-making groups and observing their effects on subsequent productivity. And Schachter (1951) conducted his seminal work on group reactions to the opinion of deviates.

Group research waxed until the mid- to late 1950s when, with the introduction of Festinger's theories of informal social communication (1950) and social comparison (1954), the individual became the primary unit of focus and analysis in social psychological research (see Jones, 1985, for a review). In a sense, social psychology turned inward, examining how states internal to the individual (e.g., his or her attitudes, values, personality, and thoughts) guided and influenced his or her social behavior. This individualistic trend was accelerated by the emergence of several other seminal theoretical perspectives during the late 1950s which treated the individual as the principle unit of psychological analysis (e.g., attribution theory: Heider, 1958; cognitive dissonance theory: Festinger, 1957; the Yale School of Communication research on persuasion: Hovland, Janis, & Kelley, 1953). As the mainstream focus of the field navigated away from reliance on group-level models of behavior during the late 1950s in favor of individual-level ones, the group movement began to wane.

Reasons for the Decline of Small Group Research

Steiner (1974, 1986) and Jones (1985) have argued that both theoretical poverty and inadequate methodological and statistical tools served to hasten the demise of group research. Once the individual became the primary unit of study, the "new" social psychological approach to research became inimical to the study of groups. Support for this new perspective was fueled by a number of factors.

First, because individuals register as salient units in social interaction much more readily than do groups, the individual appeared to be a more natural and much simpler unit on which to base the study of social interaction. Second, by virtue of their training in psychology, social psychologists were (and still are) inclined to decompose social and interpersonal actions into smaller segments rather than integrating them into larger social structures. Third, social psychologists began to develop a preference for employing proximal, single-factor explanations for behavior rather than distal, multifactor explanations (as had been popular within Field Theory). Fourth, given that Lewin himself sought to reduce group behavior to the level of individuals' thought processes, even the strongest proponents of the Lewinian tradition adopted a sympathetic stance toward the new, individualistic perspective that emerged in the late 1950s. Fifth, because group research was both extremely time-consuming and difficult to conduct, social psychologists migrated into different and less intractable areas of research more suited to individual-level analyses (e.g., attribution, cognitive dissonance, and persuasion research). And sixth, as researchers became more interested in studying group process in the early 1950s, more stringent controls concerning how group members could communicate with one another were instituted. This emphasis on control effectively rendered "group" research sterile, moving it away from the study of spontaneous, free-flowing, and bilateral patterns of communication that characterize natural groups.

One of the major group-based theories that did emerge in the wake of this revolution was Thibaut and Kelley's (1959) Theory of Interdependence. The theory attempted to explain and predict the behavior of individuals given their current reward/cost outcomes relative to those possessed by relationship partners. This theoretical model, however, was not widely adopted in group research for several reasons. First, similar to other theories in the field formulated at about the same time, interdependence theory placed the individual rather than the group as the central unit for study and analysis. Second, although Interdependence Theory could, in principle, have been applied to triads and larger social groups, it was most relevant to, and could be most easily applied to, the study of dyads. Third, even though the theory served as a rich source of hypotheses, researchers found it difficult to operationalize, quantify, and scale the reward and cost values that comprised different outcome matrices. The voluminous amount of research on the Prisoner's Dilemma Game (Rubin & Brown, 1975) is one of the few domains in which Interdependence Theory has been applied. And fourth, because the theory was associated with this game-playing paradigm, some researchers questioned the ecological validity of the results it generated. All of these factors effectively deprived group researchers of one of the major theories—and perhaps *the* major interpersonal relations theory—of the day. With few if any substitutes available, group research entered a period of theoretical dormancy.

Statistical and methodological deficiencies also may have stymied group research. Steiner (1986) has argued that the penchant of social psychologists to rely heavily on laboratory and experimental research designs placed severe limits on the kinds of research questions that typically were asked (and subsequently were answered) by group researchers. This situation was exacerbated by the fact that few simple, ecologically-valid research paradigms existed to study groups (see Jones, 1985). The highly structured interaction settings that met requirements of experimental control (e.g., communication networks) were criticized for their questionable validity in real world situations and settings. Moreover, with a few isolated exceptions (see Lewin, Lippett, & White, 1939; Sherif, Harvey, White, Hood, & Sherif, 1961), studies that involved the systematic observation of groups in naturalistic settings typically were too difficult to conduct, analyze, and interpret.

Reasons for Optimism About the Role of Groups in Social Psychology

These methodological considerations, along with the problem of theoretical poverty mentioned above, served to stifle the proliferation of group research within social psychology well into the 1970s. In his 1974 article, Steiner expressed optimism about the possibility that group research might experience an empirical re-vitalization, once again becoming a major and perhaps central area of inquiry in social psychology. His most recent assessment (Steiner, 1986) paints a much bleaker picture.

Of course, the study of groups has not ceased. As Levine and Moreland (1990) have cogently documented, group research is alive and well; it simply is not residing in mainstream social psychology. The bulk of research on small group processes is now conducted in areas such as sociology, clinical psychology, and organizational psychology.

The characteristic treatment of groups varies across these disciplines. In sociology, for example, research on the possession and use of power as well as the establishment of dominance hierarchies and other structures in groups has become prevalent (e.g., Berger, Rosenholtz, & Zelditch, 1980). Clinical research on groups has emphasized treatment of families as dysfunctional systems as well as the client-therapist dyad (e.g., Wolman & Stricker, 1983). And organizational research has identified determinants of work-group productivity and modes of effective leadership in them (e.g., Hackman & Oldham, 1980).

We clearly recognize the importance of multiple views on group phenomena. Group life is rich in complexity and demands investigation from a variety of perspectives. Important among these is a social psychology of groups. It is unlikely that group research conducted in other disciplines will duplicate the unique contributions that a social psychological perspective can bring to the field. The kinds of questions featured in such a perspective might include the personal functions served by group membership (e.g., Mackie & Goethals, 1987; Wegner, 1987), how reference groups strengthen members' attitudes and self-concepts (e.g., Hovland, Harvey, & Sherif, 1957), and how group members construe their role in group functioning (e.g., Sherif & Sherif, 1964).

Because the proliferation of group research in other disciplines does not obviate the need for a social psychological approach to groups, we hope that Steiner's (1986) most recent reflections are overly pessimistic. Indeed, there may be signs that the research climate for the study of groups in social psychology is changing.

Many of the pragmatic, methodological, and statistical difficulties that thwarted group research in the 1950s and 1960s have been either ameliorated or largely overcome in the past decade. The use of audio-video recording equipment, for instance, not only has produced more reliable measurement of group interactions, it also has allowed researchers to study subtle, microscopic patterns of behavior and interaction (e.g., facial reactions, subtle patterns of interaction that evolve between discussants) that often cannot be discerned by *in vivo* observers (e.g., see Dabbs & Ruback, 1987; Gottman, 1979). Recent advances in statistics and methodology also have made group research more feasible to conduct. Problems associated with statistical dependency in dyads and larger groups now can be dealt with directly (e.g., see Mendoza & Graziano, 1982). Procedures for identifying and testing the most probable causal "pathways" or "models" underlying correlational data now exist (e.g., structural equation modeling; see Bentler, 1980; Kenny, 1979, 1985). And a generalized model designed to study the source of effects that occur in dyadic interaction—the Social Relations Model (Kenny & LaVoie, 1984)—recently has been developed.

Even though the individual remains the primary unit of theoretical and empirical analysis in social psychology, several recent theories have sought to situate, study, and understand the individual within larger group structures. Examples include theoretical work pertaining to social impact theory (Latané & Wolf, 1981), minority influence (Moscovici, 1985), member socialization (Moreland & Levine, 1982), choice dilemmas (Messick et al., 1983), and nominal groups and inter-group relations (Brewer & Kramer, 1985; Tajfel, 1981). It is interesting that the impetus for several of these perspectives came from Europe. American social psychologists have been less ready than their European counterparts in recent years to expand beyond a conservative focus on the individual.

We hope that these recent technological advances and empirical trends will redress the malaise that has afflicted small group research in social psychology since the late 1950s. We believe that this volume and the conference from which it originated are an indication of the renewed interest in group dynamics. Hopefully, this volume will hasten and promote this process. Indeed, if its contents are an accurate indicator of the current state of group research in social psychology and in other fields, better times may lie ahead.

References

Asch, S. E. (1951). Effects of group pressure upon the modification and distortion of judgments. In H. Guetzkow (Ed.), *Groups, leadership, and men* (pp. 177-190). Pittsburgh, PA: Carnegie Press.

Allport, G. W. (1985). The historical background of social psychology. In G. Lindzey & E. Aronson (Eds.), *Handbook of social psychology* (Vol. 1, 3rd ed., pp. 1-46). New York: Random House.

Bales, R. F. (1950). *Interaction process analysis.* Cambridge, MA: Addison-Wesley.

Bales, R. F. (1953). The equilibrium problem in small groups. In T. Parsons, R. F. Bales, & E. A. Shils (Eds.), *Working papers in the theory of action* (pp. 111-162). Glencoe, IL: Free Press.

Bales, R. F., & Slater, P. E. (1955). Role differentiation in small decision-making groups. In T. Parsons & R. F. Bales (Eds.). *The family, socialization, and interaction process* (pp. 259-306). Glencoe, IL: Free Press.

Bavelas, A. (1948). A mathematical model for group structure. *Applied Anthropology, 7,* 16-30.

Bentler, P. M. (1980). Multivariate analysis with latent variables: Causal modeling. In M. R. Rosenzweig (Ed.), *Annual review of psychology* (Vol. 31). Palo Alto, CA: Annual Reviews.

Berger, J., Rosenholtz, S. J., & Zelditch, M., Jr. (1980). Status organizing processes. *Annual Review of Sociology, 6,* 479-508.

Brewer, M. B., & Kramer, R. M. (1985). The psychology of intergroup attitudes and behavior. *Annual Review of Psychology, 36,* 219-243.

Campbell, A., Converse, P. E., & Rodgers, W. L. (1976). *The quality of American life.* New York: Russell Sage Foundation.

Dabbs, J. M., & Ruback, R. B. (1987). Dimensions of group process: Amount and structure of vocal interaction. In L. Berkowitz (Ed.), *Advances in experimental social psychology* (Vol. 20, pp. 123-169). San Diego, CA: Academic Press.

Davis, J. H. (1969). *Group performance.* Reading, MA: Addison-Wesley.

Festinger, L. (1950). Informal social communication. *Psychological Review, 57,* 271-282.

Festinger, L. (1954). A theory of social comparison processes. *Human Relations, 7,* 117-140.

Festinger, L. (1957). *A theory of cognitive dissonance.* Stanford, CA: Stanford University Press.

Gottman, J. M. (1979). *Marital interaction: Experimental investigations.* New York: Academic Press.

Hackman, J. R., & Oldham, G. R. (1980). *Work redesign.* Reading, MA: Addison-Wesley.

Harkins, S. G., & Szymanski, K. (1987). Social loafing and social facilitation: New wine in old bottles. In C. Hendrick (Ed.), *Review of personality and social psychology: Group processes and intergroup relations* (Vol. 9, pp. 167-188). Newbury Park, CA: Sage.

Heider, F. (1958). *The psychology of interpersonal relations.* New York: John Wiley.

Hovland, C. I., Harvey, O. J., & Sherif, M. (1957). Assimilation and contrast effects in reactions to communication and attitude change. *Journal of Abnormal and Social Psychology, 55,* 244-252.

Hovland, C. I., Janis, I. L., & Kelley, H. H. (1953). *Communication and persuasion.* New Haven, CT: Yale University Press.

Jones, E. E. (1985). Major developments in social psychology during the past five decades. In G. Lindzey & E. Aronson (Eds.), *Handbook of social psychology* (Vol. 1, 3rd ed., pp. 47-107). New York: Random House.

Kenny, D. A. (1979). *Correlation and causality.* New York: John Wiley-Interscience.

Kenny, D. A. (1985). Quantitative methods for social psychology. In G. Lindzey & E. Aronson (Eds.), *Handbook of social psychology* (Vol. 1, 3rd ed., pp. 487-508). New York: Random House.

Kenny, D. A., & LaVoie, L. (1984). The social relations model. In L. Berkowitz (Ed.), *Advances in experimental social psychology* (Vol. 18, pp. 141-182). New York: Academic Press.

Kerr, N. L., Atkin, R. S., Stasser, G., Meek, D., Holt, R. W., & Davis, J. H. (1976). Guilt beyond a reasonable doubt: Effects of concept definition and assigned decision rule on the judgments of mock jurors. *Journal of Personality and Social Psychology, 34,* 282-294.

Latané, B., & Wolf, S. (1981). The social impact of majorities and minorities. *Psychological Review, 88,* 438-453.

Leavitt, H. J. (1951). Some effects of certain communication patterns on group performance. *Journal of Abnormal and Social Psychology, 46,* 38-50.

Levine, J. M., & Moreland, R. L. (1990). *Progress in small group research.* Unpublished manuscript, University of Pittsburgh.

Lewin, K. (1943). Forces behind food habits and methods of change. *Bulletin of the National Research Council, 108,* 35-65.

Lewin, K. (1948). *Resolving social conflicts: Selected papers on group dynamics.* New York: Harper & Row.

Lewin, K. (1951). Problems of research in social psychology. In D. Cartwright (Ed.), *Field theory in social science: Selected theoretical papers by Kurt Lewin.* New York: Harper & Row.

Lewin, K., Lippett, R., & White, R. (1939). Patterns of aggressive behavior in experimentally created "social climates." *Journal of Social Psychology, 10,* 271-299.

Mackie, D. M., & Goethals, G. R. (1987). Individual and group goals. In C. Hendrick (Ed.), *Review of personality and social psychology: Group processes* (Vol. 8, pp. 144-166). Newbury Park, CA: Sage.

Mendoza, J., & Graziano, W. G. (1982). The statistical analysis of dyadic social behavior: A multivariate approach. *Psychological Bulletin, 92,* 532-540.

Messick, D. M., Wilke, H., Brewer, M. B., Kramer, R. M., Zemke, P. E., & Lui, L. (1983). Individual adaptations and structural change as solutions to social dilemmas. *Journal of Personality and Social Psychology, 44,* 294-309.

Moreland, R. L., & Levine, J. M. (1982). Socialization in small groups: Temporal changes in individual-group relations. In L. Berkowitz (Ed.), *Advances in experimental social psychology* (Vol. 15, pp. 137-192). New York: Academic Press.

Moscovici, S. (1985). Social influence and conformity. In G. Lindzey & E. Aronson (Eds.), *Handbook of social psychology* (Vol. 1, 3rd ed., pp. 347-412). New York: Random House.

Myers, D. G. (1978). Polarizing effects of social comparison. *Journal of Experimental Social Psychology, 14,* 554-563.

Rubin, J. Z., & Brown, B. R. (1975). *The social psychology of bargaining and negotiation.* New York: Academic Press.

Schachter, S. (1951). Deviation, rejection, and communication. *Journal of Abnormal and Social Psychology, 46,* 190-207.

Sherif, M., Harvey, O. J., White, B. J., Hood, W. R., & Sherif, C. W. (1961). *Intergroup conflict and cooperation.* Norman, OK: Institute of Group Relations.

Sherif, M., & Sherif, C. W. (1964). *Reference groups.* New York: Harper & Row.

Steiner, I. D. (1974). Whatever happened to the group in social psychology? *Journal of Experimental Social Psychology, 10,* 94-108.

Steiner, I. D. (1986). Paradigms and groups. In L. Berkowitz (Ed.), *Advances in experimental social psychology* (pp. 251-289). Orlando, FL: Academic Press.

Tajfel, H. (1981). *Human groups and social categories.* Cambridge, UK: Cambridge University Press.

Thibaut, J. W., & Kelley, H. H. (1959). *The social psychology of groups.* New York: John Wiley.

Triplett, N. (1898). The dynamogenic factors in pace-making and competition. *American Journal of Psychology, 9,* 507-533.

Wegner, D. M. (1987). Transactive memory: A contemporary analysis of the group mind. In B. Mullen & G. Goethals (Eds.), *Theories of group behavior* (pp. 185-208). New York: Springer-Verlag.

Wolman, B. B., & Stricker, G. (Eds.) (1983). *Handbook of family and marital therapy.* New York: Plenum.

Zajonc, R. B. (1965). Social facilitation. *Science, 149,* 269-274.

Zander, A. (1979). The psychology of group processes. In M. R. Rosenzweig & L. R. Porter (Eds.), *Annual review of psychology* (Vol. 30, pp. 417-451). Palo Alto, CA: Annual Reviews.

PART I

Small Group
Decision Making

Introduction

Charles D. Samuelson

Research on small group problem solving and decision making has deep historical roots in social psychology. In particular, interest in the relationship between group process and group productivity can be traced back to some of the earliest empirical studies in the field. For example, Marjorie Shaw's (1932) classic experiment was perhaps the first systematic attempt to investigate how small group processes affect a group's performance on a problem-solving task. Testing the popular hypothesis of the day, that groups were superior to individuals in solving problems, Shaw observed and recorded members' behaviors during the experimental sessions to provide measures of process. Her conclusion was that groups performed better than individuals because groups engaged in checking errors and eliminating incorrect answers. Subsequent theoretical work by Lorge and Solomon (1955) provided mathematical baselines for optimal group performance which allowed for more rigorous comparisons between individual and group performance. In the 1960s, however, interest in the process-performance relationship waned as social psychologists became fascinated with the "risky shift" phenomenon by Stoner (1961). Consequently, theoretical and empirical progress in this area remained slow during this era.

The publication of Ivan Steiner's seminal book, *Group Process and Productivity,* in 1972 marked a resurgence of interest in group processes. In many respects, this monograph was the first explicit theoretical statement on how internal group processes influence group productivity. Adopting a somewhat pessimistic view of process, Steiner (1972) argued that actual group productivity should be conceptualized

13

as the group's potential productivity minus losses from faulty group process. Potential productivity was hypothesized to be a function of task demands and member resources. Steiner also provided the first systematic group task typology, which has proved extremely useful in subsequent research on group performance.

A year later, James Davis (1973) published an important article in *Psychological Review* that introduced the social decision scheme (SDS) model of group decision making. Taking a different tack than Steiner (1972), Davis (1973) showed how complex social processes in small groups could be represented mathematically. The SDS approach uses formal models to predict group decisions from the initial individual preferences of the group members. The primary focus in this research is on accounting for the group output, given the individual inputs. Although not concerned with process per se, Davis's (1973) SDS theory allows logical inferences to be made about the social interaction processes that produce the observed group decisions. SDS theory has stimulated numerous empirical studies on group decision making over the past 15 years, particularly using mock juries (see Stasser, Kerr, and Davis, 1989, for a review.)

A third important development in the literature on group performance was the review chapter by Hackman and Morris (1975). Building on the work of Steiner (1972) and others, Hackman and Morris focused more directly on the process-performance relationship and proposed a model that synthesized the available theoretical and empirical literature. They were more optimistic than Steiner (1972) about the possible beneficial effects of group interaction process on productivity. Hackman and Morris (1975) suggested that group process affects task performance through three "summary" variables—member efforts, task performance strategies, and member knowledge and skill. They argued that the key to enhancing group productivity is in designing interventions to change the group's interaction processes that affect the summary variables most relevant to the group's task demands. The Hackman-Morris (1975) model also suggested some possible input variables (e.g., group norms, task redesign, group composition) that may serve as "levers" for improving group performance. Their conceptual approach has been highly influential in subsequent group performance theory and research in social and organizational psychology.

The three chapters in this section explore various aspects of the group process-performance relationship. In Chapter 1, Moreland and Levine focus directly on process issues in the context of problem recognition in problem-solving groups. Chapter 2, by Stasser, deals with two important determinants of group performance according to Steiner (1972) and Hackman and Morris (1975), member resources and group process, to demonstrate how the sharing of information during group discussion influences final group decisions. In Chapter 3, Kerr addresses an important aspect of the group's task, issue importance, and shows how this variable can moderate group decision outcomes in a choice shift paradigm.

In the first chapter in this section, Moreland and Levine address a topic that has been relatively unexplored in social psychology, that of problem identification in small groups. They provide an excellent summary of the existing literature by discussing several key research issues, such as how groups identify problems, the conditions under which group problems will be identified successfully, which group member(s) will be likely to identify them, members' options for dealing with problems, and methods for studying group problem identification experimentally in the laboratory. The goal of this chapter is to clarify the processes involved in group problem identification and, in doing so, to stimulate greater interest in this topic among researchers.

The second chapter in this section deals with a critical aspect of group process: the sharing of information among group members during discussion. One common rationale for using groups to make decisions is that groups can benefit from pooling members' knowledge and expertise, presumably leading to higher quality decisions. Stasser questions this often cited advantage of groups and shows that, in many cases, the group's potential remains unfulfilled because members typically talk about information that all members already know instead of exchanging unique knowledge held by single members. He proposes a theoretical model to account for these results that explains how members sample information during group discussion. Stasser introduces the concept of *hidden profiles*—cases in which the superiority of one decision alternative over others is obscured because each member possesses only a portion of its supporting information—and analyzes the conditions under which information sampling dynamics within the group work against discovery of such hidden profiles. Another noteworthy aspect of this chapter is Stasser's informed speculation about how the information sampling model of the discussion process can be used to develop some practical guidelines for improving the quality of group decisions.

The final chapter in this section, by Kerr, focuses on a different, yet often neglected, feature of group decision-making studies, the importance of the issue facing the group. He argues and presents some suggestive empirical evidence for the thesis that both the process and outcome of group decision making can be systematically influenced by issue importance during group discussion. His research suggests that, as issue importance declines, the power of majority factions within the group also decreases. One interesting consequence of this effect is that the typical polarization effect (Myers & Lamm, 1976) observed during group discussion may be attenuated, or possibly reversed, leading to group depolarization in the extreme case. Kerr's chapter further illustrates the usefulness of Davis's (1973) SDS theory as a powerful analytic tool.

References

Davis, J. H. (1973). Group decision and social interaction: A theory of social decision schemes. *Psychological Review, 80*, 97-125.

Hackman, J. R., & Morris, C. G. (1975). Group tasks, group interaction process, and group performance effectiveness: A review and proposed integration. In L. Berkowitz (Ed.), *Advances in experimental social psychology* (Vol. 8, pp. 45-99). New York: Academic Press.

Lorge, I., & Solomon, H. (1955). Two models of group behavior in the solution of Eureka-type problems. *Psychometrika, 20*, 139-148.

Myers, D. G., & Lamm, H. (1976). The group polarization phenomenon. *Psychological Bulletin, 83*, 602-627.

Shaw, M. E. (1932). Comparison of individuals and small groups in the rational solution of complex problems. *American Journal of Psychology, 44*, 491-504.

Stasser, G., Kerr, N. L., & Davis, J. H. (1989). Influence processes and consensus models in decision-making groups. In P. Paulus (Ed.), *Psychology of group influence* (2nd ed.). Hillsdale, NJ: Lawrence Erlbaum.

Steiner, I. D. (1972). *Group process and productivity.* New York: Academic Press.

Stoner, J.A.F. (1961). *A comparison of individual and group decisions involving risk.* Unpublished master's thesis, Massachusetts Institute of Technology. Cambridge.

1   Problem Identification by Groups

Richard L. Moreland
John M. Levine

Every group encounters problems from time to time. Some of these problems clearly are worse than others. A major problem, such as the sudden resignation of several members, can threaten almost any group. And some groups are clearly worse than others at solving problems. For these groups, even a minor problem, such as a procedural disagreement among members, can become threatening. The productivity of a group often depends on its ability to solve problems (major and minor) quickly and efficiently. By improving that ability, it should be possible to make a group more productive.

Several field studies have focused on how natural groups try to solve their problems (e.g., Burnstein & Berbaum, 1983; Gore, 1956; Mintzberg, Raisinghani, & Theoret, 1976; Nutt, 1984). The results suggest that group problem solving is a rather complex process. Mintzberg and his colleagues, for example, studied the strategic decisions made by small groups of executives within large corporations. They found that problem solving in those groups involved three distinct activities. First, group members had to *identify the problem* that they faced. This required detecting the problem's existence and then diagnosing its probable nature. Second, group members had to *develop*

AUTHORS' NOTE: The authors would like to thank Linda Argote, Mike Berbaum, Marie Cini, and Janet Schofield for their insightful comments on earlier versions of this chapter. Dan Grech also deserves our thanks for his help in preparing the chapter.

17

alternative solutions for the problem. This required searching for existing solutions and/or designing new ones. Finally, group members had to *select a solution* from the alternatives available to them. This required evaluating the probable effectiveness of those alternatives and then implementing whatever solution seemed best.

Clearly, all three of these activities could affect the productivity of a group. Groups are likely to succeed if they can (a) identify their problems quickly and accurately, (b) develop good solutions for their problems, and (c) select the best solutions and then implement them effectively. If groups perform these three activities poorly, they are likely to fail. It is surprising, therefore, that most laboratory research on group problem solving has focused on just one of these activities. Elaborate theoretical models, derived from extensive empirical evidence, have been developed to explain how groups select solutions for their problems (see Stasser, Kerr, & Davis, 1989), but very little theoretical or empirical work has been done on how groups develop solutions for their problems or how they identify those problems in the first place.

Problem identification is an especially important activity because it often initiates the process of group problem solving. Later activities in that process thus may depend on how a problem is first identified by a group. There is some evidence, for example, that the person who identifies a problem for his or her group is more active than other members in developing alternative solutions for that problem and then in selecting and implementing whatever solution seems best (Davis & Rigaux, 1974; Wegner, 1987). And of course, the ability of a group to identify problems quickly and accurately can constrain later problem-solving activities in ways that affect group productivity. A group that detects problems too slowly or diagnoses them inaccurately will probably fail, whatever solutions it develops for those problems and however it evaluates and implements those solutions (D'Zurilla & Goldfried, 1971; Mitroff & Featheringham, 1974).

The purpose of this chapter is to clarify problem identification by groups and promote greater interest in this topic among researchers. We will begin by analyzing how group members identify their problems. Then we will discuss when a group's problems are likely to be identified, who tends to identify those problems, and what people can do about a problem after identifying it. Finally, we will suggest some ways in which problem identification by groups might be studied.

How Do Groups Identify Problems?

Several theoretical models of problem identification have been proposed (e.g., Cowan, 1986; Dutton, Fahey, & Narayanan, 1983; Kiesler & Sproull, 1982; Lyles, 1981; Pounds, 1969; Smith, 1989). None of these models has been tested extensively; most have not been tested at all. As a result, it is difficult to decide which model is best (e.g., see Lyles & Thomas, 1988). Rather than providing a detailed review of all the theoretical models and evaluating their relative strengths and weaknesses, we will offer a general account of problem identification that emphasizes certain concepts found in many of the models. Figure 1.1 illustrates our account of how problems are identified by groups.

Problems usually betray themselves by producing symptoms that attract the attention of group members. These symptoms involve unusual and often unpleasant events within the group. A problem is detected when group members notice its symptoms and realize that something is wrong. They may not understand the exact nature of the problem, but they do know that it exists. Problems vary in their symptomatology, so some are easier to detect than others (cf. Kiesler & Sproull, 1982; Leventhal, Leventhal, & Van Nguyen, 1985; Mintzberg et al., 1976). For example, some problems produce more symptoms than others and thus are more likely to be detected by group members. And when a problem produces multiple symptoms, they can seem more or less congruent with one another. The more congruent the symptoms of a problem seem, the more likely group members are to detect the problem. Finally, each symptom has its own pattern of occurrence. Some symptoms occur more often than others, and when a symptom occurs repeatedly, the intervals between those occurrences can be short or long and regular or variable. Symptoms that occur more often and at shorter, more regular intervals attract more attention from group members. Problems that produce such symptoms thus are more likely to be detected.

Once a problem has been detected, group members may or may not be motivated to do something about it. Their motivation depends on the levels of arousal produced by the symptoms associated with the problem. Every symptom embodies a contrast between realism and idealism; members realize that conditions within the group are not what they ought to be (cf. Cowan, 1986; Pounds, 1969; Smith, 1989). As a result, feelings of uncertainty and anxiety arise. As the real group diverges from the ideal group, members become increasingly aroused

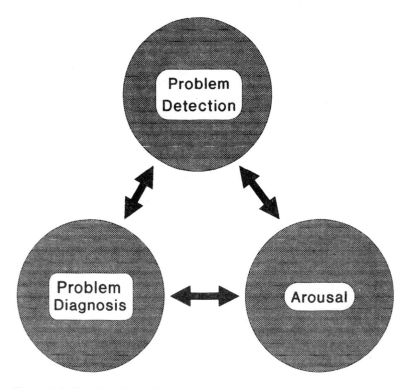

Figure 1.1. How Do Groups Identify Problems?

and are more likely to do something about their problem. Many theorists (e.g., Billings, Milburn, & Schaalman, 1980; Lyles, 1981; Turner, 1976; Yarrow, Schwartz, Murphy, & Deasy, 1955) claim that there is a threshold of arousal that must be reached before any problem-solving activity takes place. Until that threshold is reached, group members may feel vaguely uneasy, but they do not understand why they feel that way. A *triggering event*—some symptom that finally produces enough cumulative arousal to exceed the threshold—is often needed. Only then do group members acknowledge that the problem needs to be solved.

The first step that most group members take toward solving a problem is to diagnose its probable nature (Weiner, 1985). Diagnosis involves developing, through a complex cognitive process involving both induction and deduction (Dutton et al., 1983; Ramaprasad & Mitroff, 1984), a "problem representation" that incorporates whatever information (from actual events to plausible assumptions to wild hunches) seems relevant to group members. A problem representation is a mental model that includes a label for the problem, some ideas about why the problem occurred and how it might be solved, and a prediction about what will happen if the problem is ignored (cf. Dutton et al., 1983; Lau & Hartman, 1983; Smith, 1988, 1989). Once a representation has been developed, the process of group problem solving can proceed. That process is often shaped by the problem representation, because the kinds of alternative solutions that are developed for a problem and the ways in which those solutions are evaluated and implemented depend on how the problem is diagnosed by group members (Dutton & Jackson, 1987; Jervis, 1976; Lyles, 1981; Nezu & D'Zurilla, 1981).

This brief account of how group members identify problems raises several interesting issues. One such issue involves the social nature of problem identification in groups. Problems are always identified by individuals. Only a *person* can actually notice the symptoms of a problem, feel sufficiently aroused to try to solve it, and perform the cognitive processes needed to develop a problem representation. Yet group members clearly collaborate with one another while identifying problems (Anderson, Hughes, & Sharrock, 1987; Jackson, 1956; Lyles, 1987; Lyles & Mitroff, 1980). For example, members of a group can share information about recent events that might be symptomatic of underlying problems or argue about how those events should be interpreted. Even when the symptoms of a problem are apparent to everyone, some people may feel more aroused than others (because the problem affects them more deeply) or have lower arousal thresholds for problem-solving activities. These differences among group members can produce arguments about whether anything is really wrong with the group or not. Finally, agreement that a problem exists does not guarantee that it will be diagnosed in the same way by every group member. People can develop very different representations of the same problem, leading to further arguments about why the problem occurred, how it might be solved, and so on. All of this indicates that in many groups problem identification can be a social as well as a personal activity.

Another interesting issue involves the holistic nature of problem identification in groups. According to our account, the experience of identifying a problem occurs in a series of distinct phases: Detection of the problem produces feelings of arousal among group members, which motivate them to diagnose its probable nature. But experience suggests that these phases are seldom so distinct, at least while the problem is actually being identified. They often occur so rapidly that it becomes difficult or impossible to determine when one phase ends and another begins. And, as Figure 1.1 indicates, those phases need not occur in the order that we described. After experiencing one phase of problem identification, group members often return to an earlier phase, creating complex cycles of activity (cf. Cowan, 1986; Dutton et al., 1983; Lyles, 1981). For example, someone who has just diagnosed a problem may reinterpret prior events as symptomatic of that problem or try to produce new events that will confirm the diagnosis. And when the diagnosis for a problem alarms group members, because they fear the consequences of the problem but cannot readily solve it, people may try to cope by "forgetting" the problem's symptoms or discounting them in some way. They may also become less idealistic about the group, so that any remaining symptoms become less arousing. If the problem fails to produce sufficient arousal among group members, it may no longer seem problematic to them. All of this indicates that problem identification can be a very complex activity in many groups.

When Will Group Problems Be Identified?

As a complex social activity, the identification of problems by groups is susceptible to many kinds of errors. Some of these errors involve the detection of problems. For example, a group may fail to detect an existing problem or "detect" a problem that does not really exist. Delays in detecting a problem can make its proper diagnosis irrelevant. Other errors involve the feelings of arousal associated with a problem. If a problem produces too little or too much arousal among group members, or if their arousal thresholds are too high or too low, attempts to diagnose the problem can begin too late or too soon. Finally, errors often occur in the diagnosis of problems. Misdiagnoses, such as attributing a problem to the wrong cause or overlooking some of its consequences, are common and can be quite harmful to a group, especially when its members refuse to admit that they were mistaken (cf. Jervis, 1976; Schwenk, 1984; Staw & Ross, 1989). When will a problem be identified successfully by group members? A variety of factors, involving the problem itself, the group, and the environment in which problem identification takes place, may be important. A few examples of these different factors are shown in Figure 1.2.

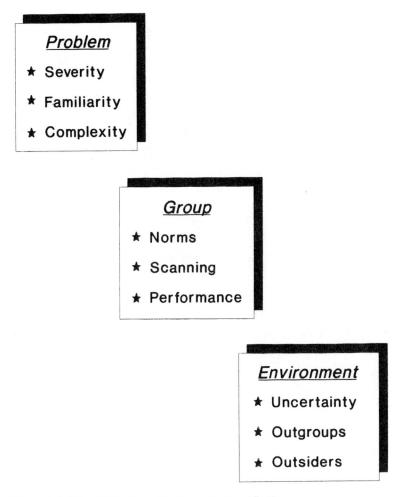

Figure 1.2. When Will Group Problems Be Identified?

Some problems are clearly easier than others for a group to identify. One important factor may be the *severity* of a problem (Billings et al., 1980; Cowan, 1986; Nutt, 1984). As a problem becomes more severe, its symptoms grow more noticeable and evoke stronger feelings of arousal. Group members thus are more likely to detect the problem and devote time and energy to its diagnosis. More severe problems also tend to be diagnosed more accurately, because their importance is appreciated by everyone in the group. However, if the diagnosis is too alarming, denial or distortion of the problem may occur as group members try to cope with their anxieties about it (Turner, 1976).

Another factor that may be important in identifying a problem is its *familiarity* (Cowan, 1986; Kiesler & Sproull, 1982; Mazzolini, 1981). The first time a problem is encountered by a group, it is relatively difficult to identify. But with each recurrence of the problem, identification becomes easier because group members are familiar with the problem's symptoms and have already considered its possible causes, consequences, and cures. Eventually, the identification of a familiar problem can become a routine activity within the group. This may save group members effort, but can be dangerous if the nature of the problem changes or different problems with similar symptoms begin to occur.

Finally, the *complexity* of a problem also may be an important factor in its identification (Smith, 1989; Taylor, 1975; Watson, 1976). Complex problems often are more difficult than others to detect because they produce ambiguous or (apparently) incongruent symptoms. Complex problems also tend to have multiple causes that are interdependent and can change over time. As a result, such problems can be especially difficult to diagnose. Group members may try to simplify complex problems in various ways, such as focusing on their short- rather than long-term consequences, but these efforts almost always involve distortions that make such problems less likely to be solved.

Just as some kinds of problems are more likely than others to be identified by a group, some groups are better than others at identifying problems. One important factor may be a group's *norms* regarding problem solving. Some groups regard all problems as threats to morale and thus discourage the identification of any problems by their members (Janis, 1982; Miceli & Near, 1985; Smircich, 1983). In these groups, people who discover problems are reluctant to talk about them because they expect to be ignored or rebuffed. As a result, the detection of problems is delayed. When problems are finally detected in these groups, the tension that they produce often precludes the sort of detailed, objective analyses that adequate diagnoses seem to require (cf. Lyles, 1981; Schwenk & Thomas, 1983). Misdiagnoses are thus common in such groups.

Identifying a problem often requires a considerable amount of information about events occurring both inside and outside of the group. Information of this sort allows problems to be detected more quickly and can also produce more accurate problem diagnoses. Groups that engage in more extensive *scanning* of their environments are thus better than others at identifying problems (Ancona & Caldwell, 1988; Billings et al., 1980; Cowan, 1976; Main, 1989). Of course, it is possible for a group to acquire more information than its members can process adequately (cf. Feldman & March, 1981; Kiesler & Sproull, 1982). Proper scanning of the environment should thus include some efforts by the group to separate relevant from irrelevant information.

Finally, the group's ability to identify problems may also depend on its level of *performance*. Groups that consistently succeed at achieving their goals often become complacent and that complacency can delay the detection of problems. People who belong to such groups rarely expect problems to arise, so they overlook or ignore many symptomatic events (Hedburg, Nystrom, & Starbuck, 1976). Complacency can also delay the diagnosis of problems because group members develop rather high arousal thresholds for problem-solving activity; only the most serious problems seem threatening enough to warrant the effort required for solving them (Frederickson, 1985). Misdiagnoses of problems often occur in successful groups, whose members attribute most of their problems to external causes, tend to underestimate the consequences of their problems, and often feel overly confident about their problem-solving abilities (Leary & Forsyth, 1987). The positive moods experienced by members of successful groups also may lead to misdiagnoses of problems. These moods can interfere with the systematic processing of information about a group, thereby limiting the ability of its members to identify problems accurately (cf. Isen, 1987; Mackie & Worth, 1989).

What about groups that are consistently unsuccessful at achieving their goals? They may have difficulty identifying problems as well. People who belong to unsuccessful groups have so many problems already that they are reluctant to discover any new ones (Burnstein & Berbaum, 1983). And they are so busy trying to solve old problems that new ones may develop without being noticed (Lyles & Mitroff, 1980). As a result, problem detection is often delayed in unsuccessful groups. Problem diagnoses may be delayed in these groups as well, because their members also have rather high arousal thresholds for problem-solving activity; time and effort can be spared only for solving the most serious problems (Mintzberg et al., 1976). Finally, misdiagnoses are common in unsuccessful groups, whose members may be so anxious that they have trouble thinking clearly about their problems. If these problems seem too severe, because they have few clear solutions or solutions that are difficult to implement, then group members may simply panic (cf. Rogers, 1983; Stein, 1976). All of this suggests that a problem is more likely to be identified successfully in groups whose levels of performance are moderate rather than extreme.

The ability of a group to identify a problem depends not only on the characteristics of that group and its problem, but also on the environment in which problem identification takes place. One important factor may be the general level of *uncertainty* associated with events in that environment. Both an environment's complexity (the number and variety of factors affecting the group) and stability (the amount and rate of change in those factors) can affect its perceived uncertainty (Duncan, 1972; Smart & Vertinsky, 1984). As the environment becomes more uncertain, problem identification becomes more difficult for the group (Hedburg et al., 1976; Kiesler & Sproull, 1982). Delays in problem identification often occur because symptomatic events are overlooked or misinterpreted. In an effort to minimize tiresome "false alarms," group members may also develop rather high arousal thresholds for problem solving, thereby delaying problem diagnoses as well. Finally, misdiagnoses are common in an uncertain environment because it is so difficult for anyone to be sure why problems occur or how they might be solved.

The presence of relevant *outgroups* in the environment may be another important factor in problem identification. Groups that are similar in important ways often compare themselves to each other, and these comparisons could affect (positively or negatively) their ability to identify problems. Some of those effects may involve direct imitation. For example, if the members of one group become aware of another group's efforts to identify a problem, they may engage in similar activities, especially if those activities seemed to benefit the other group (cf. Galaskiewicz & Wasserman, 1989). Subtler effects of outgroups on problem identification may also occur (cf. Nutt, 1984; Pounds, 1969). For example, comparisons with an outgroup could affect the detection of a problem by focusing the attention of group members on particular events or by causing them to interpret those events differently. The feelings of arousal produced by a problem's symptoms could also be affected by an outgroup comparison if that comparison leads people to change their images of the ideal group. Finally, comparisons with an outgroup could shape the diagnosis of a problem by providing evidence for or against various problem representations.

It is worth noting that groups can make temporal as well as social comparisons (Levine & Moreland, 1987). Aside from comparing their own group to some other group, people can compare their group as it is now to what it was in the past or is expected to become in the future. These temporal comparisons also could affect problem identification in many ways. For example, people often compare current events within their group to events that occurred there in the past. If past events were symptomatic of some problem, then similar events in the present are likely to be viewed as symptoms of the same problem (Kiesler & Sproull, 1982; May, 1973; Milburn, Schuler, & Watman, 1983). When people think about how their group might change in the future, they often have certain goals for the group in mind. These goals can affect which problems are detected, how those problems are diagnosed, and how hard group members work at identifying problems (Billings et al., 1980; Pounds, 1969).

A final environmental factor that may be important in problem identification is the potential involvement of *outsiders*. Outsiders are people who do not actually belong to a group, but are still concerned about its outcomes (see Hackett & Cassem, 1969; Kilmann & Mitroff, 1979; Lau & Russell, 1980; Levine & Moreland, 1985; Milburn et al., 1983; Nutt, 1984; Pounds, 1969). They include the friends and relatives of group members, prospective and ex-members of the group, the group's enemies, customers or suppliers of the group, special consultants, and regulatory agencies or other authorities (including owners). Outsiders can become involved in every phase of problem identification. They may, for example, aid in the detection of a problem by pointing out some of its symptoms or try to motivate group members to solve the problem by making its symptoms seem more arousing or by lowering their arousal thresholds for problem-solving activity. Outsiders also may help with diagnosing a problem by offering suggestions about why it has occurred or how it might be solved.

Several points regarding the involvement of outsiders in problem identification are worth noting. First, outsiders are not always helpful; whether they mean to or not, outsiders sometimes delay the detection of a problem or cause it to be misdiagnosed. Second, even though group members sometimes ask outsiders to become involved in problem identification, their involvement is often unsolicited. Finally, outsiders who are involved in problem identification can vary in their impact on the group. Most outsiders merely offer advice to the group about its problems, but some outsiders have enough power to control the identification of a problem by group members or even to require them to solve a problem that the outsiders have already identified.

Who Will Identify Group Problems?

The kinds of factors that we have just considered are important because they affect the probability that *anyone* in a group will identify a problem. A problem thus is more likely to be identified when it is severe, group members are encouraged to identify problems, there is little uncertainty in the group's environment, and so on. If we can assume that a problem will be identified by at least one group member, then it becomes important to consider just who that person might be. Perhaps some group members are more likely than others to identify problems. A few individual factors that might predict who will identify a group problem are shown in Figure 1.3.

One factor that may be important in problem identification is a person's *status* within the group. People with higher status, especially the group's leader, are more likely than others to identify problems (cf. Carter, Haythorn, Shriver, & Lanzetta, 1950; Goodman, 1968). Status can facilitate the identification of problems in several ways. First, people with higher status usually know more about what is happening in the group because they speak more often to other group members and are spoken to more often by those members (Goetsch & McFarland, 1980). Of course, efforts are sometimes made to hide problems from people with higher status (see Jablin, 1979), but those efforts often fail, because status also allows a person to demand information from other members. Because they are more knowledgeable about the group than others, people with higher status can detect its problems more quickly and diagnose them more accurately. Second, people with higher status usually are more motivated than other members to help the group succeed (cf. Leary & Forsyth, 1987; Zander, 1971). As a result, they probably have lower arousal thresholds for problem-solving activity. Finally, people with higher status usually are expected by other members to identify problems for the group (Hosking & Morley, 1988; Phillips & Lord, 1982). In fact, in many groups problems simply do not "exist" until they are detected and diagnosed by someone with relatively high status (Pfeffer, 1981). Problem identification thus can become a duty or a privilege reserved for certain members of the group.

The identification of a problem often requires special *expertise* that only a few members of the group may possess. Expertise includes personal knowledge, talent, or skill that can help someone detect a problem quickly and then diagnose it accurately. The effects of expertise on problem identification might involve cognitive and/or motivational

Figure 1.3. Who Will Identify Group Problems?

processes. At a cognitive level, expertise could improve problem detection by increasing the availability and accessibility of problem symptoms for the person (cf. Carroll, 1978; Gilovich, 1981). And expertise could improve problem diagnosis by providing the person with a more complex schema relating various aspects of the problem to one another (cf. Chi, Glaser, & Farr, 1988). At a motivational level, it is important to remember that expertise often reflects personal interests in particular problem domains and that self-esteem often depends on displaying competence in those domains (cf. Bandura, 1977). Someone with special expertise in a group thus may devote more effort to detecting and diagnosing relevant problems.

As this analysis suggests, people tend to identify problems that fall within their own areas of expertise (cf. Aguilar, 1967; Davis, 1976; Dearborn & Simon, 1958; Herden & Lyles, 1981; Mazzolini, 1981; Wegner, 1987). Task-oriented members of the group, for example, tend to identify technical problems, whereas relationship-oriented group members tend to identify social problems. Once a problem has been successfully identified by some member of the group, others begin to associate that person with problems of that sort. If a similar problem arises later on, that person is expected to detect and diagnose that problem as well. Eventually, a new role is created in the group, so that the person feels responsible and is held accountable for identifying all problems that seem relevant to his or her area of expertise.

Another factor that might be important in identifying problems is the strength of a person's *commitment* to a group. Commitment is an emotional bond between a person and a group. Many theorists (e.g., Farrell & Rusbult, 1981; Moreland & Levine, 1982; see also Rusbult, Farrell, Rogers, & Mainous, 1988) argue that commitment depends primarily on the outcomes (rewards or costs) associated with membership in a group, adjusted for whatever outcomes are available to a person from real or potential memberships in other groups. People thus are committed to a group insofar as it generates more rewards and fewer costs than do other groups to which they already belong or that they could join. Other theorists argue that commitment depends primarily on how important a group is to someone's "social identity" (e.g., Tajfel & Turner, 1986; see also Stryker & Serpe, 1982). Whereas personal identity reflects the individual characteristics that set one person apart from others, social identity reflects each person's unique pattern of group memberships. A basic need for self-enhancement leads people to feel more committed to groups that seem (to themselves and/or others) more successful.

In general, people who feel stronger commitment to a group (because of the rewarding outcomes and improved social identity that it provides) should be more concerned about its well-being. As a result, they should devote more effort to detecting and diagnosing group problems (cf. Dean, 1985; Micelli & Near, 1988). Extreme levels of commitment, however, could interfere with problem identification. Someone whose commitment to a group is very strong might view its problems as personally threatening, because those problems indicate the potential loss of valuable outcomes and possible damage to social identity. Such a person would be slow to detect problems in the group, feel reluctant to diagnose them, and make various kinds of misdiagnoses (e.g., attributing most of the group's problems to external/unstable causes). But someone whose commitment to a group is very weak might view its problems with a certain satisfaction, because they provide private and/or public justification for that person's complaints about the group. Such a person would be (too) quick to detect problems in the group, feel eager to diagnose them, and make misdiagnoses of related kinds (e.g., attributing most of the group's problems to internal/stable causes).

Finally, a variety of *personality* characteristics could affect whether and how someone in a group identifies a problem. Group members with higher self-esteem, for example, may be more likely to detect and try to diagnose problems because they feel more confident about their problem-solving abilities (Billings et al., 1980; Milburn et al., 1983). And group members whose locus of control is relatively internal may be more likely than others to detect problems because they engage in more extensive scanning of the environment (Miller, Kets deVries, & Toulouse, 1982; Wallston & Wallston, 1982). The same group members may also try to diagnose problems more often because they believe it is their responsibility to do so. Of course, the problem diagnoses of people with high self-esteem or an internal locus of control need not be especially accurate; such persons may underestimate the severity of a problem and/or overestimate their chances of solving it alone.

Problems *are* more likely to be diagnosed accurately by people with greater intelligence and cognitive complexity (Taylor, 1975), and there is some evidence that problem identification can be shaped by certain broad cognitive styles (Herden & Lyles, 1981; Malley & Davis, 1988; Mitroff & Kilmann, 1975; Ramaprasad & Mitroff, 1984; see also Lyles & Mitroff, 1980) associated with personal emphases on sensation versus intuition (in the detection of problems) and thinking versus feeling (in the diagnosis of problems). These stylistic differences seem to influence the kinds of problems that are detected and the ways in which those problems are diagnosed, rather than the speed of problem detection or the accuracy of problem diagnosis.

What Can Be Done About Group Problems?

Suppose that at least one member of a group notices the symptoms of a problem, feels sufficiently aroused to try to solve it, and performs the cognitive processes needed to develop a problem representation. What happens next? What can someone do about a problem after he or she has detected and diagnosed it? We believe that several options are available to the person who first identifies a group problem. These options are summarized in Figure 1.4.

One option that a person might choose is *denying and distorting* the problem he or she has identified (see Jackson, 1956; Lyles & Mitroff, 1980; Raymond, Slaby, & Lieb, 1975; Turner, 1976; Watson, 1976; Yarrow et al., 1955). This option is likely to be chosen when (a) the problem seems severe, but also difficult or impossible to solve; (b) the person feels responsible for causing the problem and may be held accountable for it; and (c) the group is very successful, evokes strong commitment among its members, and discourages problem

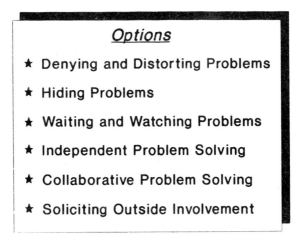

Figure 1.4. What Can Be Done About Group Problems?

identification. Under these conditions, a problem can seem so threatening that someone will prefer to deny its existence as long as possible and then distort the problem in ways that weaken its emotional impact. Of course, denying and distorting a problem may not always be feasible. It is easier if the problem is unfamiliar and complex, the environment is uncertain, and the person lacks expertise. Otherwise, the problem may be so clear and compelling that it must be accepted.

Several tactics could be used by someone trying to deny a problem's existence. For example, the person might avoid situations in which symptomatic events are likely to occur and ignore or discount such events when they do occur. The person could also become less idealistic about the group, so that any symptoms that are acknowledged seem less arousing, or raise his or her arousal threshold for problem-solving activity. Several tactics are also available for distorting a problem in ways that make it seem less threatening. The person might, for example, attribute the person to external/unstable causes (Leary & Forsyth, 1987; Rejeski & Brawley, 1983). If the problem must be attributed to internal causes, blame can often be shifted away from the person onto other group members (Turner, 1976), or excuses may be found that make the person seem less culpable (Snyder, 1985). Other tactics for distorting a problem include minimizing its consequences and imagining that it can be solved easily (Jackson, 1956; Raymond et al., 1975).

Rather than denying and distorting a problem, someone could prefer *hiding* it instead. This option is also likely to be chosen when a person feels responsible for causing the problem and may be held accountable for it (Lyles & Mitroff, 1980). Under these conditions, guilt or fear can overcome any feelings of commitment that the person has for the group. And identifying a problem can sometimes seem more harmful than helpful to a group, by weakening the morale of its members or creating conflicts among them about such issues as who caused the problem or who should solve it (cf. Ancona, 1987; Leary & Forsyth, 1987; Lyles & Mitroff, 1980; Tesser & Rosen, 1975; Watson, 1976). In fact, if problems are viewed as sufficiently disruptive, some group members may assume the role of "mind guards," whose duty is to prevent problem identification from taking place at all (Janis, 1982). But it may not be feasible to hide a problem from other group members. If the problem is familiar and severe, the group engages in extensive scanning of its environment, and many people have the expertise to identify the problem, then it probably cannot be hidden for long.

Someone trying to hide a problem could use a variety of tactics. Detection of the problem might be delayed by preventing symptomatic events from occurring, concealing those events from other group members (by denying or failing to reveal their occurrence), and inducing people to ignore or discount any symptomatic events whose occurrence is noticed. Diagnosis of the problem might be delayed by persuading other members to become less idealistic about the group or raising their arousal thresholds for problem-solving activity. Once a problem has been acknowledged, someone could subvert its diagnosis by offering incorrect diagnoses for the problem or disparaging anyone who diagnoses it correctly. Finally, a general tactic for interfering with the identification of a problem might be to distract group members by identifying other (real or imaginary) problems for them.

Another option that someone could choose after identifying a problem is simply *waiting and watching* to see how it develops. There are several conditions under which this option is likely to be chosen. First, the group may already be faced with other problems that are more urgent. A person who identifies a new problem may thus prefer to put it aside for a while, especially if it seems mild and relatively stable (Cowan, 1986; Gore, 1956; Nutt, 1979). Second, the person may lack confidence in his or her discovery of the problem. Confidence tends to be low when the problem is unfamiliar or complex, the environment is uncertain, and the person lacks expertise or has such personality traits as low self-esteem or intelligence. Waiting and watching a problem can provide valuable information to prove that the problem has been identified correctly. Such information can also be reassuring if the person expects other group members to be skeptical about the problem or is concerned about alarming them unnecessarily (Lyles, 1981; Lyles & Mitroff, 1980; Turner, 1976). Third, there are times when a person might prefer to have someone else in the group identify a problem. For example, if the problem falls within the purview of a particular group member (because of that person's status or expertise), then he or she probably should be the first one to identify it. Someone who has already identified many problems in the past may also feel reluctant to identify new ones, for fear of being labelled as a "troublemaker" (Kiechel, 1990). Finally, the leader of a group may try to evaluate his or her followers by watching how quickly they detect a problem and how accurately they diagnose it.

In principle, waiting and watching a problem are relatively easy. The person simply monitors events within the group, devoting special attention to those that seem symptomatic of the problem. Efforts also may be made to produce events that could confirm the problem's diagnosis. The reactions (or nonreactions) of other group members to symptomatic events might also be informative and thus are likely to be considered. However, in practice, waiting and watching a problem can be more difficult than it seems. The person may feel uneasy about not solving a problem that he or she has already identified. And if other group members later realize that someone identified the problem but failed to inform them about it, the person may be punished in some way. Considerable discretion is thus required to collect useful information about a problem without betraying one's discovery of it.

The three options we have discussed so far are rather unproductive, at least in terms of problem solving. A problem cannot be solved very quickly or efficiently if it is denied or distorted, hidden, or simply watched by group members. Fortunately, there are three other options available to someone who has identified a problem in a group. The remaining options are more productive, because they involve actual attempts by the person to solve the problem.

One option that the person could choose is to conduct *independent problem solving* activities—attempts to solve the problem alone, without seeking any help from other group members. This option is likely to be chosen when the person feels capable of solving the problem alone and thus does not need (or perhaps want) others' help in solving it

(Billings et al., 1980). Such confidence is characteristic of a person with special expertise or high self-esteem. Independent problem solving also is likely to occur when someone feels responsible for causing the problem or would be expected by other group members to solve the problem anyway. These expectations often arise because the person has high status or expertise (Leary & Forsyth, 1987). If the person suspects that other group members will reject his or her discovery of the problem or has tried but failed to win their acceptance of that "discovery," a sense of personal concern might lead again to independent problem solving. Group members may refuse to acknowledge a problem when it is complex and unfamiliar, the group discourages problem identification, the environment is uncertain, and the person who "discovered" the problem has low status and no expertise. Finally, some people choose to solve a problem independently because they hope to be rewarded for their efforts later on (Leary & Forsyth, 1987). This hope is founded on two general beliefs, namely that the person can indeed solve the problem alone and that the group (or certain outsiders) will someday acknowledge that he or she discovered the problem.

Like waiting and watching a problem, independent problem solving is easier in principle than in practice. One major issue to consider is whether the group will ever acknowledge the problem. If acknowledgment seems impossible, attempts to solve the problem need not be concealed from other group members, as long as their personal activities are not disturbed by those attempts. Of course, the person will never be rewarded by the group for solving the "problem," but self-praise can often be just as motivating, especially when the person is strongly committed to the group. However, if acknowledgment of the problem by the group seems possible, independent problem solving becomes much more complicated. The person must consider a second major issue: Can he or she indeed solve the problem alone? The less confident someone is about solving a problem without the help of others, the more careful he or she should be to conceal any problem-solving activities. If the group later acknowledges the problem and realizes that one of its members identified that problem earlier but tried and failed to solve it alone, that person is likely to be punished in some way.

Another option that could be chosen by someone who has identified a group problem is to conduct *collaborative problem solving* activities. These activities begin by discussing with other group members how the problem was detected and diagnosed. Arguments often follow about whether the problem really exists and what its true nature might be

(Lyles, 1987; Narayanan & Fahey, 1982). Attempts to actually solve the problem become possible only when someone with sufficient authority in the group imposes a problem diagnosis on other members or a majority of the members agree on their own diagnosis of the problem.

There are several conditions under which someone might choose to conduct collaborative problem solving. First, the person may lack confidence in his or her discovery of the problem and thus value social comparison information from other group members (cf. Festinger, 1954; Latané & Darley, 1970). As we noted earlier, such confidence tends to be low when the problem is unfamiliar or complex, the environment is uncertain, and the person lacks expertise or has such personality traits as low self-esteem or intelligence. If the problem seems severe and insoluble, the person may even hope to be convinced that he or she has identified it incorrectly. Second, the person may expect to be rewarded by other members for identifying a problem in the group. Assuming that the group acknowledges that problem, the person is more likely to be rewarded when the problem is severe (but soluble) and the group encourages problem identification. Group members also may be more impressed if the person's discovery surprises them (e.g., no one else was aware of the problem or the person never identified problems before). Finally, the person may feel confident about identifying the problem correctly, but doubtful about his or her ability to solve the problem alone. Doubts of this sort can arise because the problem is severe, other group members have more expertise, or the person has low self-esteem.

If the person wants to convince the group that he or she has identified a problem correctly, a variety of tactics can be used. Someone who has sufficient authority can simply impose his or her diagnosis of the problem on the group. Someone who has enough allies in the group (or among outsiders) can achieve the same goal by mustering their support (Narayanan & Fahey, 1982). Otherwise, more subtle tactics may be required (see Kiechel, 1990; Lyles, 1981; Smith, 1989; Volkema, 1986).

The existence of a problem often can be verified by providing the group with evidence of symptomatic events. Facts and figures usually are more effective in this regard than anecdotes about personal experiences (cf. Taylor & Thompson, 1982). Once group members agree that symptomatic events have indeed occurred, the person can try to dramatize those events or idealize the group (so that the problem's symptoms seem more arousing), or lower everyone's arousal thresholds for problem solving activity. If the group agrees that a problem exists and should be solved, the person must also convince its members to accept his or her diagnosis of that problem. Some common mistakes in this regard include (a) focusing on issues of internal blame while discussing the problem's causes; (b) exaggerating the consequences of the problem without also suggesting ways to solve it; and (c) insisting that the problem can only be solved in one way. It may also be necessary to simplify diagnoses of complex or unfamiliar problems, perhaps by drawing analogies to problems that the group has solved before or by providing metaphors that group members are likely to appreciate. Of course, some people are simply more persuasive than others, regardless of the tactics they use. For example, a person whose motives seem altruistic rather than selfish (Ridgeway, 1982), who has high status and expertise, or who has helped the group to solve problems before, will generally be more persuasive.

Finally, someone who has identified a problem in a group always has the option of *soliciting outside involvement* (see Dozier & Miceli, 1985; Jackson, 1956; Yarrow et al., 1955). Like collaborative problem solving, this option requires the person to discuss with other people how the problem was detected and diagnosed. It may also involve arguments with those people about whether the problem really exists and what its true nature might be. The difference is that these discussions and arguments are with people (e.g., relatives, customers, enemies) who do not actually belong to the group.

Outside involvement often is solicited when a person fails to convince a group to acknowledge whatever problem he or she has identified. If the person cannot solve the problem alone, and the group refuses to acknowledge it, a deadlock arises. Sometimes the only way to break that deadlock is to involve outsiders in problem solving. Another condition under which outside help is likely to be solicited is when the group acknowledges a problem that the person has identified, but after repeated attempts seems unable to solve it. Failure to solve a problem can occur because it has been diagnosed inaccurately or because its solution requires resources (e.g., money, equipment, personnel) that the group does not possess or has already committed elsewhere. In either case, outsiders can help by providing a more accurate diagnosis of the problem or by supplying the necessary resources. Some groups may be capable of solving problems themselves, but solicit the help of outsiders because group members have low self-esteem or external loci of control or because outsiders seem to have more expertise. Finally, there are two other, less common conditions that might lead a person to inform outsiders about a group's problems. First, some of those outsiders, such as prospective or ex-members of the group and owners, may have considerable personal investments in the group. Thus it might seem unethical to conceal any serious problems from such persons. Second, the person might be angry at the group and seek to harm it by informing certain people, such as customers or enemies, about its problems.

Someone who hopes to involve outsiders in solving a group problem should begin by considering his or her audience carefully. Outsiders vary in several important ways, including their (a) likelihood of acknowledging the problem, (b) ability to solve the problem, (c) motivation to help the group, and (d) power over group members. These and other variables can be helpful in predicting what outsiders will do when the problem is revealed to them. Outsiders selected as an appropriate audience next must be convinced that the person has identified the problem correctly. Many of the persuasion tactics mentioned earlier could be useful here as well, but might need to be adjusted to reflect the facts that outsiders generally know less than group members about recent events in the group, are less aroused by the problem's symptoms and have higher arousal thresholds for problem solving activity, and are more objective in their opinions about the problem's causes, consequences, and cures.

Once outsiders have acknowledged a problem, they can try to help solve it. If the problem has already been acknowledged by the group, help from outsiders may be accepted, if not welcomed, by group members. However, if the problem has not yet been acknowledged, outsiders will have to impose their diagnosis of it on the group (if they have sufficient authority) or convince group members to accept their diagnosis using other, subtler tactics. In either case, help from outsiders is unlikely to be welcomed and may even be rejected. And the person's role in seeking that help will almost certainly be discovered by other group members, who may decide to punish him or her in some way (Near & Miceli, 1986).

Before we move on, two general points should be made regarding the various options that someone who has identified a group problem can consider. First, our descriptions of these options may imply that they are always pursued by an individual group member. Yet each option also could be pursued by a clique within the group. The members of that clique might help one another to deny and distort a problem or to hide that problem from the rest of the group, or they might decide to wait and watch a problem together, solve it on their own, or ask outsiders to help solve the problem. Of course, different cliques within the group might argue about whether a problem really exists or what its true nature might be.

The second point involves relationships among the various options. Our descriptions of the options may imply that they are mutually exclusive and that only one option can be pursued by a given person (or clique). Few of the options, however, actually preclude one another. For example, a person might reveal a problem to both group members and outsiders at the same time, or try to hide a threatening problem after it can no longer be denied or distorted. And, of course, several people (or cliques) could try to pursue various options simultaneously.

How Can Group Problem Identification Be Studied?

Throughout this chapter, we have attempted to support our analyses of group problem identification by citing relevant research literature, but many of our analyses were speculative because so little research has been done in this area. Field studies, in which researchers try to observe group members while they are identifying problems, are obviously impractical and thus seldom performed (but see Smircich, 1983). Most researchers have chosen to perform other kinds of studies instead. One method involves analyzing archival data that describe the efforts of a group to identify a problem (e.g., Anderson et al., 1987; Burnstein & Berbaum, 1983; Turner, 1976). Another method involves interviewing people about current or previous efforts by their group to identify a problem (e.g., Lyles, 1981; Pounds, 1969; Yarrow et al., 1955). Finally, people are sometimes asked to read a case study describing a group and then to play the role of someone trying to identify its problems (e.g., Frederickson, 1985; Herden & Lyles, 1981).

Although all of these methods are useful, each has its own limitations. The results of archival analyses, for example, depend heavily on the quality of whatever data are available about a group's activities. It can be difficult to determine whether those data are really complete or accurate, and the interpretation of such data can be quite subjective, requiring many "insights" from researchers. The results of interviews depend heavily on the ability and motivation of people to describe their group's activities accurately. Descriptive errors could easily arise from the emotional impact of problems on group members or members' self-presentational concerns. Finally, the results of role-playing studies depend heavily on the realism of the materials that are used. If the materials are unrealistic, reactions to them may not reflect how people would actually identify problems in a group.

There is also a more general methodological issue that should be considered. In order to measure the *speed* with which problems are detected and the *accuracy* with which they are diagnosed by a group, researchers must know exactly *when those problems occurred* and *what kinds of problems they were.* Yet such knowledge is rarely available, at least from archival analyses or interviews with group members. After carefully analyzing archival data, researchers and other experts may claim to know when a group first encountered a problem and what the nature of that problem was. Similar claims may be made by group members during interviews, especially when hindsight allows them to reinterpret previous events. But few of these claims can be verified; they are simply stories about group problem identification that may seem more or less plausible. A better research approach might be to *create problems* for a group and then evaluate how quickly they are detected and how accurately they are diagnosed by its members. This approach clearly would be unethical for studying natural groups in the real world, but it could be used for studying artificial groups in the laboratory. In fact, we believe that laboratory simulations may offer the best means for studying problem identification by groups. Other observers (e.g., Cowan, 1986; Ungson, Braunstein, & Hall, 1981) have expressed the same opinion.

Several kinds of laboratory simulations might be suitable for research on group problem identification. We have been especially interested in the "total enterprise games" (see Keys, 1987) used to teach management skills to students in many business schools. These computerized games require groups of players to operate small "companies" that compete against one another for shares of the consumer "market." Players must make many decisions about such issues as what "products" to offer consumers, how much to pay their "employees," whether to acquire new "equipment," and so on. These decisions affect, through complex algorithms embodied in the computer programs, the performance of the companies. Players receive periodic feedback about their company's performance and can modify their decisions accordingly. In this way, they learn to be more effective managers.

Total enterprise games vary in their sophistication, but the best ones are quite complex and realistic. Most of the games are also enjoyable and elicit considerable involvement from players. This involvement increases as the game progresses; many of the games are played for long time periods (weeks or months). But the most important feature of total enterprise games, at least from our perspective, is that they allow for the creation of problems. The algorithms in each game's computer program can be altered (covertly) by whomever controls the game. This makes it possible to create problems for companies (e.g., decreasing price elasticity or increasing worker turnover) and to know exactly when those problems occur and what kinds of problems they are. As a result, the speed with which problems are detected and the accuracy with which they are diagnosed can be measured more precisely.

For example, we argued earlier that personal expertise often determines which member of a group will identify a particular problem. A simple experiment, in which several groups played the same total enterprise game, could be performed to test this hypothesis. Role assignments would be made in some of the groups, so that each of their members felt responsible and was held accountable for a different aspect of company operations (e.g., production, accounting, marketing). No role assignments would be made in the remaining (control) groups. After all the groups had played the game for a while, the experimenter would create a problem (e.g., decreasing price elasticity) involving the marketing of each company's products. Control groups should detect this problem more slowly, and diagnose it less accurately, than groups whose members were assigned specific roles. In the latter groups, the problem should be identified most often by the person who was assigned the role of marketing specialist. We have recently performed a pilot study in which a total enterprise game was used in this way; the results indicate that laboratory simulation can be a very effective means of studying problem identification by groups.

Conclusions

The productivity of a group often depends on its ability to solve problems quickly and efficiently. Problem solving involves several activities, but the most important of these may be the initial identification of problems by the group. Unfortunately, problem identification is a complex social process that is susceptible to many kinds of errors. Errors in problem identification threaten group productivity, sometimes with disastrous consequences (see Hackett & Cassem, 1969; Jervis,

1976; Murphy, 1980; Turner, 1976). These errors can take several forms, but they are all potentially dangerous.

Some groups overlook problems completely, minimize their severity, or identify them slowly and inefficiently. This negligence can be dangerous, because many problems worsen over time. As time passes, the number of alternative solutions for a problem often decreases, while the difficulty of implementing those solutions increases. Problems that are overlooked, underestimated, or identified ineptly thus can become quite costly to solve. In some cases, they may become insoluble.

Other groups exaggerate the severity of their problems or identify "problems" that may not really exist. This vigilance also can be dangerous, because it produces unnecessary problem solving activities. These activities absorb resources (e.g., time, energy, operating funds, equipment) that could otherwise be devoted to more productive pursuits. The stress associated with trying to solve so many problems may also limit the productivity of group members by creating feelings of anxiety or despair among them.

Finally, many groups misidentify their problems (Lyles, 1981), mistaking one problem for another. This confusion may be the most dangerous error of all (Mitroff & Featheringham, 1974), because it compounds many of the risks already discussed. When problems are misidentified, a group not only wastes valuable resources by conducting unnecessary problem solving activities, but also fails to conduct whatever activities are necessary to solve its real problems. When those real problems are finally identified, the group may be too weak to solve them.

Several observers have offered advice about how groups can avoid these and other errors of problem identification (e.g., Delbecq & Van De Ven, 1971; Kilmann & Mitroff, 1979; Schwenk & Thomas, 1983). But such advice seems premature in the absence of clearer theories and firmer research evidence. The purpose of this chapter was to promote greater interest among social scientists in studying problem identification by groups. We began by analyzing how group members identify their problems. Then we discussed when a group's problems are likely to be identified, who tends to identify those problems, and what people can do about a problem after identifying it. Finally, we suggested some ways in which group problem identification could be studied by researchers.

References

Aguilar, F. (1967). *Scanning the business environment.* New York: Macmillan.

Ancona, D. G. (1987). Groups in organizations: Extending laboratory models. In C. Hendrick (Ed.), *Review of personality and social psychology* (Vol. 9, pp. 207-230). Newbury Park, CA: Sage.

Ancona, D. G., & Caldwell, D. F. (1988). Beyond task and maintenance: Defining external functions in groups. *Group and Organization Studies, 13,* 468-494.

Anderson, R. J., Hughes, J. A., & Sharrock, W. W. (1987). Executive problem finding: Some material and initial observations. *Social Psychology Quarterly, 50,* 143-159.

Bandura, A. (1977). Self-efficacy: Toward a unifying theory of behavioral change. *Psychological Review, 84,* 191-215.

Billings, R. S., Milburn, T. W., & Schaalman, M. L. (1980). A model of crisis perception: A theoretical and empirical analysis. *Administrative Science Quarterly, 25,* 300-316.

Burnstein, E., & Berbaum, M. L. (1983). Stages in group decision making: The decomposition of historical narratives. *Political Psychology, 4,* 531-561.

Carroll, J. S. (1978). The effect of imagining an event on expectations for the event: An interpretation in terms of the availability heuristic. *Journal of Experimental Social Psychology, 14,* 88-96.

Carter, L., Haythorn, W., Shriver, B., & Lanzetta, J. (1950). The behavior of leaders and other group members. *Journal of Abnormal and Social Psychology, 46,* 589-595.

Chi, M.T.H., Glaser, R., & Farr, M. J. (Eds.). (1988). *The nature of expertise.* Hillsdale, NJ: Lawrence Erlbaum.

Cowan, D. A. (1986). Developing a process model of problem recognition. *Academy of Management Review, 11,* 763-776.

Davis, H. L. (1976). Decision making within the household. *Journal of Consumer Research, 2,* 241-260.

Davis, H. L., & Rigaux, B. P. (1974). Perceptions of marital roles in decision processes. *Journal of Consumer Research, 1,* 51-62.

Dean, J. W. (1985). The decision to participate in quality circles. *Journal of Applied Behavioral Science, 21,* 317-327.

Dearborn, D. C., & Simon, H. A. (1958). Selective perception: A note on the departmental identifications of executives. *Sociometry, 21,* 140-144.

Delbecq, A., & Van de Ven, A. (1971). A group process model for problem identification. *Journal of Applied Behavioral Science, 7,* 466-492.

Dozier, J. B., & Miceli, M. F. (1985). Potential predictors of whistle-blowing: A prosocial behavior perspective. *Academy of Management Review, 10,* 823-836.

Duncan, R. B. (1972). Characteristics of organizational environments and perceived environmental uncertainty. *Administrative Science Quarterly, 17,* 313-327.

Dutton, J. E., Fahey, L., & Narayanan, V. K. (1983). Toward understanding strategic issue diagnosis. *Strategic Management Journal, 4,* 307-323.

Dutton, J. E., & Jackson, S. E. (1987). Categorizing strategic issues: Links to organizational action. *Academy of Management Review, 12,* 76-90.

D'Zurilla, T. J., & Goldfried, M. R. (1971). Problem solving and behavior modification. *Journal of Abnormal Psychology, 78,* 107-126.

Farrell, D., & Rusbult, C. E. (1981). Exchange variables as predictors of job satisfaction, job commitment, and turnover: The impact of rewards, costs, alternatives, and investments. *Organizational Behavior and Human Performance, 27*, 78-95.

Feldman, M. S., & March, J. G. (1981). Information in organizations as signal and symbol. *Administrative Science Quarterly, 26*, 171-186.

Festinger, L. (1954). A theory of social comparison processes. *Human Relations, 7*, 117-140.

Frederickson, J. W. (1985). Effects of decision motive and organizational performance level on strategic decision processes. *Academy of Management Journal, 28*, 821-843.

Galaskiewicz, J., & Wasserman, S. (1989). Mimetic processes within an organizational field. *Administrative Science Quarterly, 34*, 454-479.

Gilovich, T. (1981). Seeing the past in the present: The effect of associations to familiar events in judgments and decisions. *Journal of Personality and Social Psychology, 40*, 797-808.

Goetsch, G., & McFarland, D. (1980). Models of the distribution of acts in small discussion groups. *Social Psychology Quarterly, 43*, 173-183.

Goodman, P. S. (1968). The measurement of an individual's organization map. *Administrative Science Quarterly, 13*, 246-265.

Gore, W. J. (1956). Administrative decision-making in federal field offices. *Public Administration Review, 16*, 281-291.

Hackett, T. P., & Cassem, N. H. (1969). Factors contributing to delay in responding to the signs and symptoms of acute myocardial infarction. *The American Journal of Cardiology, 24*, 651-658.

Hedburg, B.L.T., Nystrom, P. C., & Starbuck, W. H. (1976). Camping on seesaws: Prescriptions for a self-designing organization. *Administrative Science Quarterly, 21*, 41-65.

Herden, R. P., & Lyles, M. A. (1981). Individual attributes and the problem conceptualization process. *Human Systems Management, 2*, 275-284.

Hosking, D. M., & Morley, I. E. (1988). The skills of leadership. In J. G. Hunt, B. R. Baliga, H. P. Dachler, & C. A. Schriesheim (Eds.), *Emerging leadership vistas* (pp. 80-106). Lexington, MA: Lexington.

Isen, A. M. (1987). Positive affect, cognitive processes, and social behavior. In L. Berkowitz (Ed.), *Advances in experimental social psychology* (Vol. 20, pp. 203-254). New York: Academic Press.

Jablin, F. M. (1979). Superior-subordinate communication: The state of the art. *Psychological Bulletin, 86*, 1201-1222.

Jackson, J. K. (1956). The adjustment of the family to alcoholism. *Marriage and Family Living, 18*, 361-369.

Janis, I. L. (1982). *Victims of groupthink* (2nd ed.). Boston: Houghton-Mifflin.

Jervis, R. (1976). *Perception and misperception in international politics*. Princeton, NJ: Princeton University Press.

Keys, B. (1987). Total enterprise business games. *Simulation and Games, 18*, 225-241.

Kiechel, W. (1990, April 9). Breaking bad news to the boss. *Fortune*, pp. 111-112.

Kiesler, S., & Sproull, L. (1982). Managerial responses to changing environments: Perspectives on problem sensing from social cognition. *Administrative Science Quarterly, 27*, 548-570.

Kilmann, R. H., & Mitroff, I. I. (1979). Problem defining and the consulting/intervention process. *California Management Review, 21*, 26-33.

Latané, B., & Darley, J. (1970). *The unresponsive bystander: Why doesn't he help?* New York: Appleton-Century-Crofts.

Lau, R. R., & Hartman, K. A. (1983). Common sense representations of common illnesses. *Health Psychology, 2,* 167-185.

Lau, R. R., & Russell, D. (1980). Attributions in the sports pages: A field test of some current hypotheses in attribution research. *Journal of Personality and Social Psychology, 39,* 29-38.

Leary, M. R., & Forsyth, D. R. (1987). Attributions of responsibility for collective endeavors. In C. Hendrick (Ed.), *Review of personality and social psychology* (Vol. 8, pp. 167-188). Newbury Park, CA: Sage.

Leventhal, H., Leventhal, E. A., & Van Nguyen, T. (1985). Reactions of families to illness: Theoretical models and perspectives. In D. C. Turk & R. D. Kerns (Eds.), *Health, illness, and families: A life-span perspective* (pp. 108-145). New York: John Wiley.

Levine, J. M., & Moreland, R. L. (1985). Innovation and socialization in small groups. In S. Moscovici, G. Mugny, & E. Van Avermaet (Eds.), *Perspectives on minority influence* (pp. 143-169). Cambridge: Cambridge University Press.

Levine, J. M., & Moreland, R. L. (1987). Social comparison and outcome evaluation in group contexts. In J. C. Masters & W. P. Smith (Eds.), *Social comparison, social justice, and relative deprivation: Theoretical, empirical, and policy perspectives* (pp. 105-127). Hillsdale, NJ: Lawrence Erlbaum.

Lyles, M. A. (1981). Formulating strategic problems: Empirical analysis and problem development. *Strategic Management Journal, 2,* 61-75.

Lyles, M. A. (1987). Defining strategic problems: Subjective criteria of executives. *Organization Studies, 8,* 263-280.

Lyles, M. A., & Mitroff, I. I. (1980). Organizational problem formulation: An empirical study. *Administrative Science Quarterly, 25,* 109-119.

Lyles, M. A., & Thomas, H. (1988). Strategic problem formulation: Biases and assumptions embedded in alternative decision-making models. *Journal of Management Studies, 25,* 131-145.

Mackie, D. M., & Worth, L. T. (1989). Processing deficits and the mediation of positive affect in persuasion. *Journal of Personality and Social Psychology, 57,* 27-40.

Main, J. (1989, March 13). At last, software CEO's can use. *Fortune,* pp. 77-78, 80-83.

Malley, J. C., & Davis, D. L. (1988). Strategic decision making behavior: Aspects of the problem formulation phase. *Journal of Human Behavior and Learning, 5,* 44-52.

May, E. R. (1973). *"Lessons" of the past: The use and misuse of history in American foreign policy.* London: Oxford University Press.

Mazzolini, R. (1981). How strategic decisions are made. *Long Range Planning, 14,* 85-96.

Miceli, M. P., & Near, J. P. (1985). Characteristics of organizational climate and perceived wrongdoing associated with whistle-blowing decisions. *Personnel Psychology, 38,* 525-544.

Miceli, M. P., & Near, J. P. (1988). Individual and situational correlations of whistle-blowing. *Personnel Psychology, 41,* 267-281.

Milburn, T. W., Schuler, R. S., & Watman, K. H. (1983). Organizational crisis. I. Definition and conceptualization. *Human Relations, 36,* 1141-1160.

Miller, D., Kets de Vries, M.F.R., & Toulouse, J. M. (1982). Top executive locus of control and its relationship to strategy-making, structure, and environment. *Academy of Management Journal, 25,* 237-253.

Mintzberg, H., Raisinghani, D., & Theoret, A. (1976). The structure of "unstructured" decision processes. *Administrative Science Quarterly, 21*, 246-275.

Mitroff, I. I., & Featheringham, T. R. (1974). On systematic problem solving and the error of the third kind. *Behavioral Science, 19*, 383-393.

Mitroff, I. I., & Kilmann, R. H. (1975). The stories managers tell: A new tool for organizational problem solving. *Management Review, 64*, 18-28.

Moreland, R. L., & Levine, J. M. (1982). Socialization in small groups: Temporal changes in individual-group relations. In L. Berkowitz (Ed.), *Advances in experimental social psychology* (Vol. 15, pp. 137-192). New York: Academic Press.

Murphy, M. R. (1980). Analysis of 84 commercial aviation accidents: Implications for a resource management approach to crew training. *Proceedings of the Annual Reliability & Maintainability Symposium, 163*, 298-306.

Narayanan, V. K., & Fahey, L. (1982). The micro-politics of strategy formulation. *Academy of Management Review, 7*, 25-34.

Near, J. P., & Miceli, M. P. (1986). Retaliation against whistle blowers: Predictors and effects. *Journal of Applied Psychology, 71*, 137-145.

Nezu, A., & D'Zurilla, T. J. (1981). Effects of problem definition and formulation on the generation of alternatives in the social problem-solving process. *Cognitive Therapy and Research, 5*, 265-271.

Nutt, P. C. (1979). Calling out and calling off the dogs: Managerial diagnosis in public service organizations. *Academy of Management Review, 4*, 203-214.

Nutt, P. C. (1984). Types of organizational decision processes. *Administrative Science Quarterly, 29*, 414-450.

Pfeffer, J. (1981). Management as symbolic action: The creation and maintenance of organizational paradigms. In L. L. Cummings & B. M. Staw (Eds.), *Research in organizational behavior* (Vol. 3, pp. 1-52). Greenwich, CT: JAI.

Phillips, J. S., & Lord, R. G. (1982). Schematic information processing and perceptions of leadership in problem-solving groups. *Journal of Applied Psychology, 67*, 486-492.

Pounds, W. F. (1969). The process of problem finding. *Industrial Management Review, 11*, 1-19.

Ramaprasad, A., & Mitroff, I. I. (1984). On formulating strategic problems. *Academy of Management Review, 9*, 597-605.

Raymond, M. E., Slaby, A. E., & Lieb, J. (1975). Familial response to mental illness. *Social Casework, 56*, 492-498.

Rejeski, W. J., & Brawley, L. R. (1983). Attribution theory in sport: Current status and new perspectives. *Journal of Sport Psychology, 5*, 77-99.

Ridgeway, C. L. (1982). Status in groups: The importance of motivation. *American Sociological Review, 47*, 76-88.

Rogers, R. W. (1983). Cognitive and physiological processes in fear appeals and attitude change: A revised theory of protective motivation. In J. T. Cacioppo & R. E. Petty (Eds.), *Social psychophysiology: A sourcebook* (pp. 153-176). New York: Guilford.

Rusbult, C. E., Farrell, D., Rogers, G., & Mainous, A. G. (1988). Impact of exchange variables on exit, voice, loyalty, and neglect: An integrative model of responses to declining job satisfaction. *Academy of Management Journal, 31*, 599-627.

Schwenk, C. R. (1984). Cognitive simplification processes in strategic decision-making. *Strategic Management Journal, 5*, 111-128.

Schwenk, C. R., & Thomas, H. (1983). Formulating the mess: The role of decision aids in problem formulation. *Omega, 11*, 239-252.

Smart, C., & Vertinsky, I. (1984). Strategy and the environment: A study of corporate responses to crises. *Strategic Management Journal, 5,* 199-213.

Smircich, L. (1983). Organizations as shared meanings. In L. R. Pondy, P. Frost, G. Morgan, & T. Dandridge (Eds.), *Organizational symbolism* (pp. 55-65). Greenwich, CT: JAI.

Smith, G. F. (1988). Towards a heuristic theory of problem structuring. *Management Science, 34,* 1489-1506.

Smith, G. F. (1989). Defining managerial problems: A framework for prescriptive theorizing. *Management Science, 35,* 963-981.

Snyder, C. R. (1985). The excuse: An amazing grace? In B. R. Schlenker (Ed.), *The self and social life* (pp. 235-260). New York: McGraw-Hill.

Stasser, G., Kerr, N. L., & Davis, J. H. (1989). Influence processes and consensus models in decision-making groups. In P. B. Paulus (Ed.), *Psychology of social influence* (2nd ed., pp. 279-326). Hillsdale, NJ: Lawrence Erlbaum.

Staw, B. M., & Ross, J. (1989). Understanding behavior in escalation situations. *Science, 246,* 216-220.

Stein, A. A. (1976). Conflict and cohesion: A review of the literature. *Journal of Conflict Resolution, 20,* 143-172.

Stryker, S., & Serpe, R. T. (1982). Commitment, identity salience, and role behavior: Theory and research example. In W. Ickes & E. S. Knowles (Eds.), *Personality, roles, and social behavior* (pp. 199-218). New York: Springer-Verlag.

Tajfel, H., & Turner, J. C. (1986). The social identity theory of intergroup behavior. In S. Worchel & W. G. Austin (Eds.), *Psychology of intergroup relations* (pp. 7-24). Chicago: Nelson-Hall.

Taylor, R. N. (1975). Psychological determinants of bounded rationality: Implications for decision-making strategies. *Decision Sciences, 6,* 409-429.

Taylor, S. E., & Thompson, S. C. (1982). Stalking the elusive "vividness" effect. *Psychological Review, 89,* 155-181.

Tesser, A., & Rosen, S. (1975). The reluctance to transmit bad news. In L. Berkowitz (Ed.), *Advances in experimental social psychology* (Vol. 8, pp. 194-232). New York: Academic Press.

Turner, B. (1976). The organizational and interorganizational development of disasters. *Administrative Science Quarterly, 21,* 378-397.

Ungson, G. R., Braunstein, D. N., & Hall, P. D. (1981). Managerial information processing: A research review. *Administrative Science Quarterly, 26,* 116-134.

Volkema, R. J. (1986). Problem formulation as a purposive activity. *Strategic Management Journal, 7,* 267-279.

Wallston, K. A., & Wallston, B. S. (1982). Who is responsible for your health? The construct of health locus of control. In G. Sanders & J. Suls (Eds.), *Social psychology of health and illness* (pp. 189-243). Hillsdale, NJ: Lawrence Erlbaum.

Watson, C. E. (1976). The problems of problem solving. *Business Horizons, 19,* 88-94.

Wegner, D. M. (1987). Transactive memory: A contemporary analysis of the group mind. In B. Mullen & G. R. Goethals (Eds.), *Theories of group behavior* (pp. 185-208). New York: Springer-Verlag.

Weiner, B. (1985). "Spontaneous" causal thinking. *Psychological Bulletin, 97,* 74-84.

Yarrow, M. R., Schwartz, C. G., Murphy, H. S., & Deasy, L. L. (1955). The psychological meaning of mental illness in the family. *Journal of Social Issues, 11,* 12-24.

Zander, A. (1971). *Motives and goals in groups.* New York: Academic Press.

2 Pooling of Unshared Information During Group Discussion

Garold Stasser

Groups are often maligned. They are described as inefficient, un-imaginative, and unproductive (Anderson, 1978; Buys, 1978; Tillman, 1960). They are prone to various dysfunctions ranging from suppress-ing minority opinions to instilling overconfidence in members (Janis, 1982). Yet, we endure these shortcomings and continue to trust impor-tant matters to the deliberations of groups. In part, the appeal of decision-making groups stems from the democratic ideal that people should be able to impact decisions that affect them; in many contexts, this ideal is most easily realized by using committees, juries, and the like. Moreover, the notion that participation in a decision engenders commitment is frequently offered as justification for delegating deci-sions to groups. In addition to the democratic ideal and the desire to foster commitment, there is the belief that groups potentially benefit from the diversity of knowledge, experience, and points of view that their membership brings to bear on a decision. As a result, group decisions are thought to be better informed than individual decisions.

Although there seemingly is merit to the idea that groups can, in principle, benefit from pooling members' knowledge and expertise, the degree to which they, in practice, realize this benefit is open to question. The presumed benefit depends on two conditions. First, at least some

AUTHOR'S NOTE: Preparation of this manuscript was supported by National Science Foundation Grant BNS 8721844 to the author.

48

of the members must bring to the group unique information that others do not have; otherwise, there is no unique information to pool. Second, such unique information must be mentioned during discussion; otherwise, the collective decision does not benefit. The necessity of these conditions to enhancing the informational base for group decisions is self-evident, but I want to examine the second condition more closely. One implication of the research that will be discussed in this chapter is that groups tend to talk about what all the members already know rather than to exchange information that is held by single members.

Why would group members fail to disclose information that others do not have but instead rehash what everyone already knows? The group performance literature offers several possible answers. Many of these answers fit the "groups are bad" and, more aptly, "people in groups are bad" themes (Anderson, 1978; Buys, 1978). Group members may fail to disclose uniquely held information because they are lazy or uninvolved (Harkins, Latané, & Williams, 1980; Kerr, 1983; Petty, Harkins & Williams, 1980), they diffuse responsibility (Myers & Lamm, 1976), or they conform to majority pressures (Asch, 1956). These sorts of "bad things" undoubtedly occur, and when they do, they probably interfere with effective information exchange. However, this chapter considers a different explanation that is based on a model of how members sample information for group discussion. This model does not need to presume that members are loafing, conforming, or conniving to explain why group discussion can fail to effectively disseminate information.

After presenting the information sampling model, I will consider hidden profiles—cases that seem to be tailored to demonstrate the advantage of group, over individual, decision making. A hidden profile exists when the superiority of one decision alternative over others is masked because each member is aware of only part of its supporting information, but the group, by pooling its information, can reveal to all the superior option. I will review evidence suggesting that sampling dynamics counter the discovery of such hidden profiles when they exist.

Finally, I will consider some implications of viewing discussion as an information sampling process. For example, what might be the effect of explicitly linking certain kinds of unique information to salient roles within the group? That is, does it help when a committee knows that the accountant knows about financial matters, the lawyer knows the law, and the marketing director knows how to sell things? For another example, does it matter whether the group views the decision task as a problem to be solved or a judgment to be made?

Information Sampling During Group Discussion

Burnstein and Vinokur (1977; see also Burnstein & Schul, 1983) argued that group polarization (i.e., shifts of opinion to more extreme positions as a result of discussion) could be understood in terms of argument sampling during group discussion. Their persuasive arguments theory proposed that each group member brings to discussion a set of arguments that were sampled from a culturally shared pool of arguments. Their explanation of group polarization rests on the idea that what members bring to discussion determines not only their initial opinions but also their contributions to discussion. Thus, discussion will tend to bolster the dominant sentiment within the group. An important proposition in their theory is that original arguments, arguments held by one or few members, are particularly persuasive. In general, more polarization is expected when each member brings a unique set of arguments than when all members bring the same arguments.

Stasser and Titus (1985, 1987) viewed information sampling during group discussion in a similar way. When discussing decision alternatives, members sample from a pool of information that is a repository of previous experience. However, items in this pool may not be available to all members before discussion. Moreover, the likelihood that an item is mentioned during discussion depends on the number of members who have had prior exposure to the item. Thus, for example, if all of the members of a graduate admissions committee had read a reference letter that alluded to an academic dishonesty incident, this information would be more likely to be mentioned in their discussion of applicants than if only one member had read the letter.

Part of a decision-making group's task is to recall critical information. In other words, group decision making entails group remembering (Clark & Stephenson, 1989; Hartwick, Sheppard, & Davis, 1982). There is usually a large number of items that the group can recall during discussion, but for the moment, let us focus on the task of recalling one particular item. For this item to come to the immediate attention of the group, only one member needs to recall and mention it during the course of discussion. As such, the recall of an item by the group has a disjunctive quality. In Steiner's (1972) typology of group tasks, a *disjunctive task* is one that is successfully accomplished by the whole group if any one member succeeds. For such tasks the likelihood of group success increases as the number of potentially successful members increases.

Stasser and Titus (1987) stated this relationship more formally as it applies to sampling a critical item during discussion. Suppose that each individual with prior exposure to an item would mention the item with some probability, $p(M)$. Because only one group member needs to mention the item to bring it to the immediate attention of the group, the group will fail to discuss the item only if *all* members *fail* to mention it. This reasoning allows one to express the probability that a group will discuss a particular item, $p(D)$, as follows:

$$p(D) = 1 - [1 - p(M)]^n \qquad (1)$$

where n is the number of members who were exposed to the item before discussion.

The relationship expressed in equation 1 is not new. Steiner (1972), drawing on earlier work by Lorge and Solomon (1955), proposed a similar model for describing group performance on disjunctive tasks. Indeed, Lorge and Solomon (1962) used such a formulation to predict group performance on a free recall task. More recently, Clark and Stephenson (1989) reviewed evidence for such a disjunctive process in collaborative recall where the primary task of the group is to remember previously encountered material. For such tasks, groups tend to perform better than individuals but not as well as would be expected for a disjunctive task. That is, accurate recall of an item of information by one member apparently does not guarantee that the group will include that item in their collectively endorsed recall protocol.

There is, however, an important distinction between mentioning information during discussion en route to a decision (the focus in this chapter) and the more general process of collaborative recall as discussed by Clark and Stephenson (1989). Collaborative recall entails not only mentioning information during group interaction but also typically involves a collective judgment about the veracity or importance of the recalled item. For example, a collaborative recall task may require the group to develop a summary of their recall and, as a result, to decide what information to retain in that summary. The information retained in the group protocol may be considerably less than the total information mentioned during the group's discussion. The focus in this chapter is on the simpler problem of whether information is mentioned at all during the group's discussion. This focus does not imply that members' perceptions of the validity and relevance of information that is mentioned during discussion are unimportant in decision-making groups.

These are clearly important issues but they go beyond collective information sampling per se.

Figure 2.1 displays the relationship, as specified in equation 1, between the probability of an individual mentioning an item and the probability of the group discussing the item for various values of n. It is evident in Figure 2.1 that, in general, the chances of an item being discussed increase as n, the number of members who have prior knowledge of the item, increases. This increase in the probability of discussion due to more members having the item before discussion can be quite large, particularly when $p(M)$ is in the range of .1 to .5.

This way of viewing information sampling during discussion reveals a possible weakness of group discussion as a mechanism for pooling items that are held by individual members. In general, the relationships summarized in equation 1 and displayed in Figure 2.1 suggest that groups are more likely to discuss items that all (or most) members already know than items that only one (or a few) members know.

Stasser and Titus (1985, 1987) considered two extreme cases. In their terms, *shared* information is information that all members have before discussion whereas *unshared* information is available to only one member prior to discussion. We can think of information pooling as being the process of members informing one another of unshared information. However, in equation 1, n is by definition equal to 1 for unshared information while n is equal to group size for shared. Or, in Figure 2.1, the probability of discussing unshared information is given by the straight line for which $n = 1$, while the probability of discussing shared information is given by one of the higher curves for which n equals group size. Several implications of these relationships are relevant to the pooling function of group discussion.

First, other things being equal, shared information often is much more likely to be discussed than is unshared information. For example, suppose that members of a three-person group mention about 30% of the information that they bring to discussion; that is, let $p(M) = 0.3$. Then the probability of an unshared item being discussed is 0.3, but the probability of a shared item being mentioned is 0.66. In other words, shared information has a *sampling advantage* over unshared information (Stasser, Taylor, & Hanna, 1989). The size of the sampling advantage is depicted graphically in Figure 2.1 as the vertical distance between the straight line for unshared information (i.e., $n = 1$) and the applicable curved line (for n equal to group size).

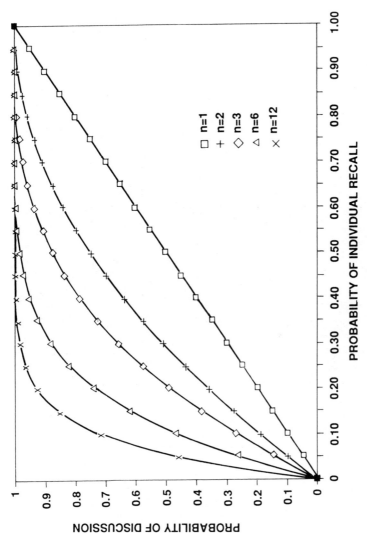

Figure 2.1. The Probability of an Item Being Discussed as a Function of the Probability That an Individual Will Recall and Mention the Item and the Number, *N*, of Individuals Who Can Recall the Item.

Second, this sampling advantage favoring unshared information depends on group size. In the foregoing example, if group size were six rather than three, the probability of discussing a shared item would be 0.88, but the probability of mentioning an unshared item would remain at 0.3. (To keep the example simple, I have assumed that increasing group size does not affect $p(M)$; in fact, increasing group size may decrease the opportunities that individual members have to contribute and, thus, decrease $p(M)$. But this possibility does not change the point that I have; it only suggests another way in which group size may impact the relative probabilities of mentioning shared and unshared items.)

Third, the degree to which shared information has a sampling advantage over unshared depends on the level of $p(M)$. The advantage can be quite substantial for low to moderate values of $p(M)$ but disappears in the extremes (as $p(M)$ approaches 0 or 1). Moreover, as Stasser and Titus (1987) noted, the range that yields the largest sampling advantage to shared information depends partly on group size.

Stasser, Taylor, and Hanna (1989) examined these relationships by noting the relative frequencies with which shared and unshared items were discussed in three- and six-person groups. Before discussion, they gave university students descriptions of three hypothetical candidates for student body president. These descriptions were constructed so that some information about the candidates was read by every member in a group (shared information) whereas other information was read by only one of the members (unshared information). Groups discussed the candidates and decided which candidate was the best qualified. Overall, groups discussed 45% of the shared information but only 18% of the unshared information. This difference between the percentages of shared and unshared information discussed was larger for six-person than for three-person groups.

Stasser et al. (1989) also instructed some of their groups to follow a structured discussion procedure that increased the amount of information discussed. What is interesting about this manipulation is that it had only a slight effect on the proportions of unshared information discussed but had a substantial effect on the proportions of shared information discussed. This was particularly true for six-person groups. When discussions were unstructured, six-person groups discussed 15% of unshared and 48% of shared information. In comparison, structuring discussions increased the percentage of unshared information discussed to a modest 23% but increased the percentage of shared information discussed to an impressive 67%. In terms of Figure 2.1, the net effect of structuring discussion was to move $p(M)$ into a range where the sampling advantage to shared information was greater.

Although these results were anticipated by the information sampling model of discussion, they are nonetheless disconcerting if one believes that a major virtue of group decision making is the opportunity to exchange unshared information. These groups spent most of their time talking about information that all members already had and relatively little time exchanging unshared information. In fact, most of the unshared information was never mentioned during their discussions. Equally disconcerting is the finding that structuring discussion, which seemingly should improve matters, actually led to discussions being more dominated by already shared information. Urging groups to discuss more or invoking procedures that encourage a more systematic review of information will not necessarily alleviate the problem and may even aggravate it.

Hidden Profiles

What I have said could be much ado about nothing if information was always distributed among members before discussion so that shared and unshared items tended to favor, in the balance, the same decision alternative. In such cases, the degree to which groups discussed shared versus unshared information would have little impact on their decision. Of course, if shared and unshared information led to the same outcome, the presumed advantage that pooling information gives groups, relative to individuals, in decision making would also diminish. That is, if members' commonly held information favored the same decision as their uniquely held information, individuals and groups would tend to endorse the same outcome. In such a case, group discussion might increase confidence or make people feel more involved, but it would not lead to an emergent consensus that differed from the predominant individual sentiment.

However, it is not difficult to imagine a situation in which unshared information supports a different outcome than shared information. Suppose that a corporate board, a small board of three to keep the example manageable, was to decide between two mutually exclusive courses of action, A and B. Furthermore, as depicted in Table 2.1, suppose that all three members knew of three reasons to favor B (denoted b_1, b_2, and b_3) but only one reason to favor A (a_1); that is,

Table 2.1
A Simple Example of a Hidden Profile

Group Member	Information Supporting A	Information Supporting B
X	$a_1\ a_x$	$b_1\ b_2\ b_3$
Y	$a_1\ a_y$	$b_1\ b_2\ b_3$
Z	$a_1\ a_z$	$b_1\ b_2\ b_3$

shared information favored B three to one. If each member also had an additional unshared reason to favor A, (a_x, a_y, and a_z for members X, Y, and Z, respectively), then B would still appear to be better to each of them but collectively they would have information that favored A on the whole. Of course, for them to recognize the superiority of A, they would need to exchange their unshared items.

Stasser (1988) labeled such situations *hidden profiles* because individuals in the group cannot see that the collective profile of information favors an alternative that to each individual appears to be inferior. Hidden profiles can be revealed if members do, in fact, pool their unshared information. When faced with a hidden profile, the group potentially can make a better decision than any one of the members alone. Unfortunately, the information sampling model suggests that groups will often fail to discover a hidden profile precisely because they tend to discuss already shared information and fail to exchange unshared information.

Stasser and Titus (1985) constructed hidden profiles that were more complex than the one illustrated in Table 2.1. Students read descriptions of three candidates for student body president. One of these candidates, A, had a larger number of positive attributes (characteristics that were regarded as desirable by an independent sample) than the other two candidates. In fact, when students were given all of the information about the three candidates, 67% of them favored A with the remaining 33% split evenly between the other two candidates. When groups were composed of members who had complete information before discussion, 83% picked A as their group decision.

In other conditions, hidden profiles were realized by giving each member of a four-person group one fourth of the positive information about A. (Adding to the hidden profile, negative information about the other two inferior candidates was also unshared.) The hidden profile distribution of information reduced prediscussion support for A to 23% as intended. It is critical to note, however, that groups collectively had all of the information about the candidates and were in a position to discover the superiority of A if they exchanged unshared information. In contrast to the 83% of groups who picked A when all information was shared before discussion, only 18% of the groups given a hidden profile chose A.

There are at least two explanations of this result. One is provided by the sampling model and the results of Stasser et al. (1989): Group discussions may have been dominated by already shared information, and thus most of the critical unshared information was not mentioned. It is inherent in the nature of hidden profiles that discussion of shared information will interfere with discovering the decision alternative that is favored by the total pool of information.

Stasser and Titus (1985) offered another explanation. Group members may have adopted an advocacy role. That is, they may have attempted to justify or defend their initial preferences. Because a hidden profile is structured so that members initially tend to favor the alternative(s) supported by shared information, an advocacy stance would have unwittingly led them to select information that was already shared and to avoid discussing the unshared information that favored the best, but initially unpopular, candidate.

These two explanations of groups' failures to discover hidden profiles are not mutually exclusive. Indeed, an advocacy approach may tend to enhance the sampling advantage to shared information in the face of a hidden profile. Stasser (1988) used a simulation model of group decision making, DISCUSS, to determine whether the sampling advantage to shared information was sufficient to explain Stasser and Titus's (1985) results or whether one needed to assume that members were also biasing their contributions to support their extant preferences.

DISCUSS is a computer model that simulates the processes of members sampling information during discussion and revising their preferences in light of new information received. Two versions of the model were used. A *nonadvocacy* version simulated a process whereby each member sampled randomly from memory for items to discuss whereas an *advocacy* version biased their sampling in favor of information that supported their current preferences. In both versions, members' preferences were updated as they received new or forgotten information during the course of discussion, and the simulated discussions stopped when a consensus was reached. When fed the patterns of information that Stasser and Titus (1985) used to create hidden profiles, both versions were able to reproduce the distributions of prediscussion preferences and group decisions observed in their study. The success of both the nonadvocacy and the advocacy versions of the model does not allow us to rule out the possibility that members biased their contributions to discussion. However, the fact that the nonadvocacy version was able to account for the results suggests that, even if members were unbiased in selecting their contributions to discussion, the groups would have still failed to discover the hidden profiles.

Hidden profiles seemingly represent a critical class of problems for studying group decision-making effectiveness. In Steiner's (1972) terminology, the group's potential is greater than the potential of any member (even its best member) when a hidden profile exists. But the available empirical evidence suggests that face-to-face discussion en route to a decision is an ineffective way of realizing this potential. Of course, one might wonder if hidden profiles are merely laboratory curiosities and not of much practical concern. Unfortunately, we do not know how often they arise naturally in nonlaboratory decision environments. By their very nature, hidden profiles that are not revealed during group interaction remain hidden, and thus, as far as the group members know, never existed.

The Fate of Unshared Information

I have argued that group discussion is not a reliable means of pooling diverse information, a process that is often thought to be a primary function of decision-making groups. Moreover, we need not presume that group members are performing badly to account for the fact that group discussion seems to focus on already shared information. In fact, we need only presume that members do not discuss all of the information that they have at their disposal (i.e., $p(M)$ in equation 1 is substantially less than 1) to understand why shared information is more likely than unshared to enter discussion. There are many things that work against complete recall of information during discussion. Human memories are faulty at best, and the distractions that accompany group interaction undoubtedly interfere with recalling and communicating information (Diehl & Stroebe, 1987). Discussion time must be shared, and as a result, opportunities to contribute are curtailed. Moreover, attention is often focused on reaching a consensus, and naturally members may be more concerned with understanding and assimilating information that is mentioned early in discussion than with searching for more information. In sum, many things conspire to keep recall during discussion less than complete; we need not assume that members are unmotivated, irresponsible, or shortsighted.

Maintaining that cooperative and well intentioned groups can unwittingly overlook hidden profiles is not meant to suggest that motivational factors are irrelevant. For example, many issues and social contexts may elicit mixed motives. A member may want the group to make a good decision, but he or she may oppose some decision alternatives for personal reasons. In this event, the member may strategically withhold unshared information to avoid the group's endorsing the personally undesirable option. Additionally, there are often incentives to hoard information, either because it can be used to one's advantage later or because ownership of specialized knowledge enhances one's social status (Bonacich, 1987; Hackman & Morris, 1983). Such individualistic motives undoubtedly hamper the effective pooling of information.

Moreover, to this point, I have been primarily concerned with whether information is mentioned during discussion and have said little about what happens after it is mentioned. There are reasons to believe that, even when it is mentioned, unshared information may have limited impact on a group's decision. For example, Stasser et al. (1989) found that discussions were less likely to return to unshared, than to shared, items. That is, unshared items were not only less likely to be brought up in the first place, but if they were brought up, they were also less likely to be repeated during subsequent discussion. In addition, Clark and Stephenson (1989) noted that collective recall often entails an element of consensual validation. If one member recalls an item that no other member can corroborate, the group may omit that item when generating a written account of their recall. Similarly, in decision-making groups, members may discount or ignore an unshared item after it is mentioned because no one else can attest to its validity.

In sum, many processes, in addition to collective information sampling, can diminish the impact of unshared information on collective decisions. To say the least, presuming that decision-making groups effectively pool their members' specialized knowledge is risky. This conclusion seemingly fits the "groups are bad" theme that I mentioned earlier. However, I prefer to think of groups as being bad for doing some things in some situations. As Hackman and Morris (1983; see also Murnighan, 1981) noted, we should be more attuned to the limitations

of group performance and not so disappointed when groups fail to do
what they are not well designed to do. A worthwhile goal for group
research and theory is to identify task, situational, and procedural
factors that enhance as well as diminish group performance. In this
spirit, the remainder of this chapter uses the information sampling
model to identify some conditions that may facilitate the exchange of
unshared information during discussion.

Facilitating the Exchange of Unshared Information

Extensive Information Recall

One thing that is evident from examining Figure 2.1 is that modest
increases in the likelihood that information will be discussed can benefit shared more than unshared information. For example, increasing
$p(M)$ from 0.2 to 0.3 will not help much if the goal is to facilitate the
exchange of unshared information. However, Figure 2.1 also suggests
that increasing $p(M)$ to and beyond 0.5 should enhance the sampling of
unshared more than shared information, particularly for groups of more
than two members. The lesson is that modest increases in low levels of
recall during discussion may not help much whereas conditions that
lead to high levels of recall should help considerably when the goal is
to promote the exchange of unshared information.

One implication is that when members have little information to
remember, they may recall and discuss more unshared information during discussion. Stasser and Titus (1987) obtained indirect evidence for
this implication. They constructed four different versions of a task
which varied the amount of information given to members before discussion. At one extreme, each member received only six items (low
information load); at the other extreme, each member received 18 items
(high information load) about each of three decision alternatives. As a
measure of information dissemination, Stasser and Titus (1987) computed the proportion of unshared items that members recalled after
discussion that they had *not* received before discussion. To recall such
an item, a member would have had to hear it during discussion. When
information load was low, members recalled 24% of the items that they
did not receive before discussion, but under high load, they recalled
only 8% of such items. This result is not a direct test of the patterns
predicted by Figure 2.1 because discussion content was not recorded.

Undoubtedly postdiscussion recall provided a somewhat insensitive measure of the frequency with which unshared items were mentioned during discussion. Additionally, there was no way to determine how much information was discussed overall (and, thus, no way to estimate $p(M)$ in Figure 2.1). Nonetheless, it seems that groups were better at disseminating unshared information when information load was low.

Of course, many decision tasks involve high information loads, and knowing that groups pool information more effectively when information load is light provides little comfort in these cases. Still any procedure that promotes discussing most of the information that is held by members should help. Under high information loads, promoting such an extensive discussion entails several problems. One is the problem of ensuring that members can recall large quantities of information under the deleterious conditions provided by group discussion. Another is the problem of giving members ample time to contribute what they can recall. To solve both of these problems may require a highly structured, multifaceted technique such as the Nominal Groups Technique (NGT) (Delbecq, Van de Ven, & Gustafson, 1975). NGT uses several procedures that may substantially improve recall: writing down ideas before discussion starts and using memory aids such as personal notes and flip charts that summarize points of discussion. Moreover, NGT prescribes a round-robin discussion process which ensures that each member has an opportunity to communicate his or her ideas. Indeed, Taylor (1990) found that using personal notes during discussion increased the number of ideas considered by decision-making groups and using flip charts to summarize ideas increased the number of ideas incorporated in their final decisions.

The relevance of information load and use of memory aids to promote extensive discussion is fairly obvious. However, there is another factor that is less obvious but perhaps just as critical to promoting extensive discussion: Group members must believe that sharing information is necessary for them to reach a good decision. In most of the research that I have described (Stasser & Titus, 1985, 1987; Stasser et al., 1989), we were careful to forewarn participants that they would not necessarily have identical information about the decision alternatives. In part, this forewarning was given so that group members would not question the validity of unshared information when it was mentioned during discussion, but we also did not want members to assume that they had all read the same information and, as a result, to disregard the need to exchange information. In retrospect, I question whether this forewarning that unshared information existed had the intended impact of emphasizing the importance of exchanging information.

What people make of such a forewarning may depend on whether they think the group is solving a problem or making a judgment. This distinction between solving a problem and making a judgment is related to Laughlin and Ellis's (1986) distinction between intellective and judgmental tasks. In their analysis, the distinction is based on the degree to which responses to the task can be demonstrated to be correct or incorrect. Intellective tasks have demonstrably correct answers; judgmental tasks do not. Laughlin and Ellis (1986) discussed the conditions that effect the degree of demonstrability and thus the location of a group task on a continuum anchored on one end by purely intellectual and on the other by purely judgmental tasks. Their analysis is theoretically and conceptually useful, but the distinction that I want to make between solving a problem and making a judgment is concerned more with how the group members view the task.

From a group member's perspective, a problem to be solved presumably has a correct answer, and the group's task is to identify the necessary information and reasoning to discover the correct answer. In this case, knowing that each member has information that the group as a whole does not have may induce extensive discussion, particularly when no decision alternative has emerged as a defensibly correct answer. That is, in solving a problem, there is presumably a critical set of information that, when considered in the right way, leads to the solution.

In contrast, making a judgment seems to invoke a different intuitive model of how information should be used. Judgments are based on the "weight of the evidence," and one does not expect that a judgment, once made, can be logically defended based on a critical set of information. Thus, there is no apparent need to search for a critical set of information and the group may discuss only long enough to obtain a sense of which decision alternative is favored by the preponderance of information. In this case, knowing that others have different information may not induce further discussion. Indeed, when the group agrees, knowing that each member has different information may enhance their confidence that they have identified the alternative favored by the preponderance of the information. That is, group members may use an information sampling heuristic: The more diverse the sets of information that group members have, the more confident one can be that the consensus choice is supported by the weight of the available evidence. Thus, knowing that members have unshared information may make their agreement seem more compelling and further exploration of information seem unnecessary.

This line of reasoning leads to the tentative hypothesis: When group members believe that their task requires a demonstrably correct answer rather than a subjective judgment, they will engage in more extensive information search, mention more unshared information in their discussions, and be less likely to overlook hidden profiles. It is likely that group members viewed the political candidate task that was used by Stasser and Titus (1985, 1987) and by Stasser et al. (1989) as a judgmental rather than a problem-solving task. Using a task that group members would tend to presume had a correct answer (e.g., a mystery or "brain teaser" task) may motivate more extensive discussions and thus the exchange of more unshared information.

Enhancing the Salience of Unshared Information

Another feature of the studies that I have reviewed is that group members did not know what information was unshared. They were forewarned that unshared information existed, but they had no way of determining which items they had that others did not. Additionally, they had no clues as to the kinds of information that others had that they did not. Thus, the information sampling model as expressed in equation 1 assumes that unshared information is no more or less likely to be mentioned by any one individual than is shared information. However, one can think of conditions that may make unshared information more salient than shared, which in effect implies that the probability of an individual mentioning unshared information, $p(M_u)$, is greater than the probability of mentioning shared information, $p(M_s)$. However, this difference in the probabilities of an individual mentioning unshared versus shared information will, in many cases, have to be substantial for the probability of the group discussing unshared information, $p(D_u)$, to equal the probability of their discussing shared, $p(D_s)$. For example, if group size is six and $p(M_s)$ is 0.2, then $p(M_u)$ would have to be slightly greater than 0.8 for $p(D_u)$ to equal $p(D_s)$. Nonetheless, conditions that would promote the recall and mentioning of unshared information without increasing the likelihood of mentioning shared information should help.

In many circumstances, members of a decision-making group may be recruited precisely because they have certain kinds of information that others do not. Indeed, particular members may fill identifiable roles (e.g., lawyer, accountant, production manager, marketing director) that are associated with known expertise and specialized knowledge. In these cases, members would be able to ascertain what relevant information they had that others lacked and, as a result, might focus their contributions on such unshared information. Moreover, the other group members might have a sense of the kinds of information that a person in a given role could contribute and probe for that information. The net effect should be to substantially increase the likelihood that unshared information would be mentioned during discussion.

In fact, any clues that help to identify the specific items and kinds of information that are unshared may help to redirect the focus of group discussion away from belaboring already shared information. The clues need not be as obvious as having specialized roles that are explicitly defined or assigned. Wegner's (1986) account of transactive memory suggests that people who have a history of working together on memory tasks develop ways of delegating the responsibility for remembering and recalling specific kinds of information. In a similar way, decision-making groups that have a history of working together on similar kinds of tasks may develop an efficient and effective division of responsibility for accumulating before discussion, and communicating during discussion, various kinds of information. Such strategies would create unshared information before discussion but also should promote its dissemination during discussion.

Therefore, when group members have clues that help identify who holds what kinds of unshared information, they may exchange more unshared information and, thereby, be more likely to discover hidden profiles when they exist.

Summary

The information sampling model and studies of information flow through group discussion (Stasser & Titus, 1985, 1987; Stasser et al., 1989) emphasize that group discussion is often an ineffective way of disseminating unshared information. As a result, I have argued that decision-making groups risk overlooking decision alternatives that are favored by their collective knowledge; that is, they often may fail to discover hidden profiles.

However, certain features of the studies I have reviewed may have impeded the exchange of unshared information. In these studies, participants chose the best qualified of several candidates for a student government position. Although groups typically discussed the relative merits of the candidates for some time, they never seemed to presume that there was, in any sense, a correct answer; that is, they likely felt that they were making a judgment rather than solving a problem. Moreover, group members could not easily distinguish unshared from shared information and they were, in most cases, given rather large amounts of information about the decision alternatives. I have considered ways in which a judgment set, indistinguishable shared and unshared information, and large amounts of information work against exchanging unshared information and discovering hidden profiles. Although these conditions undoubtedly resemble many that occur in natural decision environments, it is also easy to think of counterexamples.

A product design team for which members are explicitly recruited because they have known domains of expertise is a good counterexample. Members of such a team may feel that by pooling their expertise they can design a product that is demonstrably effective. Each member should know what she or he can contribute that others cannot and, conversely, what others' unique contributions are likely to be. Finally, members should be very familiar with their domains of expert knowledge, and high levels of discussion recall should be feasible. This example suggests a recipe for effective information pooling: (a) establish the expectation that the available information leads to a demonstrably correct answer; (b) keep information loads low or invoke procedures that lead to high recall in the face of high information loads; (c) make each member aware of the unique information that he or she can contribute; and (d) make members aware of the kinds of unique information that others are likely to have. Although there is as yet little empirical evidence to demonstrate that these ingredients do facilitate the exchange of unshared information and the discovery of hidden profiles, there are reasonable theoretical grounds for expecting that they would help.

References

Asch, S. E. (1956). Studies of independence and submission to group pressure: I. On minority of one against a unanimous majority. *Psychological Monographs, 70* (9 Whole No. 417).

Anderson, L. R. (1978). Groups would do better without humans. *Personality and Social Psychology Bulletin, 4,* 557-558.

Bonacich, P. (1987). Communication networks and collective action. *Social Networks, 9,* 389-396.

Burnstein, E., & Schul, Y. (1983). Group polarization. In H. H. Blumberg, A. P. Hare, V. Kent, & M. F. Davies (Eds.), *Small groups and social interaction* (Vol. 2, pp. 57-64). New York: John Wiley.

Burnstein, E., & Vinokur, A. (1977). Persuasive argumentation and social comparison as determinants of attitude polarization. *Journal of Experimental Social Psychology, 13,* 315-332.

Buys, B. J. (1978). Humans would do better without groups. *Personality and Social Psychology Bulletin, 4,* 123-125.

Clark, N. K., & Stephenson, G. M. (1989). Group remembering. In P. B. Paulus (Ed.). *Psychology of group influence* (Vol. 2, pp. 357-391). Hillsdale, NJ: Lawrence Erlbaum.

Delbecq, A. L., Van de Ven, A. H., & Gustafson, D. H. (1975). *Group techniques for program planning: A guide to nominal group and delphi processes.* Glenview, IL: Scott, Foresman.

Diehl, M., & Stroebe, W. (1987). Productivity loss in brainstorming groups: Toward the solution of a riddle. *Journal of Personality and Social Psychology, 53,* 497-509.

Hackman, J. R., & Morris, C. G. (1983). Group tasks, group interaction process, and group performance effectiveness. In H. H. Blumberg, A. P. Hare, V. Kent, & M. F. Davies. (Eds.), *Small groups and social interaction* (Vol. 1, pp. 331-345). New York: John Wiley.

Harkins, S., Latané, B., & Williams, K. (1980). Social loafing: Allocating effort or taking it easy? *Journal of Experimental Social Psychology, 16,* 1214-1229.

Hartwick, J., Sheppard, B. H., & Davis, J. H. (1982). Group remembering: Research and implications. In R. A. Guzzo (Ed.). *Improving group decision making in organizations* (pp. 41-72). New York: Praeger.

Janis, I. L. (1982). *Groupthink.* Boston: Houghton Mifflin.

Kerr, N. (1983). Motivation losses in small groups: A social dilemma analysis. *Journal of Personality and Social Psychology, 45,* 819-828.

Laughlin, P. R., & Ellis, A. L. (1986). Demonstrability and social combination processes on mathematical intellective tasks. *Journal of Experimental Social Psychology, 22,* 177-189.

Lorge, I., & Solomon, H. (1955). Two models of group behavior in the solution of Eureka-type problems. *Psychometrika, 20,* 139-148.

Lorge, I., & Solomon, H. (1962). Group and individual behavior in free-recall verbal learning. In J. H. Criswell, H. Solomon, & P. Suppes (Eds.), *Mathematical methods in small group processes* (pp. 221-231). Stanford, CA: Stanford University Press.

Myers, D. C., & Lamm, H. (1976). The group polarization phenomenon. *Psychological Bulletin, 83,* 602-627.

Murnighan, J. K. (1981). Group decision making: What strategies should you use? *Management Review, 70,* 55-62.

Petty, R., Harkins, S., & Williams, K. (1980). The effects of group diffusion of cognitive effort on attitudes: An information-processing view. *Journal of Personality and Social Psychology, 38,* 81-92.

Stasser, G. (1988). Computer simulation as a research tool: The DISCUSS model of group decision making. *Journal of Experimental Social Psychology, 24,* 393-422.

Stasser, G., Taylor, L. A., & Hanna, C. (1989). Information sampling in structured and unstructured discussions of three- and six-person groups. *Journal of Personality and Social Psychology, 57,* 67-78.

Stasser, G., & Titus, W. (1985). Pooling of unshared information in group decision making: Biased information sampling during group discussion. *Journal of Personality and Social Psychology, 48,* 1467-1478.

Stasser, G., & Titus, W. (1987). Effects of information load and percentage of shared information on the dissemination of unshared information during group discussion. *Journal of Personality and Social Psychology, 53,* 81-93.

Steiner, I. D. (1972). *Group processes and productivity.* New York: Academic Press.

Taylor, L. A. (1990). *Program planning effectiveness: Improving the quantity and quality of idea generation with memory aids and structured interaction.* Unpublished doctoral dissertation, Miami University, Oxford, OH.

Tillman, R. (1960, May-June). Committees on trial. *Harvard Business Review,* pp. 4-5, 8, 11-12, 162-164, 166, 168, 171-173.

Wegner, D. M. (1986). Transactive memory: A contemporary analysis of the group mind. In B. Mullen & G. Goethals (Eds.), *Theories of group behavior* (pp. 185-208). New York: Springer-Verlag.

3 Issue Importance and Group Decision Making

Norbert L. Kerr

Those of us who study group decision making are prone to justify our research preoccupation by reminding readers that groups are routinely called upon to make extremely important decisions. For example, boards of directors make decisions that determine the fates of large corporations and their employees, the decisions of legislative bodies and appellate courts define the law of the land, and juries sometimes literally make life-or-death decisions.

Not all group decisions are so momentous. Groups are also routinely called upon to make relatively unimportant decisions, a fact to which, for example, veterans of faculty meetings of academic departments can readily attest. The central premise of this chapter is that both the process and product of group decision making is systematically affected by the importance of the decision task to the members of the group. In particular, it is suggested that (a) as issue importance declines, the power of numerically larger factions to prevail declines and, as a consequence, (b) the usual polarizing effect of group discussion (see Myers & Lamm, 1976) is attenuated or, if the issue is sufficiently unimportant, even reversed, producing group depolarization.[1] The chapter also presents the results of an experiment performed to examine these hypotheses.

AUTHOR'S NOTE: I would like to express my thanks to James Davis, David Myers, Maryla Zelska, Alonzo Anderson, and the editors of this volume for their comments on earlier drafts of this chapter. Support for the research reported in this chapter was provided by NIMH Grant R01-MH29919.

The Social Decision Scheme Model and Issue Importance

These hypotheses were suggested by previous work utilizing Davis's (1973) social decision scheme (SDS) model. A *social decision scheme* is a probabilistic rule which specifies the likelihood that a group will reach any particular decision given that it begins discussion with any particular distribution of member opinion. It is summarized by a $m \times n$ matrix, D, where n is the number of decision alternatives, r is the size of the group, and m is the number of possible initial distributions of opinion $[(n + r - 1)!/(n!(r - 1)!)]$; d_{ij} is the probability that a group beginning discussion with the ith possible distribution of member opinion across the n alternatives ends up choosing the jth decision alternative. For example, an averaging decision scheme would predict that the group will choose with certainty that alternative closest to the average of the members' initial preferences. The applicable social decision scheme serves as a useful summary of the processes by which the group moves from initial disagreement to whatever level of agreement is required at the completion of deliberation to authorize a group decision, the group's *decision rule* (e.g., unanimity, majority rules, and so on; see Miller, 1989). The goal of a social decision scheme analysis is to identify the applicable D matrix, either by constructing one or more D matrices from theoretical principles and testing their goodness of fit, or by deriving a direct estimate of D from individual and group choice data (see Kerr, Stasser, & Davis, 1979). (See Davis [1973, 1980], Stasser, et al. [1989] for a more detailed description of the SDS model.)

A sizable number of studies applying the SDS model have found that one or more social decision schemes can provide an acceptable fit of the data, but that the best fitting scheme can vary across studies (see Davis, 1980; Laughlin, 1980; Stasser, Kerr, & Bray, 1982; Stasser et al., 1989, for reviews). The interesting questions suggested by these results are (a) which features of the task, subjects, and so forth affect the predictive accuracy of various social decision schemes and (b) what does variation in optimal social decision scheme tell us about the group decision-making process? Regarding the first question, inspection of previous research suggests certain regularities. For most of the decision tasks that have been studied using the SDS model, including duplex bets (Davis, Kerr, Sussman, & Rissman, 1974), attitudinal judgments (Kerr, Davis, Meek, & Rissman, 1975), and jury decision making (see Davis, 1980; Stasser et al., 1982), some variant on a majority-wins decision scheme has provided the best fit to the group decision data. That is, those alternatives initially supported by the relatively larger factions are much more likely to emerge as the group's choice than the initially unpopular alternatives.

For a few studies, however, a majority decision scheme is not optimal. In a number of studies, Laughlin and his colleagues (e.g., Laughlin & Adamopoulos, 1982; Laughlin & Ellis, 1986; Laughlin, Kerr, Davis, Halff, & Marciniak, 1975; Laughlin, Kerr, Munch, & Haggarty, 1976) have shown that for certain tasks, relatively small, nonmajority factions can prevail. These tasks are what Laughlin terms *intellective* tasks. They are "problems or decisions for which there exists a demonstrably correct answer within a verbal or mathematical conceptual system" (Laughlin & Ellis, 1986, p. 177). For example, the correct answer to a simple arithmetic problem would be demonstrably correct to group members if they all have a basic knowledge of mathematics. Laughlin suggests (and has shown, e.g., Laughlin et al., 1976; Laughlin & Ellis, 1986) that, for purely intellective tasks like simple arithmetic problems or verbal "Eureka" or insight problems, a *truth-wins* social decision scheme provides the best fit to group performance data. That is, a single advocate of the correct answer in the group is sufficient to ensure that the group selects the correct answer. For tasks with somewhat less obviously "correct" answers (such as vocabulary, world knowledge, or analogies), a *truth-supported wins* scheme applies; two correct members are necessary and sufficient to ensure that the group endorses the correct answer.

Laughlin suggests that a majority-wins decision scheme applies for what he terms *judgmental tasks*, ". . . evaluative, behavioral, or aesthetic judgments for which there does not exist a demonstrably correct answer" (Laughlin & Ellis, 1986, p. 177). Most jury trials represent judgmental tasks; the "correct" verdict is objectively unknowable, and jurors can honestly disagree about the credibility, meaning, and relevance of evidence. Without some "objective" means of evaluating verdict preference, based on a shared and applicable conceptual system, alternative verdicts must, of necessity, be evaluated through social consensus for such judgmental tasks (cf. Festinger, 1954). This offers an explanation of why relatively large factions (e.g., majorities) tend to prevail at a wide range of judgmental tasks.

There is also another, smaller set of studies that show a departure from a majority-wins decision scheme. These do not involve clearly intellective tasks, and further, they do not find that some variant of a truth-wins decision scheme fits well. Davis, Hornik, and Hornseth

(1970) and Johnson and Davis (1972) found that an *equiprobability* decision scheme—for which every decision alternative with at least one advocate is equally likely to become the group decision—produced good fits for sequential probability-matching tasks (on which subjects decided which of several lights would be lit on each of several trials) (cf. Zajonc, Wolosin, Wolosin, & Sherman, 1968).

To what might the accuracy of the equiprobability decision scheme plausibly be attributed in these studies? There are many features which might distinguish them from the studies for which majority- and truth-wins type models have predominated. For example, Davis (1982) suggests that the crucial task feature may be high task uncertainty. This is certainly a distinctive feature of the probability matching tasks. Groups did not know (but rather had to infer) the key task parameters—the probabilities that the various lights would be lit on each trial. Indeed, on roughly comparable tasks involving considerably less uncertainty (e.g., Davis et al., 1974), a majority decision scheme provided the optimal fit.

Another possibly relevant variable is the importance of the decision task (Kerr, 1983; Kerr, 1985; Laughlin & Ellis, 1986). Studies for which a majority scheme have been optimal have tended to use rather interesting, ego-involving judgmental tasks, such as discussion of a set of current social issues or engaging in mock jury deliberations. In contrast, the Johnson and Davis (1972) and Davis et al. (1970) studies, for which the equiprobability scheme was optimal, employed tasks which, on their face, would likely be viewed by subjects as rather sterile and uninvolving. It also seems likely that group members had relatively little commitment to their preferences; the extremely high level of uncertainty, stressed by Davis (1982), would also probably contribute to a general indifference among alternatives.

Issue Importance and Group Decision-Making Process

To understand the significance of this pattern for the group decision-making process, consider a three-person group that begins discussion of a two-alternative decision task with a (2:1) split. The majority decision scheme would predict that the group will choose the first alternative; the equiprobability scheme would predict that the group is equally likely to choose either alternative. One way of thinking about the differences between these two decision schemes is that there is "strength in numbers" in the majority scheme, whereas there is none in the equiprobability scheme (for which only the existence and not the relative frequency of advocates determines the probability of the group choosing an alternative) (cf. Johnson & Davis, 1972). This analysis suggests that, with respect to influence on the group's decision, there is less of an advantage in having a numerical superiority at the outset of group deliberation as the decision task becomes less important. This direct relationship between task importance and strength in numbers will be termed the *majority-if-important hypothesis*. It holds that the probability that an initial majority will ultimately prevail increases as task importance increases.

The interesting process question suggested by the majority-if-important hypothesis is: Why should decision making on less important issues be characterized by reduced strength-in-numbers? One possibility considered in this study is that the relative importance of task versus social motives varies with issue importance. Following Erickson et al. (1974), issue importance is conceptualized as the degree to which the subjective utility of endorsement varies across response alternatives. In other words, one really does not care very much which alternative one or one's group endorses for unimportant issues, but one does care about one's personal or group endorsement of various alternatives for important issues. This suggests that task motives should predominate in group discussion of important issues; a member should become committed to the preferred alternative and abandon it only when faced with many opponents (e.g., majorities). However, for unimportant tasks, members' relative indifference toward response alternatives might make social motives (e.g., avoiding conflict) relatively more salient. The willingness of a faction to abandon a numerically superior position (inherent in the equiprobability scheme) is consistent with this analysis. Thus, if the majority-if-important hypothesis is valid, it may be because groups have more of a *task-set* for important issues and a *group-set* for unimportant issues (cf. Thibaut & Strickland, 1956).

Issue Importance and the Product of Group Decision Making

The majority-if-important hypothesis also has implications for a phenomenon involving the product of group discussion or decision making—*group polarization*. A sizable body of research has shown that group discussion will produce a shift of both individual and group opinions relative to prediscussion values. This has been termed the "choice shift" phenomenon. Most of this research has been concerned with shifts on a risk dimension, but choice shifts have also been observed for many other judgments (e.g., attitudes, jury sentences). Myers and Lamm (1976) reviewed the choice shift literature and suggested that nearly all choice shifts were instances of group polarization, that is, the average post-group response tends to be more extreme in the same direction as the average of the prediscussion responses.

Several previous studies have examined the effects on choice shifts of decision task features which appear to be related to issue importance as conceptualized here. Unfortunately, there has been little consistency across studies in either conceptualization or operationalization of issue importance (cf. Madsen, 1978), nor much consistency in results. Some studies have found stronger polarization effects for important issues (e.g., Baron, Baron, & Roper, 1974); some have found weaker polarization effects (e.g., Baron, Roper, & Baron, 1974; Madsen, 1978); whereas in others, issue importance did not alter the degree of polarization (e.g., Spector, Cohen, & Penner, 1976). Some of the empirical confusion may stem from the fact that the degree and direction of polarization depends on the extremity of the mean prediscussion opinion. Several studies have clearly confounded issue importance with initial extremity, and many more studies have reported only shift data so that the issue degree of confounding cannot be determined. Care was taken in the experiment reported in this chapter to match high- and low-importance issues on prediscussion extremity.

Prior work has also been characterized by a lack of theory linking issue importance and polarization. A notable exception to this rule is the work of Moscovici and Zavalloni (1969). They suggest that whenever group discussion increases one's commitment to one's position and increases the salience of socially dominant values and attitudes, polarization should occur. This should be more likely when the task is ". . . ego involving or is regarded as a meaningful issue" (p. 128). When the task has little significance or is not involving, they suggest that group discussion will produce a "convergence phenomenon" wherein members average their opinions. Since, by definition, polarization requires that groups are more extreme after discussion than the average of their prediscussion opinions, this logic predicts little, if any, polarization for unimportant, uninvolving issues. The results of several studies conducted by Moscovici and his colleagues to test this prediction have tended to support it, although the support is inconclusive due to several methodological problems (Moscovici & Zavalloni, 1969; Moscovici, Zavalloni, & Louis-Gúerin, 1972; Moscovici, Zavalloni, & Weinberger, 1972).

If issue importance and the power of initial majorities are directly related, as suggested earlier, should issue importance affect group polarization? The operation of a majority decision scheme (or any decision scheme with high strength-in-numbers) tends to enhance in groups the popularity of alternatives that are relatively popular among individuals and to depress in groups the popularity of the unpopular alternatives among individuals (Davis, 1973; Davis & Kerr, 1986; Kerr & Huang, 1986). Whenever extremity of the mean preference of individuals is accompanied by skew in the opposite direction (the usual pattern), one consequence of a majority-wins decision scheme is the "pulling in the tail" of the distribution and movement of the mean toward the mode of the distribution—that is, group polarization (cf. Kerr et al., 1975).[2]

An equiprobability scheme (low strength-in-numbers) signals the opposite effect. Compared to the distribution of individual preference, the distribution of group preferences for groups operating under such a scheme will be "flattened" (Davis, 1973). This tends to extend the tail of a skewed distribution and should move the mean away from the mode—that is, a choice shift toward the neutral point of a bipolar response scale or group depolarization. Thus, like Moscovici and Zavalloni's formulation, the majority-if-important notion also predicts that reducing the importance of an issue will attenuate the polarization effect, but unlike Moscovici and Zavalloni, it also predicts that for sufficiently unimportant tasks group discussion should actually produce depolarization in opinion (i.e., post-discussion shifts toward, rather than away from, the scale's neutral midpoint).

An Experimental Test of the
Majority-If-Important Hypothesis

To explore the effects of issue importance on both the process and product of group decision making, we conducted an experiment. Examination of polarization effects requires a response scale with a psychologically neutral zero point. Likert-type attitudinal scales were used in our study. Based on the responses of pilot subjects, five high- and five low-importance issues were chosen from a larger set. Since the strength of polarization effects seems to depend on the extremity of the mean prediscussion opinion and possibly on other distributional characteristics (e.g., skewness), the 10 selected items constituted five pairs matched as closely as possible on the mean, variance, and skewness of the pilot subjects' responses. An item consisted of a statement to which the subjects responded on a six-point bipolar scale anchored by *strongly disagree* and *strongly agree*. The item statements for the 10 items are listed in Table 3.1, along with descriptive labels.

Experimental Method

The subjects were 200 students (100 males, 100 females) drawn from introductory psychology classes. Following the standard choice shift paradigm, subjects first responded to several items individually, then discussed them in groups, and then considered them again individually. The basic design was a 2×2 (Issue Importance × Subject Sex) factorial. Sex of subjects was included as an experimental factor in light of some research (e.g., Bond & Vinacke, 1961) suggesting sex differences in group versus task set; females seem more likely than males to adopt a group set. There were 10 five-person groups in each condition.

Subjects were typically scheduled in groups of about 25. Their first task was providing their personal opinions on either the five high-importance or five low-importance issues (Table 3.1). The experiment was presented as a study of the group decision-making process. The choice of the issues and the use to which the group's decisions were to be put were then described. Under the present conceptualization of issue importance, any of several individual, group, or task factors might affect the utilities of endorsing various alternatives and, hence, issue importance. To further supplement the differences in personal importance between the high- and low-importance items, the instructions purported differences in the importance of the items as judged by peers and in the import of the group decisions. Specifically, the subjects in the high-importance condition were told that the issues they were considering had been rated by another group of students as the five most important of a set of 50 issues, and that their group decisions would be provided to a statewide student lobbying organization to indicate local student opinion. In the low-importance condition subjects were told that the issues had been rated as the least important of the 50 issue set and that the experiment was a pilot study for which the data of

Table 3.1
Item Statements

High Importance

1. Eighteen-year-olds should be able to purchase hard liquor in the state of California. (Liquor)

2. The present UCSD course load requirements are not too high. (Course load)

3. Abortions should be prohibited except in cases where the life of the mother is in danger. (Abortion)

4. All laws prohibiting the use and sale of marijuana should be repealed. (Marijuana)

5. In order to combat inflation, President Ford should reimpose wage and price controls. (Inflation)

Low Importance

1. Intercollegiate sports should be promoted at UCSD. (Sports)

2. The water supply of Los Angeles should be fluoridated. (Fluoridation)

3. San Diego should build a new airport near the Mexican border. (Airport)

4. The tariff on imported beef should be reduced. (Tariff)

5. The United States should give up its control of the Panama Canal. (Canal)

---

principal interest were checks on the clarity of instructions, timing, and so forth.

Subjects were randomly assigned to five-person all-male or all-female groups which assembled in nearby smaller rooms. Groups were instructed to discuss the issues and to try to reach a unanimous decision. Each group was given a total of 25 minutes. The groups paced themselves and could consider the issues in any order they liked; the order in which issues were presented was randomized for each group. If the group decided that unanimous agreement on an item was unlikely, they were permitted to skip the item and come back to it later if time allowed. When the group finished or the available time expired, group members individually completed a questionnaire containing the following items of interest: the five attitudinal items, each followed by a rating of the personal importance of the issue; a rating of the importance of the group decisions; ratings of the subject's interest and involvement in his or her group's decisions; a rating of the ease with which members changed opinions; and a dichotomous choice between a social- versus task-emphasis in the groups.

Experimental Results

Checks on the Experimental Manipulation

Unless otherwise indicated, the unit for all analyses was the group, not the individual group member. Mean group ratings of the personal importance of the five issues considered by the group (averaged across issues and members within each group) and mean group ratings of the importance of the decisions made (averaged across members within each group) were both analyzed in 2 × 2 (Importance × Sex) least-squares analyses of variance. The only significant effect for these variables was the Importance main effects; on average, groups in the high-importance conditions considered their issues more important to them personally, $F(1,32) = 20.23, p < .001$, and also felt that their group decisions were more important, $F(1,32) = 5.29, p < .05$. Groups also reported being significantly more interested in their decisions in the high-importance condition $(p < .01)$. The Importance manipulation did not affect ratings of involvement in the group discussion.

Group Polarization/Depolarization

Before discussion-induced shifts were considered, the prediscussion distributions of individuals' opinions were examined to verify that there were reliable prediscussion tendencies for these issues and also to verify that the high- and low-importance issues had been matched effectively. Descriptive statistics on prediscussion opinions appear in Table 3.2. The overall prediscussion mean was significantly different from the ostensibly neutral midpoint of the response scale for every item. Thus, for none of the issues considered here was the direction of the prediscussion opinion indeterminate. Also, with respect to the first three moments of the distributions, the high- and low-importance item pairs seemed to be fairly well matched.

To examine the general effect of issue importance on choice shifts, the following polarization measure was computed. The difference between the post-discussion and prediscussion group averages was computed on each issue. The sign of this difference was taken so that a positive difference reflected a polarization effect (relative to the prediscussion mean for all subjects). These differences were then averaged

Table 3.2
Item Statistics

	Prediscussion			
Issues	Mean[a]	Polarity[b]	s	Skew
High importance				
Liquor	4.51	1.01***	1.41	−1.01
Course load	4.27	0.77***	1.17	−0.88
Abortion	2.30	−1.20***	1.63	1.05
Marijuana	4.02	0.52***	1.42	−0.67
Inflation	3.23	−0.27*	1.18	−0.04
Low importance				
Sports	4.54	1.04***	1.08	−0.80
Fluoridation	4.16	0.66***	1.37	−0.65
Airport	2.85	−0.65***	1.42	0.46
Tariff	3.94	0.44***	1.13	0.03
Canal	3.13	−0.37**	1.12	−0.08

NOTES: a. Prediscussion means are based on all subjects. Post-discussion means are based on those subjects who actually discussed the issue.
b. Tests were of the null hypothesis that (mean − 3.5) = polarity = 0, where 3.5 = the scale midpoint.
*$p < .05$; **$p < .01$; ***$p < .001$.

across the items discussed by a group to yield an overall index of group polarization.

Both the Importance main effect and the Sex × Importance interaction were significant, $F(1,36) = 12.2$, $p < .001$ and $F(1,36) = 5.27$, $p < .05$, respectively. As expected, discussion of unimportant issues led to depolarization of opinion, whereas the mean choice shift for important issues was a polarization effect. The observed means were as follows: males/high-importance, −.078; males/low-importance, −.225; females/high-importance, .224; females/low-importance, −.171. Constructing the 95% confidence intervals for each of these means indicated that for males there was no significant choice shift for important issues but a significant depolarization shift for the unimportant issues, whereas for females both the polarization shift for important issues and the depolarization shift for unimportant issues were statistically significant. It is somewhat puzzling why only females polarized on the high-importance issues. It is interesting to note that individual females tended ($p < .09$) to rate the set of issues and their decisions as more important than males. We have suggested that the tendency to polarize is directly related to the importance of the decision task. There is evidence that males tended to see all of the present tasks as less important than females. Females polarized significantly on the important issues and depolarized significantly on the unimportant issues. Taken together these premises imply a weaker or no polarization effect on the important issues and a stronger depolarization on the unimportant issues for males, which was just the observed pattern.

Majority-If-Important Hypothesis

One way to test the majority-if-important hypothesis would be to test both majority and equiprobability social decision schemes against the group decision data for the high- and low-importance issues. The hypothesis predicts that the relative accuracy of the equiprobability scheme should improve as issue importance decreases. However, because of time limitations and/or lack of compromise, groups often were unable to unanimously endorse a position. Thus, rather than using the model-testing strategy common in most previous SDS research, a model-fitting strategy was employed (Kerr, Stasser, & Davis, 1979).

The objective was to estimate separately the best fitting social decision schemes for the high- and low-importance conditions. Basically, this required a crosstabulation of observed group decisions for each possible initial distribution of member preference within each Importance condition. There are 252 possible initial distributions of opinion, given six response alternatives and five-person groups. Obviously, the maximum of 100 (5 issues × 20 groups/conditions) observations available in the present study were not adequate to estimate the entries of a $252 \times 6 = 1512$ cell table. To make estimation feasible, the first three decision alternatives (strongly disagree, moderately disagree, slightly disagree) were combined, as were the last three (slightly agree, moderately agree, strongly agree) to make the response scale dichotomous. The resultant data are presented in Table 3.3.

As one can see in the table, the data provided support for the majority-if-important hypothesis in the "minority of one" cases (i.e., initial 4-1 and 1-4 splits). In the high-importance condition, out of 20 instances in which the group began discussion with a minority of one and eventually reached a group decision, 19 were for the alternative favored by the majority. However, in the low-importance condition, the minority of one prevailed in six out of 17 such instances. This direct relationship between issue importance and strength-in-numbers was statistically significant ($p < .03$ by Fisher's exact test). There was no such relationship for the only other relevant case, the "minority of two" (i.e., 3-2 and

Table 3.3
Initial Distribution to Final Decision Frequencies

Initial Individual Distribution		Group Decisions							
		High Importance Condition				Low Importance Condition			
Disagree	Agree	Disagree	Agree	Hung	Not Discussed	Disagree	Agree	Hung	Not Discussed
5	0	5	0	2	0	3	0	4	0
4	1	7	0	5	0	5	1	3	0
3	2	7	1	3	1	8	1	8	1
2	3	6	8	12	4	6	11	13	0
1	4	1	12	13	0	5	6	5	0
0	5	0	11	0	1	0	15	3	1

NOTE: In each condition, one group could not be classified due to a group member's failure to respond to an item prior to group discussion.

2-3 splits); here, the majority won in 15 of 22 cases for high-importance issues and in 19 of 26 cases for low-importance issues, $\chi^2(1) = .003$.

Group Versus Task Set

Several aspects of the group discussions and post-experimental responses were examined to test the validity of the "group- versus task-set" idea. First, if for low-importance issues groups adopted a group set that prompted easier compromise, one would expect that groups would be more likely to achieve consensus and would do so sooner in this condition. These predictions were not confirmed (e.g., see the "hung" group rate data in Table 3.2). The data for the post-experimental questionnaire also provided little support. Groups did not feel that group members changed their minds more easily in the low-importance condition. Subjects were also asked to indicate whether their groups were characterized more by an interest in the decision reached (task set) or in getting along with one another (group set). Although the latter, group set, was endorsed slightly more frequently by subjects in the low-importance condition (29 out of 78 subjects, or 37%) than in the high-importance condition (33 out of 99, or 33%), this effect was not significant.

Issue Importance and Group Process and Product: A Re-Examination

Practically all previous work on choice shifts has shown that group discussion tends to polarize opinion (Myers & Lamm, 1976). The results of the experiment reported here suggest an interesting exception to this general rule. When groups were called upon to make decisions with little significance on issues of low importance to themselves and their peers, group discussion actually was followed by a *de*polarization of opinion.[3]

A review of the social decision scheme literature suggested that decision making on important issues was characterized by strength-in-numbers, but that there was less strength-in-numbers when unimportant issues were being considered. The present experiment did provide some support for this majority-if-important hypothesis. A minority of one was significantly more likely to prevail over the rest of the group for the unimportant issues than for the important issues. Although the support for this hypothesis was neither uniformly strong nor without plausible alternative interpretations,[4] the suggestive evidence is still quite interesting for two reasons. First, it may contribute to the depolarization effects observed here on the unimportant issues. Second, and more importantly, it suggests another factor (viz., issue importance) besides the demonstrability of a "correct" answer which may moderate the applicable social decision scheme. And since variations in decision scheme reflect variations in the underlying process of group decision making, issue importance is likewise implicated as a moderating variable for this process.

We also conjectured that groups might become less task- and more group-oriented as issues decreased in importance. Several plausible implications of this conjecture were tested in the present study. Self reports of the orientation of the group were not affected by issue importance. It is possible, though, that subjects were generally reluctant to admit to a group set—it could be tantamount to admitting that one's group did not take its task seriously. In addition, the time required to reach a decision and perceptions of the readiness of group members to yield were likewise unaffected by issue importance. These patterns suggest that group members tended to become committed to their initially stated opinions, even on issues of very low personal importance. However, these results are far from conclusive. A group set may be manifested in other, more subtle ways than immediate defection from an initial position (which may be precluded in any case by the wish not to appear inconsistent or pliable) (Cialdini, 1984; Tedeschi, 1981). For example, subjects might be less vigorous or adamant advocates for less important issues. Or they may be more willing to compromise on a position acceptable to all group members. The latter possibility gains credence from an interpretation of the depolarization results discussed below.

It may be that the present manipulation of issue importance was not sufficiently strong to undermine dramatically the usual task set and corresponding power of majorities. All of the issues were judgmental attitude items, a class of task for which initial majorities typically prevail (cf. Kerr et al., 1976). It is also instructive to compare the present operationalization of low importance with the previous studies providing the clearest evidence for an equiprobability social decision scheme (viz., Davis et al., 1970; Johnson & Davis, 1972). In the latter studies, there was far less opportunity or likelihood for group members expressing and becoming committed to a particular alternative. Unlike the present study, there was no explicit assessment of an initial, pre-group-discussion preference in Davis's studies. Furthermore, because there were only a few seconds between each probability-matching trial, there was little opportunity to formulate, let alone defend, a clear individual preference. Future research aimed at exploring the relationship of issue importance to group decision process and product should systematically examine the roles that time pressures and initial assessments of individual preference might play.

One key issue that remains unresolved by the present research is why depolarization occurred in the low-importance condition. The attenuation of the power of majorities in the low-importance conditions was not sufficient to explain this effect; although the power of the majority was attenuated somewhat by issue importance, Table 3.3 indicates that for all issues initial majorities still prevailed in most cases.[5] This suggests that the majority-if-important mechanism is, at best, only a partial explanation of the observed depolarization for low-importance issues. This effect also seems to be incompatible with currently viable theories of choice shift. In its current form, Moscovici's commitment theory and the social comparison theories (see Pruitt, 1971) would predict an attenuation but not a reversal of polarization as issues became less important. Burnstein and Vinokur's persuasive argument theory (e.g., Burnstein & Vinokur, 1973) appears not to relate issue importance to choice shifts in a consistent way (Madsen, 1978). However, with some modification, these theories might account for depolarization. For example, if one's initial consideration of an unimportant issue tended to exhaust the pool of persuasive arguments for one's favored alternative, then new arguments raised in group discussion would tend to favor unadvocated alternatives, producing depolarization.

Two additional explanations were suggested by our data. The observed choice shifts were predominantly toward the *strongly disagree* end of the response scale; examining shifts item by item, of the seven items with nontrivial shifts, five were of these type. It was also more likely for a majority favoring a *disagree* response to prevail in group discussion than one favoring an *agree* response. In particular, Table 3.2 indicates that whenever a non-unanimous majority (i.e., three or four out of five) advocated disagreement and a group decision was achieved, it usually was a decision for disagreement (on 26 out of 29 occasions, or 90% of the time), but when such a majority favored agreement, they were much less likely to prevail (on 37 out of 55 occasions, or only 67% of the time) ($\chi^2(1) = 3.95$, $p < .05$). Even if you favor the sentiment of a statement, for any particular wording, it may be easier to come up with reasons to disagree than to agree during group discussion, especially when one is relatively uncommitted or uninterested in the issue.[6] For example, even someone who is favorably disposed to the idea of reducing prices by increasing the supply of meat might be convinced during group discussion to disagree with the statement: "The tariff on imported beef should be reduced" if he or she were convinced that the statement was inadequate ("don't just reduce the tariff, eliminate it"), too narrow ("why just beef; why not all meats?"), not forceful enough ("why not *must* be reduced'?"), less effective than other means ("maybe stimulating domestic production would be better"), and so forth. These patterns suggest that generally it may be easier to advocate disagreement than agreement with a statement. One direct way in which this explanation could be tested would be to have one condition consider a set of statements and another condition consider the opposites of the first set (e.g., "we should build a new airport" vs. "we should not build a new airport"). Whenever the initial distributions for the two conditions are mirror images of one another, this explanation suggests that choice shifts toward disagreement should be stronger than the corresponding shifts toward agreement.

The second possibility is that when disagreement exists on a low-importance issue, members will more readily accept a moderate (depolarizing) alternative as a reasonable compromise than if the issue is important to them. This explanation predicts that actual group decisions are more likely to be moderate ones for low-importance issues. This prediction was confirmed. For every matched item pair, the proportion of group decisions for one of the two "neutral" alternatives (slightly disagree, slightly agree) was higher for the low-importance item than for the high-importance item. Across all five pairs, 62% (36 of 58) group decisions were neutral in the low-importance condition, but only 40% (23 of 58) were neutral in the high-importance conditions ($\chi^2(1) = 4.97$, $p < .05$). As noted above, this greater willingness to compromise on a moderate position may be viewed as a kind of group set, and encourages even more careful and detailed analyses of the effects of issue importance on the process of group decision making. As an explanation for depolarization per se, this notion might be tested by comparing the choice shifts resulting from group discussion of low-importance issues with and without the requirement of consensus; it would predict somewhat stronger depolarization in the former case.

We have theoretically and empirically linked issue importance to the process and product of group decision making. It is interesting to speculate whether related effects might occur for problem-solving task groups. Laughlin and Ellis (1986) suggest that the "correct" answer to an intellective task is not really demonstrable unless solvers (advocates of the correct answer) are motivated to share their knowledge and nonsolvers are motivated to recognize the validity of the correct answer. Perhaps any of several aspects of the importance group members attach to their problem-solving task would reduce either or both such motivations. Such aspects might include the extrinsic incentives available for successful task performance, the intrinsic interest value of the task, and whether self-esteem is contingent on demonstrating high task ability to the self or to others. Recall that for purely or largely intellective tasks, incorrect, nonsolving majorities have disproportionately *low* influence. We are suggesting that the relative power of a correct minority might be attenuated as the task became less important to its members. This leads to a rather different prediction for task groups than we explored here for decision-making groups. For the latter, we suggested that majorities lose power as the task becomes less important. However, the power of *incorrect* majorities may well increase as the importance of a group's problem solving task increases, signaling poorer group performance. These possibilities merit research attention.

Conclusions

This chapter has argued that the usual tendencies (a) for majorities to prevail for judgmental issues and (b) for group discussion to polarize opinion are attenuated (and in the latter case even reversed) as the issue becomes less important to group members. It also presented the results of an experiment that provided some preliminary although inconclusive evidence for this argument. Clearly, much more focused research is needed on these questions.

This chapter has also re-illustrated the utility of the social decision scheme model for the study of group decision making. Most previous applications of the SDS model have tended to employ it as a descriptive or predictive tool. However, it can also serve as a powerful analytic tool. Regularities and irregularities in the optimal social decision scheme matrix across experimental conditions or studies can suggest interesting new hypotheses, like Laughlin's hypotheses concerning demonstrability and the present hypotheses concerning issue importance.

Notes

1. The term depolarization is not used here, as in Vinokur and Burnstein (1978), to mean a convergence of opinion within the group following group discussion, but signifies a mean choice shift of opinion toward the neutral point of the response scale across groups following group discussion/decision making.

2. Polarization may also reflect task demonstrability. For example, Laughlin and Early (1982) have shown that group decision making on Choice Dilemma items, that produce strong risky shifts is summarized by a risk-supported-wins social decision scheme. Similarly, strong cautious shift items evoke a caution-supported-wins scheme. Group decision making on items which produce only weak risky/cautious shifts is described by a majority-wins decision scheme. Evidently, for certain decision tasks, certain positions are demonstrably "correct" and even small factions can bring the group around to their position (also see MacCoun & Kerr, 1988).

3. This result is all the more striking in light of the general pattern of previous research (Myers, 1973) that has, on the whole, tended to favor the opposite relationship, viz., stronger polarization for unimportant issues (usually, stronger risky shifts for less important or costly Choice Dilemmas or gambles). However, a confounding of prediscussion polarity and issue importance has either been a clear or a potential problem for interpreting most of this previous research. If group members tend individually to be less extreme when the issue is an "important" one (e.g., when one's own money is being wagered), then the present findings need not be viewed as in conflict with previous research on issue importance.

4. Issue importance did not affect the power of the majorities when the five-person groups were initially split 3 to 2 (or 2-3). Furthermore, close inspection of Table 3.2 suggests that the evidence for the hypothesis in the 4-1 case could also be interpreted in terms of the drawing power of a faction advocating a "disagree" response rather than of a minority faction. This possibility is discussed in more detail later in the text of the chapter.

5. Generally, in order for groups to depolarize, the probability that initial minority factions should prevail needs to be greater than the minority faction's relative size (cf. Davis, 1973; Kerr et al., 1976). For example, the probability that the group will endorse the preference of a two-person minority in a five-person group should be greater than 2/5 = .40. With only one exception (viz. the 1-4 splits, see Table 3.2), minorities in the low-importance groups did not exert this degree of power in the present study.

6. See footnote 5, Supra.

References

Baron, P., Baron, R. S., & Roper, G. (1974). External validity and the risky shift: Empirical limits and theoretical implications. *Journal of Personality and Social Psychology, 30,* 95-103.

Baron, R. S., Roper, G., & Baron, P. (1974). Group discussion and the stingy shift. *Journal of Personality and Social Psychology, 30,* 538-545.

Bond, J., & Vinacke, W. (1961). Coalitions in mixed sex trials. *Sociometry, 24,* 61-75.

Burnstein, E., & Vinokur, A. (1973). Testing two classes of theories about group-induced shifts in individual choice. *Journal of Experimental Social Psychology, 9,* 123-137.

Cialdini, R. B. (1984). *Influence: How and why people agree to things.* New York: William Morrow.

Davis, J. H. (1973). Group decision and social interaction: A theory of social decision schemes. *Psychological Review, 80,* 97-125.

Davis, J. H. (1980). Group decision and procedural justice. In M. L. Fishbein (Ed.), *Progress in social psychology* (Vol. 1, pp. 157-229). Hillsdale, NJ: Lawrence Erlbaum.

Davis, J. H. (1982). Social interaction as a combinatorial process in group decision. In H. Brandstätter, J. H. Davis, & G. Stocker-Kreichgauer (Eds.), *Group decision making* (pp. 27-58). New York: Academic Press.

Davis, J. H., Hornik, H., & Hornseth, J. (1970). Group decision schemes and strategy preferences in a sequential response task. *Journal of Personality and Social Psychology, 15,* 397-408.

Davis, J. H., & Kerr, N. L. (1986). Thought experiments and the problem of sparse data in small-group performance research. In P. Goodman (Ed.), *Designing effective work groups.* San Francisco: Jossey-Bass.

Davis, J. H., Kerr, N. L., Sussmann, M., & Rissman, A. K. (1974). Social decision schemes under risk. *Journal of Personality and Social Psychology, 30,* 248-271.

Erickson, B., Holmes, H., Frey, R., Walker, L., & Thibaut, J. (1974). Functions of a third party in the resolution of conflict: The role of a judge in pretrial conferences. *Journal of Personality and Social Psychology, 30,* 293-306.

Festinger, L. (1954). A theory of social comparison processes. *Human Relations, 1,* 117-140.

Johnson, C. & Davis, J. H. (1972). An equiprobability model of risk taking. *Organizational Behavior and Human Performance, 8,* 159-175.

Kerr, N. L. (1983). Issue importance, group polarization, and social decision schemes. Paper presented in the symposium, "Social decision schemes and opinion change," (D. Nagao & D. Vollrath, Chairs) at the 1983 American Psychological Association Convention, Los Angeles.

Kerr, N. L. (1985, June). The social decision scheme model: A missionary's position. Paper presented at the Fifth Annual Conference on Small Groups, Nags Head, NC.

Kerr, N. L., Davis, J. H., Meek, D., & Rissman, A. (1975). The group position as a function of member attitudes—Polarization effects from the perspective of social decision scheme theory. *Journal of Personality and Social Psychology, 31,* 574-593.

Kerr, N. L., & Huang, J. (1986). How much difference does one juror make in jury deliberation. *Personality and Social Psychology Bulletin, 12,* 325-343.

Kerr, N. L., Stasser, G., & Davis, J. H. (1979). Model-testing, model-fitting, and social decision schemes. *Organizational Behavior and Human Performance, 23,* 339-410.

Laughlin, P. R. (1980). Social combination processes of cooperative problem-solving groups on verbal intellective tasks. In M. L. Fishbein (Ed.), *Progress in social psychology* (Vol. 1). Hillsdale, NJ: Lawrence Erlbaum.

Laughlin, P. R., & Adamopoulos, J. (1982). Social decision schemes on intellective tasks. In H. Brandstätter, J. H. Davis, & G. Stocker-Kreichgauer (Eds.), *Group decision making* (pp. 81-102). New York: Academic Press.

Laughlin, P. R., & Early, P. C. (1982). Social combination models, persuasive arguments theory, social comparison theory, and choice shift. *Journal of Personality and Social Psychology, 42,* 273-280.

Laughlin, P. R., & Ellis, A. L. (1986). Demonstrability and social combination processes on mathematical intellective tasks. *Journal of Experimental Social Psychology, 22,* 177-189.

Laughlin, P. R., Kerr, N. L., Davis, J. H., Halff, H. M., & Marciniak, K. A. (1975). Group size, member ability, and social decision schemes on an intellective task. *Journal of Personality and Social Psychology, 31,* 522-535.

Laughlin, P. R., Kerr, N. L., Munch, M., & Haggarty, C. (1976). Social decision schemes of the same four-person groups on two different intellective tasks. *Journal of Personality and Social Psychology, 33,* 80-88.

MacCoun, R. J., & Kerr, N. L. (1988). Asymmetric influence in mock jury deliberation: Jurors' bias for leniency. *Journal of Personality and Social Psychology, 54,* 21-33.

Madsen, D. (1978). Issue importance and group choice shifts: A persuasive arguments approach. *Journal of Personality and Social Psychology, 36,* 1118-1127.

Miller, C. E. (1989). The social psychological effects of group decision rules. In P. Paulus (Ed.), *Psychology of group influence* (2nd ed., pp. 324-356). Hillsdale, NJ: Lawrence Erlbaum.

Moscovici, S. & Zavalloni, M. (1969). The group as a polarizer of attitudes. *Journal of Personality and Social Psychology, 12,* 125-135.

Moscovici, S., Zavalloni, M., & Louis-Gúerin, C. (1972). Studies on polarization of judgments: I. Group effects on person perception, *European Journal of Social Psychology, 2,* 87-91.

Moscovici, S., Zavalloni, M., & Weinberger, M. (1972). Studies on the polarization of judgments: II. Person perception, ego involvement, and group interaction. *European Journal of Social Psychology, 2,* 92-94.

Myers, D. G. (1973). Summary and bibliography of experiments on group-induced response shift. *Catalog of Selected Documents in Psychology, 3,* 123.

Myers, D. & Lamm, H. (1976). The group polarization phenomenon. *Psychological Bulletin, 83,* 602-627.

Pruitt, D. G. (1971). Choice shifts in group discussion: An introductory review. *Journal of Personality and Social Psychology, 20,* 339-360.

Spector, P., Cohen, S., & Penner, L. (1976). The effect of real vs. hypothetical risk on group choice shifts. *Personality and Social Psychology Bulletin, 2,* 290-293.

Stasser, G., Kerr, N. L., & Bray, R. (1982). The social psychology of jury deliberation: Structure, process, and product. In N. Kerr & R. Bray (Eds.), *The psychology of the courtroom* (pp. 221-256). New York: Academic Press.

Stasser, G., Kerr, N. L., & Davis, J. H. (1989). Influence processes and consensus models in decision-making groups. In P. Paulus (Ed.), *Psychology of group influence* (2nd ed., pp. 279-326). Hillsdale, NJ: Lawrence Erlbaum.

Tedeschi, J. T. (Ed.) (1981). *Impression management theory and social psychological research.* New York: Academic Press.

Thibaut, J., & Strickland, L. (1956). Psychological set and social conformity. *Journal of Personality, 25,* 115-129.

Vinokur, A., & Burnstein, E. (1978). Depolarization of attitudes in groups. *Journal of Personality and Social Psychology, 36,* 872-885.

Zajonc, R. B., Wolosin, R. J., Wolosin, M. A., & Sherman, S. J. (1968). Individual and group risk taking in a two-choice situation. *Journal of Experimental Social Psychology, 4,* 89-106.

PART II

Group Member
Attributes and Status

Introduction

Nancy Rhodes

Group members can differ from one another along a variety of dimensions, and these differences may affect the group's ability to perform tasks essential to its goals. One framework for understanding the complex effects of group composition on group member interaction and group productivity is McGrath's (1964) input-process-output model of group interaction (see also Hackman & Morris, 1975; McGrath, 1984). According to this view, input variables such as the composition of the group and the nature of the group's task affect the interaction of the group members, that is, the group process. The group process in turn affects such output variables as the quality of the group's solution to a task, the group members' satisfaction with the group process, and changes in the group members' attitudes.

One input variable that has received much attention is the diversity of group member attributes. According to Shaw (1983), increasing the diversity of the group might enhance or hinder performance, depending on the nature of the attributes being considered. Enhanced performance might result, for example, when a group working on a complex task is composed of members having diverse abilities that are relevant to the task. The effects of diversity of personality, attitudes, and demographics are less clear. Some evidence indicates that heterogeneity of personality enhances performance (Hoffman, 1959). However, diversity along any of a number of variables may impair the development of cohesiveness, and subsequent performance.

The chapters in this section explore the effects of diversity of group member attributes on process and output. They consider a variety of dimensions on which the group members might vary, from attitudes to personality variables to demographics. Additionally, the chapters consider the type of tasks that might or might not be facilitated by increased diversity of group membership and document the effects of diversity on a number of process and output variables.

Diversity of attitudes in a group may result in a minority of group members holding a position that differs from the majority. Chapter 4 by Nemeth investigates the conditions under which group members having minority status will be influential within the group. Nemeth makes the case that a dissenting minority results in a different type of group process than would occur in a group without dissent. Furthermore, the type of task the group must complete will dictate whether the process resulting from a dissenting minority will be effective. Thus, in this chapter, the input variables of group composition (i.e., the presence of a dissenting minority) and the nature of the task (i.e., the type of process most likely to result in the best solution) are both important in determining the quality of the solution.

These ideas were tested in a series of experiments which are particularly valuable because they utilize a variety of methodologies and tasks. These experiments demonstrate persuasively that a dissenting minority prompts the group to consider the solution to the task from a variety of viewpoints, and in most cases the group settles on a better quality solution than would be the case in the absence of dissent. However, the studies also demonstrate that some tasks yield a better quality solution in the absence of dissent. Thus, Nemeth argues for the interdependence of the input variables, that is, the task requirements must be taken into account when considering whether a dissenting minority will be beneficial.

In Chapter 5, Brandstätter and Waldhör focus on diversity of personality variables in a group context. They argue that insufficient attention has been paid to the personalities of the participants in studying group phenomena. People may differ in the degree to which they are exchange or reinforcement oriented such that an individual having an exchange orientation is likely to reciprocate friendly or unfriendly behavior, whereas a reinforcement-oriented person will avoid an unfriendly partner and respond emphatically to friendly behavior. They examine how group members varying in exchange or reinforcement orientation will react to a discussion partner who is either friendly (rewarding) or hostile (punishing). Their approach also considers the emotional stability of the subjects, and examines the experience of emotion in the group situation as a process variable.

Brandstätter and Waldhör describe a number of studies which they and others have conducted to examine these issues. In general, they have found that among emotionally unstable subjects reinforcement-oriented individuals yield to unfriendly partners, whereas exchange-oriented individuals yield to friendly partners. These results are consistent with the model that they have proposed. However, for the stable subjects the pattern of influence was opposite of that for unstable subjects.

In this chapter, we see the benefits of taking into account input variables such as the group context (friendly versus unfriendly partner) and the personality traits (reinforcement versus exchange orientation) of the group members. Although the model proposed by Brandstätter and Waldhör awaits revision to account for the results for the emotionally stable subjects, it provides an interesting combination of group process research and personality theory. Furthermore, the model takes a unique approach to the study of group process by focusing on the emotional experiences of group members as they interact. This chapter provides an initial view of the group members' experience when the tone of a group's discussion is either friendly or hostile.

Chapter 6 by Jackson takes an applied view of diversity in group composition. Current trends indicate that the work force of the future will become increasingly diverse with the greater integration of women into roles previously assigned to men, the increasing ethnic diversity of our society in general, and the greater range of ages in the work force. In planning for this greater diversity of work groups, Jackson contends that we must consider the apparent trade-off between the benefits to group productivity and the decrement to group cohesiveness of heterogeneity in work groups.

The chapter reviews the results of social psychological research and concludes that, in general, heterogeneity among abilities and attributes of group members facilitates performance of most tasks assigned in laboratory research. Unfortunately, at the same time, this increased heterogeneity results in less group cohesiveness. Lowered cohesiveness has been associated with lower group productivity, lower group member satisfaction, and higher rates of absenteeism and turnover in employment settings.

Field research conducted by Jackson and her colleagues was designed to address these issues in the context of work groups in applied settings.

Utilizing questionnaire and archival data, they report the results of two studies that evaluated the heterogeneity of top management teams in banks and the performance and turnover rates of these teams. Consistent with the results of the laboratory work reviewed, they found that diversity is related to enhanced task performance. Additionally, Jackson and her colleagues found evidence that diversity in work groups is associated with a lack of cohesiveness. They found that greater heterogeneity was associated with higher turnover rates; dissimilar members were the most likely to turn over; and homogeneous teams were the most likely to fill positions from within the organization, thereby perpetuating the group members' similarity.

This chapter highlights the implications of group composition for both task performance and the satisfaction of group members. In coming years organizations will need to know how best to manage an increasingly diverse work force to enhance productivity and minimize turnover. The work reported in this chapter advances our understanding of the effects of diversity on these variables.

In general, the chapters in this section present a variety of perspectives on how diversity among group members affects group functioning. The chapters highlight the importance of considering both group composition and task demands on the group process. The breadth of methodological approaches and the variety of group member attributes considered here provide a rich basis for understanding these processes.

References

Hackman, J. R., & Morris, C. G. (1975). Group tasks, group interaction process, and group performance effectiveness: A review and proposed integration. *Advances in Experimental Social Psychology, 8,* 45-99.

Hoffman, L. R. (1959). Homogeneity of member personality and its effect on group problem-solving. *Journal of Abnormal and Social Psychology, 58,* 27-32.

McGrath, J. E. (1964). *Social psychology: A brief introduction.* New York: Holt.

Shaw, M. E. (1983). Group composition. In H. H. Blumberg, A. P. Hare, V. Kent, & M. F. Davies (Eds.), *Small groups and social interaction* (Vol. 1). Chichester: John Wiley.

4   Minority Dissent as a Stimulant to Group Performance

Charlan Jeanne Nemeth

We dislike arguments of any kind; they are always vulgar, and often convincing.

—Oscar Wilde

For a good many years, social psychologists have recognized the importance of opinion differences as they have attempted to understand attitude formation and change, group performance, and group decision making. We have learned that opinion differences and arguments produce a great deal of stress and irritation (Asch, 1956; Janis, 1982; Schachter, 1951) but we also have learned that some of those opinions are convincing. Other people move toward those positions, and sometimes adopt them. As a result, a good deal of our work over the past few decades has been aimed at understanding whose opinions are convincing, for what reasons, and with what effect.

One of the concerns that has repeatedly been voiced about "convincing" or successfully influencing others to one's position is that such influence is not necessarily based on the correctness of one's position. In some studies, it is apparent that attributes of the person(s) who holds

AUTHOR'S NOTE: The material in this chapter was presented as an invited address to the First Annual Conference on Group Processes and Productivity, Texas A&M University, April 1989. Preparation of this manuscript was supported by the National Science Foundation grant No. BNS85-12000 to the author, support that is gratefully acknowledged.

the position may be more important than the truth or falsity of the position itself.

In the early studies by Torrance (1955), for example, three-person Navy bomber crews consisting of a pilot, a navigator, and a gunner, were asked to solve a problem. The task was the horsetrading problem, described below:

> A man bought a horse for $60 and sold it for $70. Then he bought the same horse back for $80 and again sold it for $90. How much money did he make in the horse business?

The answer, which is not apparent to most college students, is $20. Two types of reasoning can be given. One points out that there is a $10 profit on each of two transactions; the second notes that the person paid out $140 and took in $160. Given the simplicity of the explanations and the obviousness of the solution once proferred, one would expect that, if one of the three individuals in the group knew the correct answer, the group would then adopt that correct solution. The results, however, show that not all groups adopted the correct answer even when one member knew it. It depended on *who* knew the correct answer. If it was the pilot, the person of the highest status, the group was quite likely to adopt it; if it was the navigator, they were less likely to adopt it; and if it was the gunner (the lowest in status), they were least likely to adopt it. In the latter situation, only 65% of the groups adopted the correct position even though one person (the gunner) knew the correct answer.

Other studies corroborate the notion that people might be more influenced by who holds the position than by the "truth" inherent in the position. In one study (Nemeth, 1976; Nemeth & Wachtler, 1983), groups of six were studied in which either a majority (of 4) or a minority (of 2) made a judgment regarding an embedded figure. Depending on the condition, that judgment was either correct or incorrect. Those researchers found that people's acceptance of the position depended more on whether a majority or minority made the judgment than on whether the judgment was correct or not. People followed the majority more than the minority, right or wrong.

Still other studies show the importance of style over substance. Thomas and Fink (1961), for example, found that when one person knew the correct answer, the group adopted that position if and only if the person holding the correct position talked more than anyone else. Other studies have pointed out the importance of talking quickly

(MacLachlan, 1979; Miller, Maruyama, Beaber, & Valone, 1976), taking the head seat (Nemeth & Wachtler, 1974), or using vivid images (Nisbett & Ross, 1980; Sherman, Cialdini, Schwartzman, & Reynolds, 1985) for persuasion. Such power to influence regardless of correctness of position has plagued researchers interested in raising the quality of decision making and problem solving. How do you increase the likelihood that "truth" will be adopted and error ignored?

The Power of the Majority

In the 1950s and 1960s, a great deal of research was directed at a specific form of influence to error, namely, the willingness of people to adopt majority views even when they were wrong. The power of that source of influence was documented brilliantly in the early studies by Asch (1956). In his studies, individuals adopted the erroneous position held by the majority of individuals, even when there was clear information from their own senses to the contrary. Alone, they made very few errors. Faced with a unanimous majority favoring another (but erroneous) position, fully one third of the responses were in agreement with that majority and against the information of their own senses.

Other studies, conducted at the group level, provide still further evidence of the power of majorities and of processes that do not necessarily favor adoption of the correct solution. Kalven and Zeisel (1966), for example, studied actual jury deliberations and found strong support for the power of majority views. When the first ballot showed 7 to 11 of the 12 people favoring "guilty," 84% of the jury verdicts were "guilty." When 7 to 11 of the 12 people favored "not guilty," 91% of the verdicts were "not guilty." Extensive and precise work by Davis, Kerr, Atkin, Holt, & Meek, (1975) and by Kerr et al. (1976) have added to our understanding of how individual judgments combine to form a final verdict. They provide evidence that the best model is a two-thirds majority scheme. When two out of three (or 8 out of the 12-person jury) favor a given position, it is highly likely to be the final outcome. Right or wrong, the majority has considerable power to persuade.

In studies of decision making that led to "political fiascoes," Janis (1972, 1982) provided evidence for a phenomenon similar to social conformity. In those groups, there was evidence of a group process, termed "groupthink," to describe when "the members' strivings for unanimity override their motivation to realistically appraise alternative courses of action" (Janis, 1982, p. 9). In many of these groups, cohesion and a directive leader provided the basis for adoption of a poor decision, one reached after poor information processing and decision making.

The question facing researchers is: Why do individuals and groups manifest such propensities to error? In most of these situations, the problem is not only the power of the majority and its view but also the relative absence, vulnerability, or weakness of dissent or minority views. Let us consider conformity research. People adopt the erroneous majority view not only because they believe it to be correct (informational influence) but also because they fear the rejection that comes from maintaining a minority view (Schachter, 1951). Thus, dissent tends not to be voiced nor deviance maintained. When dissent is expressed, conformity is drastically reduced. The greatest amount of conformity occurs when the majority is in agreement, namely, when there is no dissent. If there is a single dissenter (whether or not he or she agrees with the subject), conformity decreases sharply (Allen & Levine, 1968). Similarly, Janis's (1972, 1982) work on groupthink points to the absence of dissent coupled with the strain to uniformity as contributors to defective decision making. In fact there was evidence of repression of dissent in those deliberations. Members put pressure on others, even those who raised doubts; they even censored themselves.

The Power of Minorities

As we consider the importance of dissent, let us first consider whether the deviate or minority is necessarily as vulnerable and weak as has been suggested by the previous research. In the late 1960s and early 1970s, perhaps as a consequence of events such as the May 1968 uprising in Paris and the 1968 Democratic National Convention in Chicago, a number of researchers in Europe and in the United States investigated the possibility that minorities were not simply passive agents who said yes or no to a system of answers provided by a majority. In other words, conformity and independence were not the only possible responses to a majority. Rather, these researchers studied the possibility that minorities might forcefully argue for their own position and might exert influence on the majority (Moscovici & Faucheux, 1972; Moscovici, Lage, & Naffrechoux, 1969; Moscovici & Nemeth, 1974). The research on this phenomenon, conducted by dozens of researchers over the past 20 years, has led to a number of interesting insights, among them the following:

1. Minorities do exercise influence and those influence attempts depend on the behavioral style over time of the minority arguing its position.

Consistency over time has been found to be a very important variable for minority influence. In the early study by Moscovici et al. (1969), a minority who consistently judged blue slides to be "green" had significant influence on the majority, whereas a minority who gave inconsistent judgments (⅔ green and ⅓ blue responses to the blue slides) showed no significant influence. Nemeth, Swedlund, and Kanki (1974) refined the concept of consistency from simple repetition to include a patterning of judgments to properties of the stimulus and again found support for the contention that perceived consistency is related to influence by the minority. Numerous other studies have replicated and underscored this relationship even for attitudinal measures (Mugny, 1982; Paicheler, 1976).

2. Contrary to the notion that majorities are all-powerful, their vulnerabilities have been noted as well. Often content and comfortable with the knowledge that their views are shared by a majority of others, they appear to be subject to doubt when faced with confident and persistent opposition.

Kiesler and Pallak (1975), for example, found evidence that the members of the majority had their self-doubts accentuated by the defection of majority members to the minority. Studies by Nemeth (Nemeth et al., 1974; Nemeth & Wachtler, 1983) show evidence for a "snowball effect" whereby movement to the minority by one majority member is often followed by other majority members.

3. Minorities appear to exert their influence at a latent or private level rather than at a public or manifest level.

Moscovici et al. (1969) found that subjects exposed to a minority who consistently judged blue slides to be "green" showed little public adoption of that position. However, there was considerable evidence for changes in blue/green perceptual judgments on a subsequent task. In a jury simulation study by Nemeth and Wachtler (1974), influence to the minority view was not evident in public on the case under discussion but was apparent on the private judgments and on related cases. Mugny, Rilliet, and Papastamou (1981) show support for the proposition that minorities exert more influence on "indirect" than on "direct" items. Finally, there is evidence (Maass & Clark, 1983; Mugny, 1976) that individuals move to a majority in public but to a minority in private.

4. Liking may be relatively unimportant for minority influence.

Although some people may be able to "win friends and influence people" (Carnegie, 1952), minorities do not appear to have that luxury. Minimally, they need to maintain a consistent position but doing this is likely to engender dislike (Nemeth & Wachtler, 1983). In addition, Nemeth, Wachtler, and Endicott (1977) find evidence for a relationship between perceived competence, perceived confidence, and influence; liking, however, had no significant effect on the amount of influence exerted.

The Stimulating Role of Minority Dissent

The research emphasizing the fact that minorities can exercise influence on majorities has been very helpful as a contrast to the emphasis on influence by majorities and those in power. It has also provided important insights into the nature of influence, raising questions about the importance of behavioral styles, the possible unimportance of liking, and the relationship between public and private attitude change. Finally, it has provided information about innovation and social change. However, this work does not directly test the issue of quality of outcome or judgments.

The fact that minorities can prevail does not ensure that "truth" or correctness has been served. In fact, many studies that have focused on the ability of minorities to influence the majority to error (e.g., calling blue slides "green"). However, I will argue in the remainder of this chapter that minority views do have an important role to play in fostering quality of thought, performance, and decision making. And this is not because they are correct or because they can influence people to move toward their position or to adopt it. Rather, it is because minority views, even when they are wrong, foster the kinds of attention and thought processes that, on balance, permit the detection of new truths and raise the quality of group decision making and performance.

In the previous discussion about the role of dissent or minority views in the conformity or groupthink contexts, we emphasized the importance of dissent for preventing powerful influences to error. Dissent thwarted the power of a majority and permitted individuals to maintain their own authentic (and veridical) views. Dissent potentially prevented the "rush to judgment" evidenced in groupthink contexts in which alternative courses of action often are not considered. Although these are important contributions made by dissenting views, we propose (Nemeth, 1986) that minorities do more than retard the negative consequences of powerful influence sources. They have an active role to play; and it takes the form of stimulating divergent thought processes that, on balance, improve performance and decision making. Let us first consider the background for such a contention and then provide several experimental studies that provide evidence for these propositions.

Most of the background for considering the stimulating properties of minority dissent comes from a reconsideration of the literature on conformity and on minority influence, research that emphasized the ability of either the majority or the minority to "prevail," that is, to influence movement toward, or adoption of, their proposed positions. As we compared these literatures, several points became evident. First, individuals report being under much more stress when faced with a disagreeing majority than with a disagreeing minority. Subjects report a great deal of stress and fear when placed in a typical conformity setting (Asch, 1956). Such stress is not evident in minority influence studies; in fact, subjects in the majority appear to be amused and derisive of the disagreeing minority—at least at first (Nemeth & Wachtler, 1974, 1983). Second, people start with the assumption that truth lies in numbers, and, as such, people in the conformity setting assume that the majority is likely to be correct (Asch, 1956). In the minority influence setting, they assume that the minority is likely to be incorrect (Nemeth et al., 1974; Nemeth & Wachtler, 1983). Finally, subjects are motivated to believe that the majority is correct and the minority is incorrect. This would legitimate adopting (or maintaining) the majority viewpoint and thereby lessen the fear of disapproval and rejection for maintaining a minority viewpoint (Asch, 1956; Deutsch & Gerard, 1955; Nemeth, Endicott, & Wachtler, 1977).

From these differences, we formed what appeared to be a reasonable scenario about the reactions to majority versus minority dissent. We started with the recognition that majority views create a good deal of stress. Such stress may be assumed to be accompanied by a narrowing of focus and an underutilization of cues (Easterbrook, 1959; Kahneman, 1973; Yerkes & Dodson, 1908). The question, however, is where they will focus, however narrow that focus may be. Our assumption was that the focus would be the perspective posed by the majority. Since the majority is assumed to be correct and people are motivated to assume that, people attempt to discern whether or not the majority is correct. Thus, they focus on the issue from that perspective. The world of alternatives is reduced to two.

By contrast, we hypothesized that dissenting minority views create arousal but far less than do majority views. People are stimulated to reconsider the issue but now there is *not* an assumption of correctness. In fact, people assume the minority is incorrect. The result is that people will consider the issue from multiple perspectives, one of which is that posed by the minority. As a result, thought will be divergent in form (see Nemeth, 1986).

It is important to underscore the fact that the above predictions are not directed at whether or not the individuals will adopt a majority or minority position. We are hypothesizing that the thought processes about the issue will be quite different; and, on balance, the divergent cognitive processes stimulated by exposure to minority views will raise the quality of performance, the attitude held, or the decision reached.

The Experimental Evidence

In our original study (Nemeth, 1976; Nemeth & Wachtler, 1983), we simply varied whether a majority or minority of individuals detected a standard figure in a complex comparison figure and whether that judgment was correct or incorrect. In that study, we found evidence for better performance by individuals exposed to dissenting minority views rather than dissenting majority views. Although subjects were more likely to follow the judgment expressed by the majority than a minority, that following was regardless of the correctness of the position. When exposed to the dissenting minority, however, there was evidence for the detection of novel and correct solutions. These were solutions that were not proposed by the minority, nor detected by a control group of subjects. We hypothesized that the improved performance was a result of the divergent cognitive processes that were stimulated by the minority views. Our later work concentrated on the intervening mechanisms for such improved performance.

In one study (Nemeth & Kwan, 1987), we showed subjects in groups of four a series of letter strings consisting of six letters and asked them to name the first three-letter word that they noticed. Examples would be rSAWed or bTONag. The first word noticed by our subjects was the word formed by the capital letters from left to right (SAW and TON in the examples). After five such slides, they were given feedback as to the responses of the four individuals. In the majority condition they were told that three people first noticed a word formed by a backward sequencing of the capital letters (e.g., WAS, WAS, WAS or NOT, NOT, NOT) and that one person (themselves, they thought) first noticed the word formed by the forward sequencing. Thus the feedback for the first example would be WAS, WAS, WAS, SAW. In the minority condition, they were told that one person first noticed the word formed by the backward sequencing and that three persons (including themselves, they thought) first noticed the word formed by the forward sequencing. Here the feedback for the first example would be WAS, SAW, SAW, SAW. They were then given a series of 10 letter strings, each again consisting of six letters each, and asked to write down all the words they could form from these letter strings. They were given 15 seconds per letter string.

For this study, we first measured overall performance. As the reader may have surmised, those exposed to the dissenting minority position found more words from the letter strings than those exposed to the dissenting majority position. The latter individuals did not differ from control subjects who received no feedback. Importantly, subjects differed in the ways in which they found the words. Let us first consider the possible ways of forming words from these letter strings and their implications for the kinds of cognitive thought processes stimulated by the dissenting viewpoints.

If we take the example of rSAWed, people can form words using a forward sequencing, for example, raw, red. They can form words using a backward sequencing, for example, war, dear. They can also form words using a mixed sequencing, for example, wad, wear. Individuals exposed to majority dissent (which favored a backward sequencing of letters) tended to take the perspective posed by the majority. They found more words using a backward sequencing. While not differing from control subjects in overall performance, they found more words using a backward sequencing but this was at the expense of finding words using a forward or mixed sequencing. By contrast, those exposed to the minority dissent used all possible patterns to form the words. They utilized forward, backward, and mixed sequencing in the service of overall performance.

In a relatively recent study, we (Nemeth, Mayseless, Sherman, & Brown, 1990) found evidence for better recall by individuals exposed to minority rather than majority dissent. In this study, we played three tape-recorded lists of 14 words each to a group of four individuals. Subjects were asked to name the first category of word that they noticed. Each list consisted of four words representing the category of "fruits" and two words each from the categories of "tools," "furniture," "clothing," "birds," and "transportation." Further, the words representing "fruits" were the first two and the last two words in the list. One such list was as follows:

apple, pear, shoes, pliers, couch, hawk, bike
coat, lamp, hammer, dove, car, grapes, cherry

The first category of word noticed by our subjects was "fruits," the reason being that it is the most frequent category (4 of the 14 words) and it also enjoys primacy and recency. After three such lists, subjects were given feedback as to the responses of the four members of their group. In the majority condition, they were told that three persons first noticed "birds" and that one person first noticed "fruits" (themselves, they thought). In the minority condition, they were told that one person first noticed "birds" and that three persons first noticed "fruits." In addition, this information was given for list 1 only or for all three lists consistently. After such feedback, they heard a tape-recorded list of the same 42 words but now presented in random order. They were now instructed to write down all the words they could remember. Finally, they listened to a list of 30 entirely new words, consisting of entirely new categories (e.g., gems, sports) and again asked to write down all the words they could remember.

The results showed a significant main effect for source on the percentage of words correctly recalled. Subjects exposed to minority dissent recalled more words than those exposed to majority dissent. There was also a source by consistency interaction such that, when exposure was once, minority and majority source did not differ and neither differed from the control group. When exposure was consistent over the three trials, subjects exposed to minority dissent had significantly better recall than control subjects who, in turn, had significantly better recall than those exposed to majority dissent. Thus, there is evidence that consistent minority dissent stimulates better recall whereas consistent majority dissent hinders good recall.

The reader might already have been considering a possible "confound" or at least another aspect of our minority/majority setting. When subjects are exposed to minority dissent, they themselves are in a majority; when they are exposed to a majority dissent, they themselves are in a minority. Thus, one might hypothesize that the improved recall as a response to minority dissent might be due to the fact that one is in a majority. Being in a majority could well provide confirmation of one's own judgment and enhance morale. However, if this were the reason for the improved recall, then agreement by all three other individuals in one's group should be even more conducive to recall.

In a follow-up study, we tested this possibility and included two control groups, one involving no feedback (as in previous studies) and the second involving complete agreement (i.e., subjects were given feedback that all four individuals named "fruits" as the category first noticed). Findings showed that the latter condition was not only *not* superior to the minority dissent condition but was inferior even to the control condition involving no feedback.

When Majority Dissent Improves Performance

In most of our theorizing about the effects of exposure to minority versus majority dissent, we have emphasized the relative advantages of minority dissent. This is primarily because, on balance, the divergent thought hypothesized to result from exposure to minority views aids performance. Minority dissent appears to stimulate exactly what theorists have recommended for improved performance and decision making, that is, a consideration of the issue from multiple perspectives. However, it is important to point out that the hypotheses link majority and minority dissent to convergent versus divergent thought processes, respectively. The improved performance results from such divergent thought processes in most situations. If convergent thought was conducive to improved performance, we would hypothesize that exposure to majority dissent would have advantages relative to minority dissent.

One situation where convergent thought processes appear to enhance performance is the classic Stroop test. Here, individuals are shown the name of a color in an ink of a different color and are asked to read the color of the ink. As an example, the word *blue* written in red ink should be read as *red*. For this task, it is helpful to ignore the name of the word, that is, to think convergently about "ink."

If our hypotheses regarding the differential cognitive processes emanating from exposure to majority versus minority dissent are correct, majority dissent should foster convergent thinking from the perspective they pose. As such, majority dissent that focuses on the ink should aid performance on the Stroop test, whereas majority dissent that focuses on the name of the color should particularly impede performance. Minority dissent, hypothesized to stimulate divergent thought, would not be predicted to enhance or impede performance, and no significant differences would be predicted as a function of where the minority focused, that is, on name or ink.

To test such hypotheses, we (Nemeth, Mosier, & Chiles, 1991) showed 88 subjects in groups of four three different slides in sequence. Each slide consisted of two words. One was centrally positioned and was the name of a color printed in ink of the same color, for example, the word *blue* in blue ink. The other word was positioned much lower and was the name of a color printed in an ink of a different color, for example, the word *red* in yellow ink. When asked to indicate the color that first came to mind, subjects said the color represented by both name and color, "blue" in the example. Feedback then indicated that one person (in the minority condition) or three persons (in the majority condition) first thought of a different color. In the ink conditions, they noticed the color represented by the ink of the second word, "yellow" in the example. In the name conditions, they said the color represented by the name of the color of the second word, "red" in the example.

After the feedback, subjects were placed in separate cubicles and shown a slide consisting of a large number of names of colors printed in inks of different colors, that is, the Stroop test. They were asked to report aloud the color of ink for each word as quickly and as accurately as possible. The main dependent variable was the amount of time it took to read the ink colors. The results showed that performance was best in the majority ink condition and poorest in the majority name condition. Thus the study provides some further evidence for the proposition that majority dissent fosters convergent thought and, in particular, thought directed to the perspective posed by the majority. Although, in general, such convergence may impede performance and lead to a restriction of the consideration of alternative views, there are situations where such convergence is helpful. The Stroop test is one of those tasks where performance is aided by convergent thought, and, as such, performance can be improved by convergent thought on ink.

Some General Comments

Given the fact that these studies have been conducted with quite different paradigms and even different measures of performance (e.g., strategies of problem solving, recall of information, reading of complex stimuli), we are encouraged by the fact that the hypotheses receive repeated support. Minority dissent does appear to stimulate divergent thought, a consideration of the stimulus or issue from multiple perspectives. Majority dissent appears to stimulate convergent thought and, specifically, convergent thought from the perspective posed by the majority. Although, in principle, convergent thought should be helpful on some kinds of tasks whereas divergent thought might be more helpful on other kinds of tasks, we find that our initial emphasis on the benefits of divergent thought and the particular value of minority dissent appears to be well founded.

Majority dissent and the convergent thought processes that it stimulates rarely culminate in superior performance. The Stroop test is one such rare situation where convergent thought (on ink) is useful, but even there, the most useful form of majority dissent (emphasizing ink) was only marginally superior to the minority dissent conditions, whereas the poorer form of majority dissent (emphasizing name) led to significantly poorer performance. The fact that majority dissent can impede performance has been found in other studies as well. In the recall study, for example, exposure to consistent majority dissent led to poorer recall than evidenced by our control subjects, who had no exposure to dissent. By contrast, we have repeated evidence that exposure to minority dissent is beneficial. It stimulates the detection of correct novel solutions to problems (Nemeth & Wachtler, 1983); it fosters the use of multiple strategies to problem solution, which aids performance (Nemeth & Kwan, 1987); and it improves recall of information (Nemeth, Mayseless, Sherman, & Brown, 1990).

Although we are encouraged by the pattern of these findings, we have much to learn about why and how majority and minority dissent influence cognitive processes, decision making, and performance. For example, most of our paradigms to date have concentrated on issues of preference or the "first" category noticed. The implication is clear that the judgments are subjective. This was a starting point, because we wanted to make the dissent appear reasonable as well as to provide alternative positions to which the individual could move. However, the issue of objective versus subjective judgments is an important one. Crano (1989) has suggested that this variable may be of major importance because it may predict social comparison processes. Gorenflo and Crano (1989) offer evidence that people's preference for similar others may be stronger when the judgments are subjective; preference for dissimilar comparison partners may be greater when judgments are objective. Such findings may prove to be very important for the understanding of majority and minority influence. They may in fact relate to the kinds of conflict experienced and the kinds of reactions that result in response to dissent.

The issue of subjectivity/objectivity may be important in another context as well. Our theory about the importance of minority dissent grew out of a longstanding interest in group problem solving and decision making—in particular, jury decision making. There, our efforts were directed at finding mechanisms by which jurors would use all the evidence and arrive at an objective "truth" (Nemeth, 1977, 1981), and it became clear that whether majorities or minorities influenced the decision in the sense of "prevailing" did not answer the questions regarding the quality of the decision reached. Rather, we needed to find mechanisms by which the process of decision making would, on balance, serve the detection of truth. And it is that work, coupled with the years of studying how minorities "prevail," that led to the theory characterized herein.

Our studies to date on the value of minority dissent and its contributions to divergent thought and the detection of correct solutions are theoretically relevant to those concerns but do not address group decision making directly. Worchel (1989) has wisely counseled us to study the interactive nature of the minority and the group and, importantly, to recognize that groups are not static entities but develop, change structure, and change members as well as respond to temporal and situational demands. As such, he proposes that our findings linking minority dissent to divergent thought may be particularly evident when the group is concerned with goal attainment and the meeting of individual needs rather than when members are concerned about their identity. This is clearly an important direction and we should expand research to the study of groups over time, including the socialization of members that Moreland and Levine (1987) have so ably articulated.

If, as we learn more, it becomes apparent that minority dissent can thwart some of the deleterious consequences of the strivings for unanimity, such as the "groupthink" syndrome and the rush to the majority's judgment, it will be important. Perhaps, more importantly, should it hold true that minority dissent, even when it is wrong, stimulates the consideration of more information and more ways to think about that information in the service of the detection of correct solutions and better performance, then we may have a very important mechanism indeed. We may learn to refrain from too easily adopting the value of efficiency, improving morale, or resolving conflicts. And we may have underscored the words of Fulbright (1964) where we "learn to welcome and not to fear the voices of dissent, where we dare to think about unthinkable things because when things become unthinkable, thinking stops and action becomes mindless."

References

Allen, V. L., & Levine, J. M. (1968). Social support, dissent and conformity. *Sociometry, 31,* 138-249.

Asch, S. E. (1956). Studies on independence and conformity: A minority of one against a unanimous majority. *Psychological Monographs, 70*(416).

Carnegie, D. (1952). *How to win friends and influence people.* New York: Simon & Schuster.

Crano, W. D. (1989, June). *Judgmental subjectivity/objectivity and minority influence.* Paper presented to Third Workshop on Minority Influence, Perugia, Italy.

Davis, J. H., Kerr, N. L., Atkin, R. S., Holt, R., & Meek, D. (1975). The decision processes of 6- and 12-person mock juries assigned unanimous and two thirds majority rules. *Journal of Personality and Social Psychology, 32* 1-14.

Deutsch, M., & Gerard, H. B. (1955). A study of normative and informational social influence upon individual judgment. *Journal of Abnormal and Social Psychology, 51,* 629-636.

Easterbrook, J. A. (1959). The effect of emotion on the utilization and the organization of behavior. *Psychological Review, 66,* 183-201.

Fulbright, J. (1964). Speech to the United States Senate, March 27, 1964.

Gorenflo, D. W., & Crano, W. D. (1989). Judgmental subjectivity/objectivity and locus of choice in social comparison. *Journal of Personality and Social Psychology, 57,* 605-614.

Janis, I. L. (1972). *Victims of groupthink: A psychological study of foreign-policy decisions and fiascoes.* Boston: Houghton Mifflin.

Janis, I. L. (1982). *Groupthink.* Boston: Houghton Mifflin.

Kahneman, D. (1973). *Attention and effort.* Englewood Cliffs, NJ: Prentice-Hall.

Kalven, H., Jr., & Zeisel, H. (1966). *The American jury.* New York: Little, Brown.

Kerr, N. L., Atkin, R. S., Stasser, G., Meek, D., Holt, R. W., & Davis, J. H. (1976). Guilt beyond a reasonable doubt: Effect of concept definition and assigned decision rule on the judgments of mock jurors. *Journal of Personality and Social Psychology, 34,* 282-295.

Kiesler, C. A., & Pallak, M. S. (1975). Minority influence: The effect of majority reactionaries and defectors, and minority and majority compromisers, upon majority opinion and attraction. *European Journal of Social Psychology, 5,* 237-256.

Maass, A., & Clark, R. D., III (1983). Internalization versus compliance: Differential processes underlying minority influence and conformity. *European Journal of Social Psychology, 13,* 45-55.

Maass, A., & Clark, R. D., III (1984). The hidden impact of minorities: Fourteen years of minority influence research. *Psychological Bulletin, 95,* 428-450.

MacLachlan, J. (1979, November). What people really think of fast talkers. *Psychology Today,* pp. 113-117.

Miller, N., Maruyama, G., Beaber, R. J., & Valone, K. (1976). Speed of speech and persuasion. *Journal of Personality and Social Psychology, 34,* 615-624.

Moreland, R. L., & Levine, J. M. (1989). Newcomers and oldtimers in small groups. In P. B. Paulus (Ed.), *Psychology of group influence* (2nd ed., pp. 143-185). Hillsdale, NJ: Lawrence Erlbaum.

Moscovici, S., & Faucheux, C. (1972). Social influence, conformity bias and the study of active minorities. In L. Berkowitz (Ed.), *Advances in experimental social psychology* (Vol. 6, pp. 149-202). New York: Academic Press.

Moscovici, S., Lage, E., & Naffrechoux, M. (1969). Influence of a consistent minority on the responses of a majority in a color perception task. *Sociometry, 32,* 365-380.

Moscovici, S., & Nemeth, C. (1974). Social influence II: Minority influence. In C. Nemeth (Ed.), *Social psychology: Classic and contemporary integrations.* Chicago: Rand-McNally.

Mugny, G. (1976). Quelle influence majoritaire? Quelle influence minoritaire? *Revue Suisse de Psychologie, 4,* 255-268.

Mugny, G. (1982). *The power of minorities.* New York: Academic Press.

Mugny, G., Rilliet, O., & Papastamou, S. (1981). Influence minoritaire et identification sociale dans les contextes d'originalite et de deviance. *Revue Suisse de Psychologie, 40,* 314-332.

Nemeth, C. (1977). Interactions between jurors as a function of majority vs. unanimity decision rules. *Journal of Applied Social Psychology, 7,* 38-56.

Nemeth, C. (1976, August). *A comparison between conformity and minority influence.* Paper presented to International Congress on Psychology, Paris, France.

Nemeth, C. (1981). Jury trials: Psychology and the law. In L. Berkowitz (Ed.), *Advances in experimental social psychology* (Vol. 14, pp. 309-367). New York: Academic Press.

Nemeth, C. (1986). Differential contributions of majority and minority influence. *Psychological Review, 93,* 23-32.

Nemeth, C., Endicott, J., & Wachtler, J. (1977). Increasing the size of the minority: Some gains and some losses. *European Journal of Social Psychology, 1,* 11-23.

Nemeth, C., & Kwan, J. (1987). Minority influence, divergent thinking and detection of correct solutions. *Journal of Applied Social Psychology, 17,* 786-797.

Nemeth, C., Mayseless, O., Sherman, J., & Brown, Y. (1990). Improving recall by exposure to consistent dissent. *Journal of Personality and Social Psychology, 58,* 429-437.

Nemeth, C., Mosier, K., & Chiles, C. (1991). When convergent thought improves performance: Majority versus minority influence. *Personality and Social Psychology.*

Nemeth, C., Swedlund, M., & Kanki, B. (1974). Patterning of the minority's responses and their influence on the majority. *European Journal of Social Psychology, 6,* 437-439.

Nemeth, C., & Wachtler, J. (1974). Creating perceptions of consistency and confidence: A necessary condition for minority influence. *Sociometry, 37,* 529-540.

Nemeth, C., & Wachtler, J. (1983). Creative problem solving as a result of majority versus minority influence. *European Journal of Social Psychology, 13,* 45-55.

Nemeth, C., Wachtler, J., & Endicott, J. (1977). Increasing the size of a minority: Some gains and some losses. *European Journal of Social Psychology, 7,* 15-27.

Nisbett, R. E., & Ross, L. (1980). *Human inference: Strategies and shortcomings of social judgment.* Englewood Cliffs, NJ: Prentice-Hall.

Paicheler, G. (1976). Norms and attitude change: Polarization and styles of behaviour. *European Journal of Social Psychology, 6,* 405-427.

Schachter, S. (1951). Deviation, rejection, and communication. *Journal of Abnormal and Social Psychology, 46,* 190-207.

Sherman, S. J., Cialdini, R. B., Schwartzman, D. F., & Reynolds, K. D. (1985). Imagining can heighten or lower the perceived likelihood of contracting a disease: The mediating effect of ease of imagery. *Personality and Social Psychology Bulletin, 11,* 118-127.

Thomas, E. J., & Fink, C. F. (1961). Models of group problem solving. *Journal of Abnormal and Social Psychology, 63,* 53-63.

Torrance, E. P. (1955). Some consequences of power differences on decision making in permanent and temporary three-man groups. In A. P. Hare, E. F. Borgatta, & R. F. Bales (Eds.), *Small groups: Studies in social interaction* (pp. 482-492). New York: Knopf.

Worchel, S. (1989, June). *Minority influence in the group context: How group factors affect when the minority will be influential.* Paper presented to Third Workshop on Minority Influence, Perugia, Italy.

Yerkes, R. M., & Dodson, J. D. (1908). The relation of strength of stimulus to rapidity of habit formation. *Journal of Comparative Neurology of Psychology, 18,* 459-482.

5   Social Exchange Orientation Versus Social Reinforcement Orientation in Controversial Discussions

Hermann Brandstätter
Klemens Waldhör

Different routes of social influence. When people try to reach agreement in group decision making they try to influence each other and are influenced by each other in three different ways (Brandstätter, 1978): (a) they communicate their preferences and learn others' stands; (b) they communicate promises and threats, social rewards, and punishments for yielding or resisting the attempted influence (they learn others' demands); and (c) they communicate the reasons for their preferences and learn others' arguments.

The first facet has been studied mainly within the tradition of conformity theory (Asch, 1956; Sherif, 1936) and social comparison theory (Festinger, 1954). The second strand of influence has its sources in people's dependence on social reward and social punishment, called effect dependence by Jones and Gerard (1967). Some of the literature on bargaining and negotiation (for reviews, see Levine & Moreland, 1990; Pruitt & Rubin, 1986; Rubin & Brown, 1975) deals extensively with this aspect of social influence.

The third route of influence has been analyzed mainly within the tradition of information integration theory (Anderson & Graeser, 1976). In explaining the choice shift caused by group discussion, Burnstein (1982) although not explicitly referring to the information integration theory, has stressed the importance of the relative number of more or less persuasive pro and con arguments. Petty and Cacioppo (1986a, 1986b) have considered information integration by careful attention to and elaboration on arguments as the central route of attitude change.

The first and second modes of social influence mentioned above can be subsumed under the category of a peripheral route of attitude change, mediated by rather simple cues that suggest a positive or negative evaluation of the object under discussion. These cues are supposed to be particularly effective in situations where a person lacks of motivation and/or ability to integrate the information provided by the arguments.

The experiments to be reviewed here all focus on the effects of social reward and punishment on conformity processes in controversial group discussions. According to Petty and Cacioppo (1986b), the effects of social rewards and punishments are part of the peripheral route of attitude change, because one can assume that emotions elicited by a hostile or friendly discussion partner shift attention away from the content of the arguments to the consequences of yielding or resisting the influence attempt.

Influence in controversial discussions. Controversial discussions often provoke hostile feelings and verbal attacks. Are they detrimental or helpful in influencing an adversary? He or she may answer with anger and resistance (response type E) or with fear and yielding (response type R). How can we tell which response is more likely?

On the other hand, a discussion partner, although opposing my view and thus causing some discomfort, can also make me feel good by telling me that he or she finds my arguments interesting, precisely formulated, well informed, and so forth. What are the effects of such a friendly and polite discussion style or of other signals of readiness to compromise? Will I gratefully reciprocate these friendly gestures and cooperative moves (response type E) or, on the contrary, feel reinforced in my stance and proudly resist any influence attempt (response type R)?

There are many other social situations where our interaction partners support or obstruct our intentions, praise or blame our behavior. Will we be grateful for the other's friendliness and act in a way that pleases them (response type E) or will we just be proud of the praise and continue our behavior in a way that pleases only us (response type R)? When criticized, will we be angry and in return obstruct the other's intentions (response type E), or will we be afraid (ashamed) and comply with the other's demands (response type R)? Reinforcement theory would predict that we answer to reward and punishment, respectively, by a behavior of response type R. Social exchange theory (and related concepts like cognitive consistency, reactance, reciprocity, and equity) would suggest a behavior of response type E.

Social influence as conditioning process in controversial discussions. In a controversial discussion the opponent provides, simply by disagreeing with the subject, some contingent punishment which is often acerbated by deprecatory remarks with respect to the quality of the subject's arguments. Applying the conditioning model of learning to social behavior (Brandstätter, 1976, and Lott & Lott, 1985, for a more extensive discussion of the problem and for further references), a person who is criticized for a statement should avoid further punishment by moving away from the attacked position, most likely not only in public statements but also, perhaps to a lesser degree, in private opinion. One of the reasons why one should expect that not only utterances but also thoughts are affected by the punishment is the close association between thinking and speaking. Generally, people are criticized, and they know that they are criticized, not just for expressing a certain opinion, but also for holding it.

Being rewarded by an opponent is somewhat ambiguous and ambivalent, since contingent reward by an acknowledgment is usually followed by a counterargument which may be perceived as aversive. However, a friendly remark following and referring immediately to a preceding statement of a person can be expected to prevail over the aversive effects of the counterargument. Again according to the reinforcement concept of operant conditioning, a person who is rewarded in some way for expressing an opinion will be inclined to stick to that opinion.

Social influence in controversial discussions as social exchange. Social reward and social punishment can be looked at from a quite different viewpoint. Being criticized or complimented on an opinion statement is not just an aversive or agreeable consequence, but is perceived as an intentional act of another person that either follows or breaks social rules of reciprocity (Gouldner, 1960) and equity (Adams, 1965; cf. also Mikula, 1985). The otherwise heterogeneous theoretical concepts of social reciprocity, exchange, and equity have in common the notion that what people give and receive from each other is gauged according to some rule of social justice, and that people try to reach an equitable balance of giving and taking. Although most research in this area deals with the balance of rewards and punishments in relationships extended over longer periods of time, the basic rule also is applicable to interactions of short duration like group discussions or other short-term interactions (Gaelick, Bodenhausen, & Wyer, 1985; Helm, Bonoma, & Tedeschi, 1972; Youngs, 1986). Studies that look not only at the partners' balance of positive and negative acts but also at transition probabilities (e.g., at the probability that friendliness of partner A is immediately responded to by friendliness of partner B) usually report a certain degree of reciprocity (Gottman & Roy, 1989; Revenstorf, Hahlweg, & Schindler, 1979).

General Social Psychological Approach

Relying more on cognitive explanations than on behavioristic concepts of conditioning, Brandstätter and associates based their early experiments on controversial discussions and negotiations with a friendly or hostile adversary mainly on theories of cognitive consistency and attribution. Following a genuine social psychological tradition, they looked at individual differences as error variance by conceiving of the subjects' behavior as mere effects of specific situational characteristics like perceived similarity or perceived competence of the discussion or bargaining partner, the subject's role as actor or observer, matters of facts or matters of values as discussion topics, relative stakes of the bargaining partners, and so forth. Each of these conditions was combined with a hostile, neutral, or friendly discussion style.

A rather long series of experiments on emotional influence processes in group discussion and group decision making (for reviews see Brandstätter, 1978, 1985; Stocker-Kreichgauer & Rosenstiel, 1982; Schuler, 1982) were variations of a basic design: A subject whose initial attitude or decision preference had been measured exchanged arguments with another subject, with a confederate (face to face, via telecom, written messages, or computer terminals), or with a computer program. Attitudes or decision preferences were privately measured after each argument, or at the beginning, middle, and end of the discussion only, as well as a week or so later. Where possible, public verbal and nonverbal responses were analyzed together with the private ratings. In addition, the partner's dominance, friendliness, and competence were rated by the subject, usually immediately after the discussion and again some time later. The data were analyzed by ANOVA with covariance control or by process models representing a specific theory.

Very briefly, some general effects of hostile, neutral, or friendly styles of controversial discussions will be mentioned here, to point out the background from which the individual difference approach was later developed.

1. Schuler and Peltzer (1978) reported that nonverbal friendliness/hostility (which was not contingent on the subject's arguments but seemed to express the opposing confederate's attitude toward the subject as a person) had about the same effects as some other experimental manipulations of liking for the discussion or bargaining partner (Brandstätter & Hoggatt, 1982; Brandstätter, Kette, & Sageder, 1983; Peltzer & Schuler, 1976; Schuler, 1975; see also Schuler, 1982): An opponent who was liked by the subject (because the subject was told that he or she was liked by the other, or that he or she held similar attitudes, or because the other showed noncontingent, nonverbal friendliness) was more influential in the early stages of the interaction than an opponent who was disliked. Since liking a partner also means expecting reciprocity, disappointment with a liked partner who unexpectedly declines cooperation entails a high risk of conflict in the later stages of interaction (as to reciprocity in social interaction cf. Bierhoff, 1980, p. 214f.).

2. In discussions on matters of facts, the confederate's verbal aggression against a subject holding an opposing view provoked a more negative evaluation of the aggressor and more resistance to his or her influence attempt than in discussions on matters of values. This was particularly true for actively participating subjects who were the target of the aggression and, to a lesser degree, for subjects who observed the discussion and sympathized with the views of the attacked subject. As predicted, there were differences in attributions of the aggressive behavior: internal attribution in matters of facts, external attribution (discussion topic) in matters of values (Wagner, Glatz, & Brandstätter, 1982).

3. Although an aggressive style of discussion generally tended to diminish the influence on the directly attacked subject, as was predicted from cognitive consistency theories, the effects were rather small (Brandstätter & Klein-Moddenburg, 1982; Peltzer & Schuler, 1976; Wagner, Glatz, & Brandstätter, 1982) and not very stable. Kirchler and Brandstätter (1982) recorded higher order interactions between subject's gender, opponent's similarity, his or her friendliness, and his or her readiness to compromise, but no general superiority for a friendly discussion style. Kirchler (1984) unexpectedly found, for both men and

women, an influence advantage of the neutral style over the emotional (friendly or hostile) style in the long-term effects of the discussion.

On the whole, the general (social) psychological approach of cognitive consistency theories proved viable but the results were by no means impressive. However, the error variance, representing individual differences within experimental conditions, quite regularly was larger in responses to an emotional (hostile or friendly) adversary than in responses to an emotionally neutral adversary. Now, the question was whether these individual differences were stable and predictable from some basic personality constructs. If so, the average experimental effects, although compatible with the predictions, would not represent general functional relationships. Instead, they would hide the fact that a majority of subjects were responding consistently in one direction, and a minority of subjects the other way around. In such a case replication of the results could be expected only when the new sample happens to have the same heterogeneous composition of subjects.

Individual Difference Approach

At this stage of our research project on influence processes in controversial discussions we abandoned the general social psychological approach. We started thinking that for some people reinforcement theory might give correct predictions, whereas for others reciprocity in social exchange (friendliness and yielding for friendliness, hostility and counteracting for hostility) could be the characteristic way of responding.

Social Exchange Versus Social Reinforcement Orientation

The model of exchange versus reinforcement orientation (ERO model) implies that a person is either echange oriented or reinforcement oriented toward both social reward and social punishment. According to this model a person who is in a state of exchange orientation will retaliate against a punishing interaction partner and reciprocate the friendliness of a rewarding partner. A person who is in a state of reinforcement orientation will avoid the punished behavior and show the rewarded behavior with greater frequency or intensity.

The state of exchange versus reinforcement orientation is conceived of as an effect of both a person's disposition (trait) to respond one way or the other and the kind of social stimulation that may render one state or the other more or less likely, depending for example on power differences between the interacting persons or on social norms providing evaluation standards for specific behavior settings. This means that there may be circumstances where a person with the trait of exchange orientation may be put in the state of reinforcement orientation and vice versa. Here, we will not deal with situational conditions of exchange and reinforcement orientation, but only with the individual difference aspect.

To measure reinforcement versus exchange orientation we chose the new German version of Cattell's 16PF (Schneewind, Schröder, & Cattell, 1983) as the most comprehensive and widely used personality questionnaire, assuming that the second order factors *emotional stability (QII)* and *extroversion (QV)* would be the most promising candidates for linking the ERO construct to the broader field of personality research. There were good reasons for selecting just these two dimensions:

1. The second order factor *QII* (emotional stability; derived from the primary dimensions $C+$, $H+$, $L-$, $O-$, Q_3+, and Q_4-) seemed to be a good measure of a subject's emotional responsiveness to social reward and punishment: low emotional stability means high emotional responsiveness.
2. Most relevant seemed to be introversion/extroversion (*QV:* $A+$, $F+$, Q_2-), because according to Eysenck (1967) introverts can be more easily conditioned than extroverts; that is, they are generally more dependent on reward and punishment than extroverts. For subjects confronting an aggressive or friendly opponent in a controversial discussion this would mean that introverts yield more to an aggressive (punishing) opponent and less to a friendly (rewarding) opponent than extroverts.

Contrary to Eysenck's (1967) differential conditionability concept, which implies that introverts are supposed to be more easily conditionable than extroverts, Gray (1981, 1987) postulated that, in conditioning, introverts are more responsive to punishment, whereas extroverts are more responsive to reward, particularly when neuroticism is high. The reader should be aware of the fact that Gray's model is not equivalent to the model of exchange versus reinforcement orientation, although we identify it by the same combination of personality dimensions, that is, by neuroticism (low emotional stability) and extroversion. Although the predictions of responses to an aggressive (punishing) adversary are the same as in the ERO model, they are just opposite to ours for a friendly (rewarding) opponent. According to Gray extroverts are more responsive to reward than introverts, especially when neuroticism is high. A friendly acknowledgment of the subject's argument should induce less yielding, not more, as predicted by the ERO model.

As to differential reinforcement effects, our ERO model is in line with Eysenck's assumptions but not with Gray's. The social exchange or reciprocity aspect of the ERO model is missing in Eysenck's as well as in Gray's theory, but finds some support in Jung's original thinking about introversion and extroversion (Jung, 1921). According to Jung, introversion and extroversion can be interpreted as dispositional focus on the self and the inner world versus focus on the (social) environment. One may assume that the emotional experience of the introvert centers on the self, whereas the emotional experience of the extrovert centers on the (social) environment and the subject's relationship with others.

When social reward and punishment is a salient feature of a person's situation, introverts should focus on the target (receiver) of reward and punishment, that is, the rewarded or punished self, whereas extroverts should focus on the giver (the rewarding or punishing agent). Following this argument, one can predict that introverts, being reinforcement oriented, will yield to an unfriendly opponent more and to a friendly one less than exchange-oriented extroverts, and more so when emotional stability is low than when emotional stability is high.

We want to stress here that the notion of exchange versus reinforcement orientation was not inferred from patterns of data as a post hoc explanation, but was developed a priori as a theoretical construct for predicting and explaining individual differences in emotional and behavioral responses to social reward and social punishment.

Social Emotions as Intervening Variables

With respect to emotional responses it is assumed that a personal attack will provoke different emotions in introverts and extroverts, depending on who is perceived as the primary cause of the aversive event. The concept of introversion implies higher self-awareness, and therefore a higher probability of attributing the negative event to the self, which makes the emotional response of fear (and possibly shame) more likely than the response of anger. Extroverts, who are supposed to focus their attention on the interaction partner and to perceive him or her as the primary cause of the aversive event, are most likely to experience anger in such a situation. In the case of social reward, the self-directed emotion is pride and the other-directed emotion is gratitude.

Being confronted with an unfriendly or even aggressive adversary, a situation that is quite typical in controversial discussions, a person who responds with fear will yield; whereas a person who responds with anger will resist the influence attempt. When confronted with a friendly opponent (who, although opposing the subject's view, acknowledges the merits of his or her arguments in a friendly manner), a person who responds with complacency will resist, whereas a person who responds with gratitude will yield.

Testing the ERO Model by a Questionnaire

For a first empirical test of the ERO model Brandstätter (1988) designed the following questionnaire on exchange versus reinforcement orientation by asking (a) for the feelings of anger, fear, or indifference toward an aggressive discussion adversary and for the feelings of self-complacency, gratitude, or indifference toward a friendly discussion adversary and (b) for the respective behavioral responses (overt compliance, private attitude change, or counteractance).

Imagine you are discussing an important issue with an acquaintance of the same sex who opposes your view. How do you respond in situations where your discussion partner refuses your arguments in an unfriendly way as irrelevant or silly?

- A1 I feel intimidated
- A2 I feel angry
- A3 I stay unimpressed
- A4 I comply
- A5 I change my mind
- A6 I insist even more strongly on my view

How do you respond in situations, where your discussion partner appreciates your arguments in a friendly way, although he does not agree with you?

- B1 I feel proud
- B2 I feel grateful
- B3 I stay unimpressed

- B4 I comply
- B5 I change my mind
- B6 I insist even more strongly on my view

Subjects, 191 students of business administration and economics, half male, half female, marked each item on a 5-point scale (1 = never, 2 = rarely, 3 = occasionally, 4 = often, 5 = always). In addition, they answered the 16PF (Schneewind, Schröeder, & Cattell, 1983).

Table 5.1 shows the means and standard deviations of emotional and yielding responses to a hostile or friendly opponent as measured by the ERO questionnaire for different patterns of Emotional Stability *(QII)* and Introversion/Extroversion *(QV)*.

The ERO model predicts more fear and pride, but less anger and gratitude, for introverts than for extroverts. Only fear and anger show the predicted pattern, although it was by far not significant.

In line with the ERO model, introverts yield more to an unfriendly opponent than to a friendly one (2.7 vs. 2.65), whereas extroverts yield less to an unfriendly adversary than to a friendly one (2.55 vs. 2.65). The interaction between Introversion/Extroversion and Opponent's Friendliness is significant ($F(1,372) = 4.18$; $p = .04$). Contrary to the prediction, however, there is no three-way interaction between *QII, QV,* and Friendliness; that is, the differences in yielding between Introverts and Extroverts are about the same for unstable and stable subjects. The fact that unstable subjects report significantly more intense emotions than stable subjects fits well the concept of emotional stability.

Testing the ERO Model by Experiments

In the following section we will review four experiments on controversial discussions for which we also have measures of the subjects' emotional stability and introversion/extroversion as indicators of their exchange versus reinforcement orientation.

Only two of the four experiments were explicitly designed to test the ERO model (Kirchler & Brandstätter, 1985; Brandstätter & Cielecki, 1985). The data of the other two experiments (Grovermann, 1982; Peltzer & Schuler, 1976) have been reanalyzed by Waldhör (1987) according to the ERO model.

We will compare the effects of an unfriendly versus a friendly discussion style, because the ERO model refers only to those two

Table 5.1

Patterns of emotional stability (QII) and introversion/extroversion (QV) related to emotional and yielding responses to an unfriendly and friendly opponent in controversial discussions as measured by the ERO questionnaire.

Subjects	Unfriendly Opponent						Friendly Opponent						
	Fear (A1)		Anger (A2)		Yielding (A4)		Pride (B1)		Gratitude (B2)		Yielding (B4)		n
	M	SD	M	SD	M	SD	M	SD	M	SD	M	SD	
(A1) Unstable													
(B1) Introvert	2.6	.83	3.3	.86	2.7	.79	3.6	.80	3.1	1.23	2.5	.99	51
(B2) Extrovert	2.5	.75	3.4	.86	2.6	.83	3.5	.89	2.9	.91	2.7	.81	46
(A2) Stable													
(B1) Introvert	2.3	.78	2.9	.83	2.5	.70	3.1	1.01	2.8	.99	2.2	.94	45
(B2) Extrovert	2.2	.82	3.0	1.03	2.5	.65	3.2	.94	2.7	1.11	2.6	.94	49
$F_A(1,186)$	6.82		9.51		1.94		9.21		2.65		2.26		
p	.01		.002		.17		.003		.11		.13		
$F_B(1,186)$											5.08		
p											.03		

contrasting conditions. The experiments 1, 2, and 3 were also run with a neutral condition. The first experiment (Kirchler & Brandstätter, 1985) was performed with an unfriendly and a neutral opponent only. The results for the neutral condition can be found in Waldhör (1987).

Because the experiments did not probe directly into the subjects' emotional responses to the opponents' friendliness or hostility, we can only look at yielding responses. In the discussion section we will come back to the quite essential function of emotions in the ERO model and to ways of testing the assumptions about specific emotions.

Figure 5.1 displays the predictions derived from the ERO model: Extroverts are exchange oriented and therefore will resist an unfriendly opponent and yield to a friendly one, and more so if emotional stability is low. Introverts are reinforcement oriented and therefore will yield to an unfriendly opponent and resist a friendly one, and more so if emotional stability is low.

Experiment 1

The subjects of this experiment, performed by Kirchler and Brandstätter (1985), were 20 housewives, 20 to 25 years of age, who discussed two legal cases, one with a neutral and the other with a hostile confederate. The subject's agreement or disagreement with the confederate was measured as a dependent variable in two ways: (a) the subject's ratings of the defendant's guilt and (b) the judges' ratings of the subject's agreement with the confederate, based on transcripts of the subject's arguments.

In addition, the subjects answered the 16PF and their heart rate and electrodermal activity was measured during critical stages of the discussion. Analyzing this data, Brandstätter, Kirchler, Sananès, and Shedler (1986), as expected, found that arousal, as indicated by heart rate, magnified resistance to an aggressive opponent in extroverts, but magnified yielding in introverts. The authors saw in this result a clear support of the ERO model.

However, Waldhör (1987), testing the model for the same sample by substituting the trait measure of emotional stability (i.e., the second order factor *QII* of the 16PF) for the stated measure of arousal (heart rate), came up with less impressive results. Although unstable extroverts tended to resist, and unstable introverts tended to yield to the attempted influence of an unfriendly opponent (−.15 vs. .51 in z-scores), the difference was not significant.

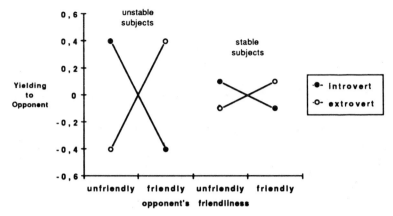

Figure 5.1. Predicted Pattern of Yielding to an Unfriendly and Friendly Opponent Dependent on Subject's Personality Structure

Unexpectedly, for emotionally stable subjects the effect was not just diminished but reversed, a phenomenon that was also observed quite regularly in the other three experiments (cf. Table 5.2).

Experiment 2

Brandstätter and Cielecki (1985) tested the ERO model with 12 women recruited by a newspaper ad. In a first session, the subjects answered an attitude questionnaire on 40 different topics and Cattell's 16PF questionnaire (Schneewind, Schröder, & Cattell, 1983) among other personality measures. A week later, each subject briefly discussed 12 topics (out of the 40 topics to which the subjects previously had responded) with three different confederates through an intercom system in a 3 × 2 × 2 partially balanced design (a confederate who was unfriendly, neutral, or friendly, either by tone of voice (nonverbal) or by verbal statements, and whose messages were received by the left or the right ear). Only the data related to verbal unfriendliness/friendliness were considered, averaged across left and right ear channel. The hemisphericity aspect of the experiment is omitted here.

The confederate who always opposed the subject's view (known from the pretest) responded to the subject's second argument with an unfriendly, neutral, or friendly remark. The discussion, initiated by the subject, ended with the subject's third argument. Thus, the confederate's unfriendly, neutral, or friendly answer could be perceived by the subject as contingent on her argument, and not as a general expression of like or dislike for her as a person.

After the end of each discussion the subject privately indicated her stance on the issue. Three to four weeks later the subjects returned to the laboratory to answer the attitude and personality questionnaires a second time.

As predicted, unstable introverts yielded most to the unfriendly opponent, whereas unstable extroverts yielded most to the friendly opponent. Again, the pattern of effects was reversed with stable subjects. For the three-way interaction (see Table 5.2): $F(1,16) = 4.62$; $p = .047$.

Experiment 3

When Grovermann (1982) was looking for individual differences in responding to an unfriendly, neutral, or friendly opponent in controversial discussions, the ERO model was not yet developed. However, Waldhör (1987) was able to reanalyze Grovermann's data according to this model.

Subjects first read the case material of a teacher who was accused before a disciplinary court of a sexual offense against a pupil. After giving a statement about his guilt or innocence, the subjects (90 male and 20 female students of economics and business administration) exchanged written arguments with a confederate of the same sex from a pool of arguments supporting their initial decision (guilty or not guilty). Each argument except the first had to be introduced by an evaluative (negative, neutral, or positive) remark about the partner's argument before the subject's argument was presented. Depending on the experimental condition, for the male subjects the confederate's remarks were unfriendly (critical), neutral, or friendly (acknowledging). With the female subjects only the neutral condition has been run.

Grovermann (1982) did not use the 16PF questionnaire for measuring personality differences, but did use several other tests, among them the extroversion scale of the Eysenck Personality Inventory (EPI) and the Freiburger Persönlichkeitsinventar (FPI), a German multidimensional personality inventory. Later, all of these tests were administered together with the 16PF to a comparable sample of 215 students. It turned out that the second order factor scores of QII (emotional stability) and QV (social extroversion) could be reconstructed by the multiple regression of the respective factor scores on the 24 EPI extroversion items with $R = .68$ for QII and $R = .67$ for QV. Therefore, Waldhör (1987) used these regression weights for estimating QII and QV with the 24 EPI extroversion items of the Grovermann study in order to test the ERO model. As Table 5.2 shows, again only the results of the unstable subjects are in line with the ERO model, whereas the pattern of the stable subjects is reversed, just as it was in the second experiment. However, this time the three-way interaction is not significant $(F(1,52) = 1.95; p = .170)$.

Experiment 4

Peltzer and Schuler (1976) had subjects communicate about a personnel decision problem via computer terminals with a partner simulated by a computer program. After reading the case material and giving an individual judgment of the applicant's aptitude, the subject received a list of arguments supporting more or less his initial decision preference (accept or reject the applicant) together with a separate list of evaluative remarks (negative, neutral, positive) by which the partner's arguments could be criticized or appreciated. Each argument except the first had to be started with such a remark on the discretion of the subject, and the alleged partner each time also communicated an evaluative remark on the subject's argument before he put forward his own argument. Depending on the experimental condition, the programmed partners were predominantly unfriendly or friendly.

Peltzer and Schuler (1976; see also the review of this experiment by Schuler, 1982) had administered the Freiburger Persönlichkeitsinventar (FPI) to their subjects without finding significant correlations with the subjects' changes in decision preferences. Now, the FPI scores could be used by Waldhör (1987) to estimate the 16PF second order factor scores of QII (emotional stability) and QV (social extroversion). In the special sample of 215 students whose answers to the various personality tests were used to establish the weights for the regression of the QII and QV factor scores on the nine FPI scores, the multiple correlations were $R = .81$ and $R = .47$, respectively.

As Table 5.2 shows, just as we found in the second and third experiment, the results support the ERO model only for unstable subjects. The interaction of Extroversion × Emotional Stability × Partner's Friendliness approaches significance $(F(1,72) = 3.36; p = .071)$.

Table 5.2

Effects of subject's emotional stability and extroversion on yielding to an unfriendly and friendly opponent in a controversial discussion.

| | Subject: | Emotionally Unstable | | | | | Emotionally Stable | | | | | | | |
| | Opponent: | Unfriendly | | Friendly | | | Unfriendly | | Friendly | | | | | |
Experiment		*1* A.M.	*2* n	*3* A.M.	*4* n	*5* d	*6* A.M.	*7* n	*8* A.M.	*9* n	*10* F	*11* df	*12* p	*13* d
1. Kirchler & Brandstätter (1985)	extrovert	-.15	4				.40	6				1.15	.340	.44
	introvert	.51	5			.66	.18	5			.97			
2. Brandstätter & Cielecki (1985)	extrovert	-.16	3	.96	3		.02	3	-.81	3		1.15	.048	.88
	introvert	.73	3	-.06	3	.96	-.73	3	.04	3	4.62			
3. Grovermann (1982)	extrovert	-.37	4	.39	7		-.05	9	-.03	13		1.51	.169	.42
	introvert	-.29	10	-.47	8	.47	-.31	7	.45	2	1.95			
4. Peltzer & Schuler (1976)	extrovert	-.40	7	.21	13		.27	11	-.28	5		1.71	.071	.43
	introvert	-.20	12	-.02	8	.22	-.40	10	.35	14	3.36			
	extrovert	a		b			e		f					
	introvert	c		d			g		h					

NOTE: Column 5 contains the effect sizes of the interaction between the subject's introversion/extroversion and the confederate's friendliness for emotionally unstable subjects. Columns 10 to 13 present F, df, p, and d (effect size) for the three-way interaction. Only the entries for the first experiment relate to the main effect of extroversion (column 5) and to the interaction extroversion × emotional stability (columns 10 to 13).

127

Combining Statistical Tests

Looking at the whole set of four experiments by which we were able to test the ERO model, partly by reanalyzing previous studies, we can estimate the overall probability of erroneously rejecting the null hypothesis.

The yielding responses to an unfriendly opponent of emotionally unstable subjects are definitely in line with the ERO model. In each of the four experiments (reinforcement oriented) unstable introverts are influenced more than (exchange oriented) unstable extroverts. Adding the one-tailed probabilities of the four studies and calculating the compound probability P according to Rosenthal (1978, p. 187), we arrive at $P = .072$.

The ERO model holds also for the interaction Extroversion × Partner's Friendliness, which could be estimated for the Experiments 2, 3, and 4. Whereas an unfriendly opponent exerts more influence on unstable introverts, a friendly opponent is more influential with unstable extroverts, just as the ERO model predicts. The compound probability is $P = .015$.

Contrary to the prediction, with emotionally stable subjects, extroversion has not just an attenuated, but a reversed effect: Extroverts yield more to an unfriendly opponent than introverts (one-tailed compound probability $P = .035$). The interaction Introversion/Extroversion × Emotional Stability on responses to an unfriendly opponent is significant with a compound probability of $P = .007$.

For the three-way interaction, Introversion/Extroversion × Emotional Stability × Partner's Friendliness, the compound probability, calculated for the Experiments 2, 3, and 4, is $P = .0005$.

Effect sizes have been calculated for differences in means representing the contrast

$$(c + b)/2 \text{ vs. } (a + d)/2$$

which characterizes the interaction Subject's Introversion/Extroversion × Partner's Friendliness for emotionally unstable subjects (see column 5 of Table 5.2).

Another contrast representing the three-way interaction Extroversion × Emotional Stability × Partner's Friendliness is given by

$$(c + b + e + h)/4 \text{ vs. } (a + d + g + f)/4$$

(see column 13 of Table 5.2). As one can see from Table 5.2, the effect sizes are substantial (cf. Cohen, 1977, p. 24) and quite consistent.

In Figures 5.2 and 5.3 the combined results (weighted means) of the four experiments are shown.

Discussion

An Unexpected Pattern of Interaction

As we have seen, all four experiments with which the ERO model was tested gave the same pattern of a two-way interaction (Extroversion × Emotional Stability) on yielding to an unfriendly opponent, and the three experiments in which the opponent's discussion style was either unfriendly or friendly showed the same pattern of a three-way interaction (Emotional Stability × Extroversion × Partner's Friendliness), although only the results of the second experiment were statistically significant ($p < .05$). Brushing aside the results of the other experiments simply because they do not reach conventional statistical significance levels would not be justified. What really counts is that all of the experiments showed the same pattern of interactions and that the one-tailed compound error probabilities vary between $P = .072$ and $P = .0005$.

A three-way interaction (Emotional Stability × Extroversion × Partner's Friendliness) was predicted from the ERO model (Figure 5.1), and we found a significant three-way interaction. Nevertheless, what we found was not what we predicted, because the stable subjects should have come up with a two-way interaction (Extroversion × Partner's Friendliness) similar to but less pronounced than the two-way interaction found with unstable subjects, and not with a mirror image of the unstable subjects' responses. Thus, the theoretical predictions from the ERO model were supported by the data of the unstable subjects only. Compared to emotionally unstable extroverts, emotionally unstable introverts yield more to unfriendly opponents, probably because they are afraid of further attacks, and they yield less to friendly adversaries, probably because of complacency, whereas unstable extroverts are supposed to feel anger and gratitude, respectively.

As yet we do not understand why emotionally stable subjects show response patterns (dependent on introversion/extroversion and partner's friendliness) that quite regularly are not just less pronounced, as

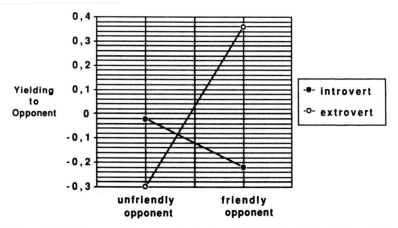

Figure 5.2. Yielding to Opponent of Emotionally Unstable Subjects Dependent on the Subject's Extroversion and the Opponent's Friendliness

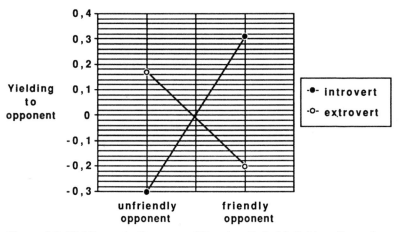

Figure 5.3. Yielding to the Opponent of Emotionally Stable Subjects Dependent on Subject's Extroversion and Opponent's Friendliness

we had expected, but opposite to the response patterns of emotionally unstable subjects. It looks as if the reinforcement orientation of introverts was a function of emotional stability, as if with increasing emotional stability reinforcement orientation turned into exchange orientation and the emotions of fear and complacency were replaced by the emotions of anger and gratitude, respectively. However, why should emotionally stable introverts react with pronounced emotions at all? Perhaps they do not respond predominantly with emotions, but rather follow social rules of reciprocity unemotionally.

On the other hand, stable extroverts may yield more to an unfriendly opponent than to a friendly one because they perceive him or her expressing a stronger need to influence them, but do not feel angered. It may well be that the yielding or resisting of emotionally excitable (unstable) subjects is mediated by social emotions, whereas the yielding or resisting of emotionally stable subjects follows social rules of reciprocity (in the case of introverts) or rules that take the other's expressed needs into account (in the case of extroverts).

As yet, these interpretations are rather speculative. Although the four experiments show remarkably consistent results, the different processes underlying the observed effects need more theoretical and empirical clarification.

Emotions as Mediating Variables

Whether the subjects really experience the emotions postulated by the ERO model is open to question. We do not exclude the possibility that various other emotions may be elicited in controversial discussions nor do we exclude the possibility that resisting or yielding to an opponent's influence attempt also may be caused by characteristics of the sender, the message, or the receiver that are not at all or only marginally related to the emotions of fear, anger, pride, and gratitude. However, we do assert that these emotions are integral components of two basically different ways of perceiving, interpreting, and reacting to social reward and punishment. Emotions are mediators between cognition and action (in our case between the social stimulation by a hostile or friendly discussion partner and the yielding or resisting response of the subject) insofar as they imply both an appraisal of the situation (in terms of its compatibility with one's needs) and a suggestion for action (cf. Klages, 1950, p. 155; see also Shaver, Schwartz, Kirson, & Connor, 1987).

Although the ERO questionnaire data suggest that feeling anxious goes with yielding to the demands of an aggressive adversary and feeling angry prompts resistance (Brandstätter, 1988), the emotional responses reported in the questionnaire correspond only partially to the pattern predicted for introversion/extroversion (cf. Table 5.1), calling for more direct empirical evidence of the model's emotional implications.

The authors of the first two experiments, which were explicitly designed to test the ERO model, were afraid that having subjects report their emotions during the discussion would interfere too much with the process, and that asking subjects for retrospective reports at the end of the discussion would result in data of highly questionable validity.

With these difficulties in mind, we have started analyzing the videotapes of one of the experiments (Brandstätter & Cielecki, 1985) using the facial action coding system FACS (Ekman & Friesen, 1975), in the hope that this will allow the emotional aspects of the ERO model to be tested more directly.

Another way of exploring emotional responses to reward and punishment and testing predictions derived from the ERO model has been tried by Brandstätter and Kirchler (1986). They reanalyzed data from seven time-sampling studies of emotions in everyday life situations in which subjects had recorded their emotional responses, behavior settings, activities, persons present, causal attributions of emotions, and motives several times a day over 30 days. They found, as predicted by the ERO model, that emotionally unstable extroverts (exchange-oriented subjects) reacted predominantly with the emotions of anger and gratitude (joy) to social punishment and social reward, respectively, whereas unstable introverts more often responded with emotions of fear and pride, respectively.

ERO Model in Relation to Other Personality Constructs

On the whole, social psychologists are reluctant to deal with individual differences. In McGuire's (1985) comprehensive review of attitude research as well as in Snyder and Ickes's (1985) chapter on personality and social behavior, nothing is said about the combined effects of the source's hostility or friendliness and the receiver's personality structure on yielding, which is the central topic of this chapter. This may be due to the fact that attitude change through group discussion has been a widely neglected field of research in the time period covered by McGuire's and Snyder and Ickes's reviews.

It is mainly in the field of bargaining and experimental games that personality characteristics like cooperativeness versus competitiveness are considered as explanatory variables (see Carson, 1979, and Rubin & Brown, 1975, p. 175, for references). For example, Kelley and

Stahelski (1970) reported that only cooperative subjects (identified as such by a questionnaire on the subjects' goals and intentions) responded in the reciprocity mode, whereas competitors were competitive irrespective of the other's cooperative or competitive behavior. The former would be exchange oriented, the latter would fit neither of the two categories.

Cacioppo, Petty, Kao, and Rodriguez (1986) provide another example of individual differences in responding to persuasive arguments. They show that a high need for cognition favors the central route of persuasion, that is, a better attention to and a more elaborate processing of the arguments. This could mean that they also are less dependent on social reward and punishment. On the other hand, people with a high need for social approval (Crowne & Marlowe, 1964; see also Snyder & Ickes, 1985, p. 887) are particularly responsive to social pressures for conformity. The conceptual and empirical relationship between the approval motive and reinforcement orientation needs closer scrutiny. One may assume that a high need for social approval is inversely related to the 16PF second order factor Independence (QIII) rather than to Extroversion (QV). If so, approval seeking would be different from reinforcement orientation, because people scoring high on independence generally are less susceptible to social influence in group discussions, irrespective of the opponent's friendliness (cf. Brandstätter, 1987).

Final Comment

The individual differences in responding to social reward and social punishment that were predicted and found in experiments on controversial discussions, although not yet fully understood, may have quite important implications for explaining the effects of reward and punishment in both education and resocialization. Differentiating between exchange- and reinforcement-oriented persons, among emotionally stable and unstable subjects, as well as between situations that provoke exchange or reinforcement orientation (Glatz & Brandstätter, 1985) should help in avoiding inefficient or counterproductive influence attempts.

The ERO model may also be useful in integrating otherwise inconsistent results in other social psychological domains like research on aggression, prosocial behavior, and conflicts in close relationships.

Focusing on the effects (or, more cautiously, on the manifestations) of social exchange versus social reinforcement orientation in unstable subjects, we did not talk about how individual differences in exchange versus reinforcement orientation come about. Should the ERO model prove valid in a variety of different social contexts, explaining these individual differences will become at least as important as studying their effects on social behavior.

Since the ERO model was not meant as a mere description of an empirical pattern of data but as a theoretical explanation, and since the predictions are in line only with the data of the unstable subjects, the theory has to be revised to account for possible functional differences in the way social-emotional influence works with the four personality types.

References

Adams, J. S. (1965). Inequity in social exchange. In L. Berkowitz (Ed.), *Advances in experimental social psychology* (Vol. 2, pp. 267-299). New York: Academic Press.

Anderson, N. H., & Graeser, C. C. (1976). An information integration analysis of attitude change in group discussion. *Journal of Personality and Social Psychology, 34,* 210-222.

Asch, S. E. (1956). Studies of independence and conformity. A minority of one against an unanimous majority. *Psychological Monographs, 70* (Whole No. 416).

Bierhoff, H. W. (1980). *Hilfreiches Verhalten* [Helping behavior]. Darmstadt: Steinkopff.

Brandstätter, H. (1976). Soziale Verstärkung in Diskussionsgruppen [Social reinforcement in discussion groups]. In H. Brandstätter & H. Schuler (Eds.), *Entscheidungsprozesse in Gruppen* (pp. 65-82). Bern: Huber.

Brandstätter, H. (1978). Social emotions in discussion groups. In H. Brandstätter, J. H. Davis, & H. Schuler (Eds.), *Dynamics of group decisions* (pp. 93-111). Beverly Hills, CA: Sage.

Brandstätter, H. (1985). Social emotions in controversial discussions and in group decision making. In E. E. Lawler (Ed.), *Advances in group processes* (Vol. 2, pp. 249-281). Greenwich, CT: JAI.

Brandstätter, H. (1987). Towards differential social psychology: Individual differences in responding to an aggressive discussant. In G. R. Semin & B. Krahé (Eds.), *Issues in contemporary German social psychology* (pp. 55-73). London: Sage.

Brandstätter, H. (1988). *Ein Fragebogen zur Messung von Ausgleichs- vs. Verstärkungsorientierung* [A questionnaire measuring social exchange vs. social reinforcement orientation]. Unpublished manuscript. University of Linz, Austria.

Brandstätter, H., & Cielecki, M. (1985). Persönlichkeitsspezifische Wirkung von Lob und Tadel in Streitgesprächen [Individual differences in responding to reward and punishment in controversial discussions]. In D. Albert (Ed.), *Bericht über den 34. Kongreß der DGfPs in Wien* (pp. 458-461). Göttingen: Hogrefe.

Brandstätter, H., & Hoggatt, A. C. (1982). The influence of social emotions on bargaining outcomes in a bilateral monopoly game. In H. Brandstätter, J. H. Davis, & G. Stocker-Kreichgauer (Eds.), *Group decision making* (pp. 279-294). London: Academic Press.

Brandstätter, H., Kette, G., & Sageder, J. (1983). Expectations and behaviour in bargaining with liked and disliked partners. In R. Tietz (Ed.), *Aspiration levels in bargaining and economic decision making* (pp. 136-152). Berlin: Springer.

Brandstätter, H., Kirchler, E., Sananès, C., & Shedler, J. (1986). Yielding to a hostile adversary: Personality and arousal as predictors of attitude change. *International Journal of Small Group Research, 2,* 1-17.

Brandstätter, H., & Kirchler, E. (1986, July). *Emotional responses to interpersonal conflict in experimental and natural behavior settings: An individual difference approach.* Paper presented at the 21st International Congress of Applied Psychology, Jerusalem.

Brandstätter, H., & Klein-Moddenborg, V. (1982). Short and long term effects of verbal aggression on observers and participants in group discussion. In H. Hiebsch, H. Brandstätter, & H. H. Kelley (Eds.), *Social psychology* (pp. 73-84). Amsterdam: North Holland.

Burnstein, E. (1982). Persuasion as argument processing. In H. Brandstätter, J. H. Davis, & G. Stocker-Kreichgauer (Eds.), *Group decision making* (pp. 103-124). London: Academic Press.

Cacioppo, J. T., Petty, R. E., Kao, C. F., & Rodriguez, R. (1986). Central and peripheral routes to persuasion: An individual difference perspective. *Journal of Personality and Social Psychology, 51,* 1032-1043.

Carson, R. C. (1979). Personality and exchange in developing relationships. In R. L. Burgess & T. L. Huston (Eds.), *Social exchange in developing relationships* (pp. 247-269). New York: Academic Press.

Cohen, J. (1977). *Statistical power analysis for the behavioral sciences* (rev. ed.). Orlando, FL: Academic Press.

Crowne, D. P., & Marlowe, D. (1964). *The approval motive: Studies in evaluative dependence.* New York: John Wiley.

Ekman, P., & Friesen, W. V. (1975). *Unmasking the face.* Palo Alto: Consulting Psychologists Press.

Eysenck, H. J. (1967). *The biological basis of personality.* Springfield, IL: Charles C Thomas.

Festinger, L. (1954). A theory of social comparison processes. *Human Relations, 7,* 117-140.

Gaelick, L., Bodenhausen, G. V., & Wyer, R. S., Jr. (1985). Emotional communication in close relationships. *Journal of Personality and Social Psychology, 49,* 1246-1265.

Glatz, W., & Brandstätter, H. (1985). Wirkung eines aggressiven Diskussionsstils auf verstärkungs- und ausgleichsorientierte Beobachter [The effects of an aggressive discussion style on reinforcement oriented vs. exchange oriented observers]. *Zeitschrift für Experimentelle und Angewandte Psychologie, 32,* 400-424.

Gottman, J., & Roy, A. (1989). *Sequential analysis: A guide for behavioral research.* New York: Cambridge University Press.

Gouldner, A. W. (1960). The norm of reciprocity. A preliminary statement. *American Sociological Review, 25,* 161-178.

Gray, J. A. (1981). A critique of Eysenck's theory of personality. In H. J. Eysenck (Ed.), *A model for personality* (pp. 246-276). Berlin: Springer.

Gray, J. A. (1987). *The psychology of fear and stress* (2nd ed.). Cambridge: Cambridge University Press.

Grovermann, W. (1982). *Person und entscheidung* [Personality and decision making]. Augsburg: Maro.

Helm, B., Bonoma, T. V., & Tedeschi, J. T. (1972). Reciprocity for harm done. *The Journal of Social Psychology, 87,* 89-98.

Jones, E. E., & Gerard, H. B. (1967). *Foundations of social psychology.* New York: John Wiley.

Jung, C. G. (1921). *Psychologische typen* [Psychological types]. Zürich: Rascher.

Kelley, H. H., & Stahelski, A. J. (1970). Social interaction basis of cooperators' and competitors' beliefs about others. *Journal of Personality and Social Psychology, 16,* 66-91.

Kirchler, E. (1984). Einstellungsänderung von Frauen und Männern in Abhängigkeit vom Diskussionsstil des Gesprächspartners [Attitude change of women and men related to discussion style]. *Archiv für Psychologie, 136,* 167-180.

Kirchler, E., & Brandstätter, H. (1982). Einstellungsänderung in Abhängigkeit von ähnlichkeit, freundlichkeit, kompromiß bereitschaft und geschlecht des Diskussionspartners [Attitude change dependent on similarity, friendliness, consensus making and sex of the discussion partner]. *Zeitschrift für Experimentelle und Angewandte Psychologie, 29,* 417-441.

Kirchler, E., & Brandstätter, H. (1985). Verstärkungs- und Ausgleichsorientierung in kontroversen Diskussionen [Reinforcement vs. exchange orientation in controversial discussions]. *Zeitschrift für Sozialpsychologie, 16,* 36-47.

Klages, L. (1950. *Grundlegung der wissenschaft vom ausdruck* [Foundations of the science of expression]. Bonn: Bouvier.

Levine, J. M., & Moreland, R. L. (1990). Progress in small group research. *Annual Review of Psychology, 41,* 585-634.

Lott, B., & Lott, A. L. (1985). Learning theory in contemporary social psychology. In G. Lindzey & E. Aronson (Eds.), *Handbook of social psychology* (Vol. 1, pp. 109-135). New York: Random House.

McGuire, W. J. (1985). Attitudes and attitude change. In G. Lindzey & E. Aronson (Eds.), *Handbook of social psychology* (3rd ed.) (Vol. 2, pp. 233-346). New York: Random House.

Mikula, G. (1985). Psychologische theorien des sozialen austauschs [Psychological theories of social exchange]. In D. Frey & M. Irle (Eds.), *Theorien der Sozialpsychologie* (Vol. 2, pp. 273-305). Bern: Huber.

Peltzer, U., & Schuler, H. (1976). Personwahrnehmung, Diskussionsverhalten und Präferenzänderung in Dyaden [Person perception, discussion behavior, and preference change in dyads]. In H. Brandstätter & H. Schuler (Eds.), *Entscheidungsprozesse in Gruppen* (pp. 105-117). Bern: Huber.

Petty, R. E., & Cacioppo, J. T. (1986a). Communication and persuasion: Central and peripheral routes to attitude change. New York: Springer.

Petty, R. E., & Cacioppo, J. T. (1986b). The elaboration likelihood model of persuasion. In L. Berkowitz (Ed.), *Advances in experimental social psychology* (Vol. 19, pp. 123-205). New York: Academic Press.

Pruitt, D. G., & Rubin, J. Z. (1986). *Social conflict: Escalation, stalemate and settlement.* New York: Random House.

Revenstorf, D., Hahlweg, K., & Schindler, L. (1979). Interaktionsanalyse von Partner-konflikten [Interaction analysis of partner conflicts]. *Zeitschrift für Sozialpsychologie, 10*, 183-196.

Rosenthal, R. (1978). Combining results of independent studies. *Psychological Bulletin, 85*, 185-193.

Rubin, J. Z., & Brown, B. R. (1975). *The social psychology of bargaining and negotiation.* New York: Academic Press.

Schneewind, K. A., Schröder, G., & Cattell, R. B. (1983). *Der 16-Persönlichkeits-Faktoren-Test. 16PF* (The 16-Personality Factor Test. 16PF.) Bern: Huber.

Schuler, H. (1975). *Sympathie und einfluß in Entscheidungsgruppen* [Liking and influence in decision making groups]. Bern: Huber.

Schuler, H. (1982). Liking and influence in group decision making: A test in four different experimental settings. In H. Brandstätter, J. H. Davis, & G. Stocker-Kreichgauer (Eds.), *Group decision making* (pp. 257-277). London: Academic Press.

Schuler, H., & Peltzer, U. (1978). Friendly versus unfriendly behavior. The effects on partner's decision-making preferences. In H. Brandstätter, J. H. Davis, & H. Schuler (Eds.), *Dynamics of group decisions* (pp. 113-132). Beverly Hills, CA: Sage.

Shaver, P., Schwartz, J., Kirson, D., & Connor, C. (1987). Emotion knowledge: Further exploration of a prototype approach. *Journal of Personality and Social Psychology, 52*, 1061-1086.

Sherif, M. (1936). *The psychology of social norms.* New York: Harper & Row.

Snyder, M., & Ickes, W. (1985). Personality and social behavior. In G. Lindzey & E. Aronson (Eds.), *Handbook of social psychology* (Vol. 2, 3rd ed., pp. 883-947). New York: Random House.

Stocker-Kreichgauer, G., & Rosenstiel, L. von (1982). Attitude change as a function of the observation of vicarious reinforcement and friendliness/hostility in a debate. In H. Brandstätter, J. H. Davis, & G. Stocker-Kreichgauer (Eds.), *Group decision making* (pp. 241-255). London: Academic Press.

Wagner, W., Glatz, W., & Brandstätter, H. (1982). Zur Wirkung verbaler Aggression in Diskussionen [Effects of verbal aggression in discussions]. *Archiv für Psychologie, 134*, 237-256.

Waldhör, K. (1987). *Modelle des sozialen einflusses in pro- und kontra-diskussionen* (Models of social influence in pro and contra-discussions]. Unpublished doctoral dissertation, University of Linz, Austria.

Youngs, G. A., Jr. (1986). Patterns of threat and punishment reciprocity in a conflict setting. *Journal of Personality and Social Psychology, 51*, 541-546.

6   Team Composition in Organizational Settings: Issues in Managing an Increasingly Diverse Work Force

Susan E. Jackson

As business leaders contemplate the future, they are realizing that tomorrow's effective organizations will be those that have learned to manage a work force characterized by demographic diversity. The results of a telephone survey of 408 opinion leaders knowledgeable about human resource issues in business (e.g., executives, consultants, faculty) illustrate the salience of work force diversity as a concern. When these leaders were asked to think ahead, to look toward the future and the strategic issues that business will face, managing a more diverse work force was the one issue that was repeatedly mentioned (Sirota, Alper, & Pfau, 1989). When business leaders state that they are concerned about how to manage a diverse work force, what do they mean? In what ways is the work force becoming more diverse? These questions will be addressed first. Then, a limited review of the empirical and theoretical literatures in social psychology will be provided to suggest the types of challenges and opportunities employers will face in managing a diverse work force. Finally, the concluding section of this chapter describes recent field research in organizational psychology that addresses the question of how group composition relates to work team outcomes.

AUTHOR'S NOTE: This chapter was originally prepared and presented as a paper for the 1989 Texas A&M Symposium on Group Productivity and Process, College Station, TX.

Demographic Trends Are Creating
a More Diverse Work Force

The changing characteristics of the work force predict the types of diversity employers will need to understand and manage in the future. (See Johnston & Packer, 1987, for an extensive description of projections.) With respect to age, the work force is getting older. This is due largely to the maturing of the baby-boom generation, but it is also due in part to the return (or entry) of middle-aged women and to part-time employment among former "retirees" who feel they need additional income to supplement their pension and social security benefits. The addition of these older workers has the effect of lengthening the upper tail of the age distribution. The lower tail of the age distribution is lengthening as well. Faced with an increasingly tight labor market for entry-level positions, due in part to the relatively small size of the post-baby-boom generation, organizations are finding creative ways to employ younger workers who traditionally might not have been available. For example, internships and apprenticeships permit high school students to work during the school year and earn academic credit for their experiences. As the upper and lower tails of the age distribution are lengthened, age diversity in the work place increases.

With respect to sex, the proportion of the work force that is female has been increasing steadily, and this trend is expected to continue. Furthermore, women have begun to enter occupations formerly dominated by men; this means that in addition to the *total* work force becoming more balanced with respect to sex, the segregation of the sexes that often occurred in organizations should be diminishing. Both of these trends will create more diversity within work groups.

The ethnic diversity of the work force also is changing. Between now and the year 2000, ethnic minorities are expected to account for 57% of the growth in the labor force. Fully 22% of new entrants are predicted to be immigrants. Thus, in addition to age- and sex-based diversity, employers must adapt to the reality of a multilingual, multicultural workplace.

Many employers are already experiencing the dramatic differences that exist between the new work force entrants and the traditional, stereotypic white male, who was once considered "the norm." These differences are not limited to the demographic characteristics of employees, because associated with the demographic differences are differences in values, attitudes, styles of interaction, physical and cognitive abilities, and nonwork commitments.

In the recent past the labor market could be characterized as a buyers' market. Labor was in abundant supply and therefore relatively cheap and easy to acquire. When "traditional" employees were abundant, employers did not *need* to recruit from the pool of nontraditional workers. However, in the near future the labor market will become more and more of a sellers' market. The shortage of labor will force employers to compete to attract, retain, and effectively manage all available employees from a shrinking labor pool.

How Are Organizations Currently Responding to These Changes in the Labor Pool?

To cope with the scarcity of potential employees, employers are responding with a number of initiatives. They are developing new recruiting strategies designed to find new sources of labor, including students, immigrants, and retirees. They are devising benefits packages that better fit the needs of the new work force in hopes of making their organizations more attractive to job applicants. They are also becoming more flexible regarding employment conditions, allowing employees more input in the determination of the length and scheduling of their work weeks, offering opportunities for extended leaves of absence, and arranging for job sharing. When successful, such initiatives mean that an organization will have more diversity not only in the types of employees it hires but also in employment conditions.

At the same time human resource planners are worrying about where they will find the employees of the future and how to prepare them for the available jobs. Many are living with the after-effects of massive organizational downsizings stimulated by the economic turmoil of the 1980s. Eager to avoid repeating the painful experiences of carrying out massive layoffs, organizations are relying more heavily on temporary employees, who are dispatched to the organization through employment agencies, as well as contract employees, who are hired only for the duration of a specific project (DeLuca, 1988). Thus, some organizations are creating diversity along yet another dimension, namely, the nature of the psychological contract that exists between employer and employees. While some employees will feel that they are central players in the organization's long-term future, others clearly will be on the periphery.

Assuming that the innovative tactics being used by organizations to cope with a tightening labor market are successful, tomorrow's work organizations will be fully staffed, albeit with a work force that is dramatically different from the work force of a decade or two ago. Yesterday's nontraditional employee hired as part of an experimental program will be tomorrow's norm.

The New Challenges Organizations Will Face

Having solved the problem of staffing their organizations with qualified employees, employers will next be confronted with the task of effectively managing the work force. Effective management involves more than finding people to fill jobs and then training them. It also involves facilitating performance to ensure that productivity is maximized and that turnover within the ranks of the most productive members is minimized. For many organizations, effective management also means facilitating creative problem solving and innovation.

The problems of maximizing employee performance, managing turnover patterns, and stimulating innovation are not new to either business leaders or to the organizational psychologists to whom they often turn for advice about how to manage such problems. Traditional solutions to these problems include using selection tests to assess the skills and abilities of job applicants so that the best applicants can be hired and placed into positions that match their talents, providing training as needed, monitoring performance, and providing rewards and sanctions—monetary and otherwise—contingent on job performance.

If the only impending change facing U.S. employers was that their work force will become more diverse, the solutions traditionally used to manage performance, turnover, and innovation could be adapted to meet the needs of the future. For example, to cope with cultural diversity, selection tests could be administered in the applicant's primary language, English courses could be offered as needed, flexible work schedules and vacation policies could be developed to accommodate differences in religious practices and traditions, and so forth. This approach to managing diversity, which might be described as business as usual plus variations on the theme, seems to be the preferred response of many organizations as they struggle to adjust to the changing work force. As many leading employers already understand, however, the most effective responses to the challenges posed by increasing diversity may include more radical changes. Employers who limit their response to work force diversity to the development of flexible and varied personnel practices address only one aspect of the employment situation, namely, the conditions surrounding the exchange of an individual's labor for compensation. Not addressed is the nature of the interactions that develop among an organization's employees. Yet these relationships can have important influences on performance, turnover, and innovation, especially in situations where there is substantial task interdependence among employees.

A hallmark of the industrial revolution was that it led organizations to design jobs in ways that kept task interdependence to a minimum (e.g., see Piore & Sable, 1984). In search of ever greater efficiency, the predominant approach to job design for most nonprofessional jobs was to break work into small tasks that individuals could repeatedly perform throughout the day, more or less independent of other employees. Under this model of job design, the performance of a work group was the consequence of the members' performances on disjunctive tasks.

During the past several years, a number of forces have pushed organizations to redesign jobs in ways that increase task interdependence. For example, the arrival of Japanese businesses as major competitors in industries traditionally dominated by the United States has stimulated many companies to experiment with group-based interventions, such as quality circles, which were believed to contain the essential aspects of successful Japanese management principles. Another impetus for redesigning work to emphasize teamwork is that such job designs are believed to facilitate the production of high quality products. For example, since the early 1980s, Ford Motor Company has been engaged in a massive organizational change to improve product quality. To produce quality automobiles, Ford believes, employees must be involved and committed to their jobs. By redesigning jobs so they are performed by interdependent team members, Ford is succeeding in its quest for quality (see Banas, 1988; see also Walton & Hackman, 1986).

Team-based job design has also been recommended as a means for facilitating innovation (Kanter, 1988). The objective is to encourage the exchange of information among experts with dissimilar knowledge bases and perspectives to encourage creative cross-fertilization of ideas. Most recently, several of this country's largest organizations have discovered that by forming multidepartment teams to develop new products and deliver them to the market, they can significantly speed up the process of shepherding a new product or service idea along the difficult road from inception to realization (Dumaine, 1989). Some observers of the American business scene are now predicting that self-managing work teams, that is, groups of interdependent employees who have control over the management and execution of their tasks (Goodman, Devadas, & Hughson, 1988) are the "wave of the future" (see Hoerr, 1989).

This trend toward greater reliance on work teams, in combination with the increasing diversity of the work force, will almost certainly force employers to find approaches to managing diversity that are substantially different from the individualistic practices they currently rely on (cf. Ilgen, 1986). In other words, employers will discover the value of management strategies that address the consequences that diversity has for productivity and interpersonal dynamics among co-workers.

Review of Social Psychological Research Relating Group Composition to Organizationally Relevant Outcomes

The question of how productivity and relationships among employees are likely to differ when the work force is relatively diverse, instead of homogeneous, and when the work is characterized by higher task interdependence, will be addressed next. The objective here is to review the empirical evidence relevant to the relationship between group composition and four outcomes of particular interest to employers: (a) performance on clearly defined production tasks, (b) performance on cognitive or intellective tasks, (c) creative idea generation and decision making related to ambiguous judgmental tasks, and (d) group cohesiveness and conflict.

In summarizing the relevant research, two classes of composition variables are considered. In some studies, group composition has been operationalized as the degree of homogeneity-heterogeneity (i.e., diversity) among members' *personal attributes,* including personality, values, attitudes, and various demographic (biographical) variables assumed or known to be associated with values and attitudes. Other studies have compared groups differing in composition with respect to members' *abilities and skills*—both technical and social. For each of the group outcomes discussed, studies relevant to these two types of composition variables will be considered. Table 6.1 provides a guide to the topics covered in this review. The cells shown in Table 6.1 are numbered to correspond to the order in which research relevant to the cells is discussed. McGrath's (1984) Group Task Circumplex, which provides a taxonomy for classifying the different types of tasks groups can engage in, is relied on to divide this review into sections.

I. Personal Attribute Composition Effects for Performance Tasks

Performance tasks are those requiring perceptual and motor skills, where the outcomes of interest are proficiency and productivity. Objective standards for performance evaluation are assumed to exist (McGrath, 1984). Haythorn (1968) provided a comprehensive review of research on group composition, covering studies conducted primarily between 1940 and 1968. Updates to the Haythorn review have since been provided by Shaw (1981), McGrath (1984), and Driskell, Hogan, and Salas (1987). As these reviews reveal, relatively few studies have assessed the impact of personal attribute composition on performance tasks, and the results of those that have are somewhat mixed. In two studies that operationalized composition using members' demographic characteristics, performance tended to be higher in the homogeneous groups (Clement & Schiereck, 1973; Fenelon & Megaree, 1971). But in a longitudinal study of student groups working on land-surveying tasks, attitude heterogeneity-homogeneity was found to be unrelated to performance (Terborg, Castore, & DeNinno, 1976).

Although the evidence is mixed, overall the few available studies tend to support the conclusion that groups composed of members who are similar with respect to personal attributes are likely to do somewhat better on performance tasks, in comparison to groups composed of members who are dissimilar. This effect has been found for tasks that require a great deal of interdependence, as well as for tasks that require relatively little interdependence.

Although more research is clearly needed before we can have confidence in the robustness and generalizability of these effects, very few recent studies have examined the effects of personal attribute composition on performance tasks. This is true despite the fact that (a) several studies have shown group process to be affected by personal attribute composition (see section VII below) and (b) most researchers assume that group process affects performance.

Table 6.1
Guide to Research Topics Covered in the Present Chapter

	Types of Composition Variables	
Types of Outcomes	*Personal Attributes*	*Abilities and Skills*
Performance tasks	I	II
Intellective tasks	III	IV
Creativity and judgmental decision making	V	VI
Group cohesion & conflict	VII	

NOTE: Roman numerals refer to chapter headings.

II. Ability Composition Effects for Performance Tasks

A few studies have provided evidence that groups composed of members with heterogeneous technical abilities do better on performance tasks in comparison to groups composed of members with homogeneous technical abilities. In an early field study, Pelz (1956) found that productivity among scientists and engineers was positively correlated with the extent to which they were in frequent contact with colleagues whose training and expertise were dissimilar to their own. The more productive scientists and engineers tended to create informal communication networks with dissimilar peers. Such networks resemble loosely structured, heterogeneous groups.

In a study of B-29 bomber crews, Voiers (1956) reported results indicating that heterogeneous abilities facilitated performance, but only when teams could take advantage of ability heterogeneity by assigning members to those tasks to which they were best suited. Professional athletic teams clearly are free to maximize performance by matching people's skills to the positions they play. Consistent with Voiers' study, Jones (1974) found that athletic teams with more diverse skills (good offensive and defensive units) outperformed teams with less diverse skills.

When the question posed is: "Do groups composed of people with diverse skills and abilities outperform those with only a single ability represented?" the intuitively obvious answer seems to be "yes." Few employers would feel they needed scientific evidence to confirm this.

It is perhaps for this reason that little empirical research has addressed this question. However, the answer is less obvious if the question is rephrased slightly to be: "Given a large number of dissimilar group performance tasks that need to be performed in an organization, and given a work force with a limited but known distribution of skills and abilities, how should employees be assigned in order to maximize the total performance of *all* groups?" This is a question that cannot be answered until scientific studies designed to address the question are conducted. Such research would be particularly valuable to employers in the manufacturing sector of our economy, because manufacturing jobs often have the characteristics of performance tasks.

III. Personal Attribute Composition Effects for Intellective Tasks

Intellective tasks are problem-solving tasks with correct answers. The availability of an objective standard for assessing performance distinguishes these cognitively based tasks from judgmental tasks and creativity tasks (McGrath, 1984). Just as there are few studies relating personal attribute composition to performance tasks, few studies have examined the impact of personal attribute composition on group problem solving for tasks with known correct answers.

In a recent review of sex differences in group performance, Wood (1987) reports findings from 12 studies in which objective performance results (accuracy or speed) could be compared for same- versus mixed-sex groups. Across all studies, there is weak support to indicate that mixed-sex groups tend to outperform same-sex groups of either males or females. As Wood pointed out, this result should be interpreted cautiously due to the small number of studies. In addition to reserving judgment about the superiority of mixed-sex groups on intellective tasks, conclusions about the appropriate explanation for any differences found must await additional research.

Although there is very little direct evidence linking personal attribute composition to performance on intellective tasks, the research of Laughlin and colleagues (see Laughlin, 1980) leads to the expectation that mixed-attribute groups should outperform homogeneous groups when attribute heterogeneity increases the probability of the group containing some members who are capable of determining the correct answer to the problems being solved. Because "truth supported wins," heterogeneous groups should have the advantage only if their heterogeneity is associated with their likelihood of determining the truth. For intellective tasks, personal attributes per se may be less important as predictor variables than the task-related abilities associated with such attributes. These are discussed next.

IV. Ability Composition Effects for Intellective Tasks

Some evidence bearing on the relationship between ability composition and performance on intellective tasks has been generated by research designed to examine what Steiner (1972) termed process losses and process gains. These studies have operationalized ability composition by composing groups with differing combinations of ability *levels* (see Laughlin, 1980). Not surprisingly, these studies support the conclusion that group performance is a positive function of the average ability of group members. The relationship is not simply linear, however. For so-called "Eureka" tasks, the group needs only one member with the ability to discover the correct answer. Otherwise, group performance is nearly maximized when at least two members have the ability to discover the correct answer.

Laughlin's research program was not intended to document or explain group composition effects on performance, although linkages can be drawn. Unfortunately, other research programs have not systematically investigated ability composition effects on intellective tasks. Thus, although many researchers would probably agree that heterogeneous groups experience more process losses than homogeneous groups, it is not at all clear that such process losses are sufficiently large to outweigh the benefits of heterogeneity of ability.

In employment settings, the people who perform intellective tasks are often referred to as "knowledge workers." Examples of knowledge workers include financial auditing teams, corporate lawyers, insurance claims representatives, teachers, and software development teams. Knowledge workers represent a growing sector of the work force (Johnston & Packer, 1987), and many of these people are employed in professional service firms. Professional service firms frequently structure work around client-centered teams of professionals with differing areas of expertise. Thus, these firms face the question: Given a large number of dissimilar (intellective) tasks, and given the distribution of skills and abilities in our work force, how should employees be assigned to teams in order to maximize the total performance of all the firm? Being curious about how this question is answered now by managers in professional service firms, I asked the personnel director of a large accounting firm how assignments to audit teams were made. He indicated that assignments were based on availability (i.e., whoever wasn't working on anything else) and the personal preferences of the team leaders. Unfortunately, the psychological literature provides no good basis for suggesting alternative methods for making such team assignments.

V. Personal Attribute Composition and Performance on Creative Idea Generation Tasks and Decision-Making Tasks

Intellective tasks typically involve some decision making, but they differ from what McGrath (1984) calls decision-making tasks in that the objective of intellective tasks is to find the correct answers whereas the objective on decision-making tasks is to reach consensus about the best solution to a problem. McGrath considers creative idea generation tasks and decision-making tasks to be separate categories. Here, creative idea generation and decision-making tasks are treated together because in most natural settings idea generation is an integral aspect of the decision-making activity.

Several reviews covering research on this topic have reached the conclusion that heterogeneous groups are more likely than homogeneous groups to be creative and to reach high-quality decisions (Filley, House, & Kerr, 1976; Hoffman, 1979; McGrath, 1984; Shaw, 1981). This finding holds for a variety of personal attributes, including personality (Hoffman & Maier, 1961), types of training (Pelz, 1956), and attitudes (Hoffman, Harburg, & Maier, 1962; Triandis, Hall, & Ewen, 1965; Willems & Clark, 1971).

Hoffman's work (Hoffman, 1961; Maier & Hoffman, 1960) epitomizes research of this type. In one study, participants were management trainees who were put into trios designed to be heterogeneous or homogeneous in values and opinions. When asked to generate alternate solutions to a problem, heterogeneous groups outperformed homogeneous groups. Another, albeit unusual, example of research showing the benefits of personal attribute heterogeneity is provided by Ziller, Behringer, and Goodchilds (1962). The task was to write cartoon captions. Heterogeneity was created in some groups by changing the people who made up the group (open groups), whereas homogeneous groups were simply those with stable membership (closed groups). Captions written by the heterogeneous groups were judged to have greater fluency and originality. Studies of research scientists similarly have shown that groups with fluid membership are likely to be more creative (Pelz & Andrews, 1966) even when groups are initially interdisciplinary. When scientists of interdisciplinary teams worked closely together on a daily basis, within three years they were found to have become homogeneous in their perspectives and approach to solving problems.

A simple explanation for why heterogeneity of personal attributes enhances performance on creative and decision-making tasks is that people who are dissimilar bring different perspectives to the task. In a sense, their differing perspectives can be considered resources available for use on the task at hand. For tasks such as these, where breadth of ideas is an important resource, heterogeneous perspectives seem to be advantageous.

It should be noted, however, that although heterogeneous groups outperform homogeneous groups on creative and judgmental tasks, face-to-face interaction is not necessarily the most effective format for heterogeneous groups to use in creative or decision-making tasks. There is substantial evidence indicating that interacting, heterogeneous decision-making groups suffer from process loss, as hypothesized by Steiner (1972). Much of this evidence is discussed in depth by Hill (1982) in her excellent review of studies addressing the question: Are $N + 1$ heads better than one? Although the focus of Hill's review is on comparing the performance of individuals to groups, she cites numerous studies that have compared the performance of a group to the group's potential, as measured by statistical pooling techniques. For both creative and decision-making tasks, the performance of interacting groups tends to be less than their potential as estimated by statistical pooling.

VI. Ability Composition and Performance on Creative and Decision-Making Tasks

As Haythorn (1968) stated, "The question is: What combinations of individuals with different skills and proficiency levels produce the most effective groups?" (p. 114). As we have seen, there have been few attempts to answer this question for intellective tasks. More evidence is available for creative and decision-making tasks. For example, on a word association task, groups composed of members with dissimilar ability *levels* outperformed individuals whose ability was equivalent to that of the member with highest ability in the mixed groups, suggesting that high-ability members can benefit from interaction with others who have less ability (see Laughlin & Bitz, 1975).

One explanation for findings like these is that high-ability group members learn during their interactions with others of lower ability because they take on the role of teacher. Playing the teacher role may lead high-ability members to sharpen their own thinking. Another possibility is that the questions and inputs of more naive members encourage the more expert members to unbundle the assumptions and rules they automatically use when dealing with issues and problems in which they are experts (Simon, 1979). This unbundling may increase the probability of discovering assumptions that warrant scrutiny and decision rules for which exceptions may be needed.

In laboratory studies of ability composition, heterogeneity of ability level is manipulated more often than heterogeneity with respect to ability content or type. Nevertheless, a general conclusion that can be drawn from the results of laboratory research is that when working on complex, nonroutine problems—a situation that presumably requires some degree of creativity—groups are more effective when composed of individuals with diverse types of skills, knowledge, abilities, and perspectives (Shaw, 1976).

VII. Group Composition Effects on Cohesion and Conflict

In the preceding sections, the focus was on the relationship between group composition and group output, including output for tasks that emphasize *doing* and tasks that emphasize *thinking.* In this section, the focus shifts to consequences of composition for what is usually called group *process,* a group's internal functioning and its viability as an ongoing system.

Factors that influence internal processes have long been of interest to psychologists because group process is assumed to affect group performance outcomes and membership retention. For groups that value productivity as a relevant group outcome, the evidence generally supports the assumption that cohesive groups outperform noncohesive groups (McGrath, 1984; Shaw, 1981). In addition, members of cohesive groups tend to be more satisfied, absent less, and more likely to remain in the group rather than leave it (Lott & Lott, 1965; Stogdill, 1972; Shaw, 1981). However, the picture is made more complex by research showing that conflict can be beneficial for complex problem-solving tasks (Cosier, 1981; Janis, 1972; Schwenk, 1983).

Because group outcomes such as satisfaction, absenteeism, and turn-over often are nearly as important as group performance in organizational settings (Nadler, Hackman, & Lawler, 1979; Schmidt, 1974), improving our understanding of the determinants of cohesion is a useful objective. This section describes research that addresses the relationship between group composition and group processes, including both cohesiveness and conflict.

Personality

When cohesion is the variable to be predicted, group composition seems to play an important role, but specifying the nature of that role has proved difficult. Haythorn's (1968) review included numerous citations of studies that showed links between group composition and group cohesiveness or related variables. Many of those studies focused on personality variables. The conclusion drawn from this research was that the effects of personality heterogeneity-homogeneity depend on a number of factors, including the personality characteristics of interest, the task characteristics, and the extent of interpersonal contact. This complexity plus the methodological and theoretical questioning that arose among personality researchers and their critics during the 1970s apparently has stifled progress on this topic (see Driskell, Hogan, & Salas, 1987), however, so clear conclusions are difficult to reach.

Attitudes

Research relating group members' attitudes to cohesiveness is, fortunately, more easily interpreted. One of the most robust social psychological principles is that people are attracted to others with similar attitudes (Byrne, 1971; Heider, 1958; Newcomb, 1961). Given that cohesiveness is often defined as attraction to other members in one's group (Shaw, 1981), it follows that groups that are homogeneous with respect to attitudes should be more cohesive. Because group members tend to become more similar in their attitudes as they interact over time (Newcomb, 1956), the relationship between attitude homogeneity and cohesiveness should be particularly strong in natural groups. Terborg et al.'s (1976) longitudinal investigation of student groups is one of the few studies in which attitudes were assessed directly and then used to assemble groups. Cohesiveness was assessed at six points in time. At each assessment, cohesiveness was greater in the groups composed of attitudinally similar members, although the magnitude of the effect of attitude similarity on cohesiveness did not approach statistical significance until the last three assessments.

Demographic Background

There is considerable empirical evidence showing that attitudes are not randomly distributed throughout the population. Instead attitudes, values, and beliefs vary systematically with several demographic variables. For example, sociological research has documented the ways in which societal conditions associated with different age cohorts (e.g., economic depressions vs. booms and periods of war vs. peace) influence attitudes and values (Elder, 1974, 1975; Thernstrom, 1973), and psychological research has found age to be correlated with personality (e.g., Bengston & Lovejoy, 1973; Vroom & Pahl, 1971). Regarding sex, there is an extensive literature showing reliable differences between males and females with respect to both cognitive functioning and interpersonal interaction patterns (Anderson & Blanchard, 1982; Eagly, 1987; Wood, 1987). Regarding education, evidence indicates that people with more formal education have more positive attitudes toward innovation (Kimberly & Evanisko, 1981; Rogers & Shoemaker, 1971) and that curriculum choices are associated with personality, attitudes, and cognitive styles (Holland, 1976). The correlations between demographic characteristics and attitudes and values explain the finding that group demographic composition predicts cohesiveness (see Lott & Lott, 1965; Zander, 1979).

Summary of Social Psychological Research Evidence to Date

Table 6.2 briefly summarizes the conclusions that can be drawn about the effects of group heterogeneity-homogeneity on the outcomes considered in this review. For psychologists interested in improving work force productivity, two patterns of results are particularly noteworthy. The first clear pattern relates to research evidence that is and is not available. Many (and perhaps most) of the tasks likely to be performed by employees in work organizations fall in the categories of performance or intellective tasks. There is very little research evidence regarding the consequences of group homogeneity-heterogeneity for these types of tasks, and there is essentially no research that addresses how group composition affects groups working on the other types of tasks in McGrath's circumplex (i.e., cognitive conflict tasks, contests, mixed motive tasks, and planning tasks).

The second pattern of results in Table 6.2 that is noteworthy relates to the composition between the results for task outcomes versus the results for group processes. Whereas heterogeneity appears to facilitate performance on some types of tasks, it generally discourages group cohesiveness.

Thus, it appears that psychologists interested in helping organizations deal with the increasing diversity of the work force will have a difficult balancing act to perform. On the one hand, organizations might be encouraged to take full advantage of the potential benefits of the growing diversity of the work force by ensuring that work groups are composed of dissimilar employees, at least when those groups will be working on tasks that require creativity and judgmental decision making. However, organizations that take this advice may soon notice more conflict and less cohesiveness among group members.

This brief summary of the social psychological literature shows that psychologists have already begun to build a foundation of knowledge relevant to helping organizations deal with the anticipated increase in work group diversity. However, any psychologist considering making recommendations for managing diversity in the workplace should realize that there are several reasons to maintain a level of healthy skepticism about how successfully lessons from the laboratory can be applied to the workplace. Some of the reasons to question whether laboratory results will generalize to work settings are described next. Then, recent field research on the relationship between work group composition and the outcomes of organizational innovation and turnover is described.

Issues in Applying Laboratory Results in the Workplace

Which Attributes Are Important?

This may be one of the first questions that anyone would ask if faced with the task of applying research results in an organizational context. In the preceding review, attributes were grouped into two broad categories: (a) personal attributes, which included demographic characteristics such as sex and race as well as psychological characteristics such as personality and attitudes, and (b) skills and abilities. When the context of discussion is managing work force diversity, the first of these

Table 6.2

Summary of Social Psychological Research Results for Group Heterogeneity Effects

| | Types of Composition Variables | |
Types of Outcomes	Personal Attributes	Abilities and Skills
Performance tasks	Few studies with mixed results. No clear effect of group composition on performance	Heterogeneity of types and levels of ability seem beneficial, but few studies
Intellective tasks	Too few studies to draw conclusions; some evidence that mixed-sex groups outperform same-sex groups	Almost no directly relevant research
Creativity and judgmental decision making	Evidence is fairly consistent in showing that heterogeneous groups outperform homogeneous groups	Moderate amount of evidence indicates that heterogeneity of ability levels is beneficial
Cohesion and conflict	The consequences of personality heterogeneity are unclear. Attitude homogeneity and demographic homogeneity are related to group cohesiveness.	

two categories is likely to be of most concern because modern personnel selection and training procedures assume that the mix of skills and abilities needed by a work group can and should be determined by the specific demands of the group's task. Thus, the question important to organizations might be phrased: Assuming that a group has represented within it the appropriate mix of skills and abilities, how important is the distribution of group members' personal attributes, and which attributes are important?

Projections about the changing nature of the work force make demographic attributes most salient. As the demographic make-up of the work force in general changes, organizations should find that the demographic composition of various units and work groups in the organization begin to reflect the new diversity. Thus, research that sheds light on how composition variables such as age, sex, and ethnic background affect interpersonal dynamics and group outcomes will be particularly useful to organizations. Which of these attributes are likely to be most important?

Our empirical knowledge is clearly inadequate to serve as a guide for judging which attributes are likely to have the greater impact. Although a trial-and-error approach to selecting attributes for study might be a feasible strategy to adopt, a theoretically guided search for important attributes would be much better. Here, Turner's (1987) discussion of self-categorization theory may be particularly useful.

Self-categorization theory represents an attempt to synthesize research on intergroup relations with recent work in the area of social cognition. Turner argues that many group phenomena, including cohesiveness and cooperation, are influenced by the self-categorizations of group members. Specifically, psychological ingroups form when people perceive themselves to be relatively similar to each other on some dimension(s) and relatively different from comparison others, who are viewed as the outgroup.

In the context of organizations, an implication of self-categorization theory is that one cannot judge whether a work team is heterogeneous or homogeneous with respect to an attribute without considering how the attribute is distributed among nonteam members. Self-categorization theory also suggests that the process through which attributes become salient, or submerged, in a group is a significant research question. Finally, it emphasizes the importance of multiattribute research. Rather than studying the effects of, for example, sex *or* age *or* race *or* cognitive style, studies that track composition along all of these dimensions simultaneously are needed.

Does the Nature of the Task Moderate the Impact of Group Composition?

Organizations employ people to perform a wide variety of tasks, which involve perceptual and motor performance, intellective performance, and creativity and judgmental decision making. The summary of results shown in Table 6.2 suggests that group composition may affect performance on different types of tasks in different ways (although no studies were found that tested this hypothesis directly). If this is the case, the recommendations made for how to compose work groups to maximize their performances should be shaped by knowledge of the specific task the group will be performing.

The evidence available at this time regarding the role of task type as a moderator variable is sufficient to indicate the need to take task type into account. However, too little is known about precisely how tasks and group composition interact to affect performance. This makes it difficult to use one's knowledge about a group's specific task responsibilities to inform one's recommendations. Furthermore, the research provides no assistance for taking into account the fact that more than one type of task is often involved in the work performed by a single team.

How Can Group Homogeneity-Heterogeneity Be Managed Effectively?

Perspectives such as that offered by Turner (1987) emphasize the fact that work groups necessarily are simultaneously both heterogeneous and homogeneous. Groups that are homogeneous on one or two attributes will almost certainly be heterogeneous with respect to other attributes. Conversely, members of groups that are heterogeneous with respect to several attributes are likely to share some common attributes. Clearly, it is unrealistic to cope with the diversity of the work force by attempting to completely control the composition of work groups. Instead, organizations need to find ways to manage groups to ensure that (a) the positive consequences of both homogeneity and heterogeneity are maximized, while at the same time (b) the negative consequences of both are minimized.

One line of research relevant to this challenge is particularly worth mentioning, namely, research on self-managing teams. The term "self-managing team" has been used to refer to work groups that are given full responsibility for making decisions relevant to their assigned task (see Goodman et al., 1988). In rare cases, work groups might also be "self-designing" in that they have control over who enters and leaves the group and over what tasks are worked on by the group (see Hackman, 1982). Studies of such groups, especially if they are operating under strong incentives to maximize their productivity, may provide excellent opportunities to learn about how teams naturally manage the coexisting conditions of homogeneity and heterogeneity.

Current Organizational Field Research on Team Composition

During the decade of the 1980s, two theoretical position papers drew attention to the need for more research on the consequences of group composition in work settings. The first of these was Pfeffer's (1983) discussion of organizational demography. The second was Schneider's (1987) discussion of the attraction-selection-attrition model.

The term *organizational demography* refers to the demographic composition of formal organizations. Pfeffer argued that (a) many attitudes and behaviors are influenced by an organization's demographic composition, including innovation, motivation, performance, intra-firm personnel movement (e.g., transfers, promotions) and turnover, and that (b) many dimensions of demographic composition are important for explaining organizational attitudes and behaviors, including age, tenure, sex, race, socioeconomic background, religion, and so on. Building on the empirical findings from sociological and psychological studies, Pfeffer offered several hypotheses about both the causes and consequences of various demographic distributions.

Most published studies of organizational demography have examined the relationship between turnover and group demography with respect to age and tenure. People belonging to different age cohorts have been shown to have differing values and attitudes (e.g., Elder, 1974, 1975; Thernstrom, 1973). Pfeffer and his colleagues (McCain, O'Reilly, & Pfeffer, 1983; Pfeffer, 1983) argued that comparable effects were likely to exist for organizational cohorts defined by date of organizational entry (tenure). Similarity of attitudes and values facilitates communication and stimulates interpersonal attraction. By extension, when members of organizational groups belong to the same age and/or tenure cohorts, group cohesiveness should be relatively high. On the other hand, when members or organizational groups are from different cohorts, strained communications and low interpersonal attraction detract from the development of a cohesive group, and higher turnover rates are likely to result.

Empirical results tend to support the hypothesis that turnover is higher for work groups composed of members who are more diverse with respect to their ages and years of organization tenure (e.g., McCain et al., 1983; O'Reilly, Caldwell, & Barnett, 1989; Wagner, Pfeffer, & O'Reilly, 1984), although the analyses reported in organizational demography studies to date make it difficult to draw conclusions about the relative importance of these two correlated demographic characteristics. One recent study (Zenger & Lawrence, 1989) suggests that when communication is the outcome of interest, age cohort effects may be more powerful than tenure cohort effects.

Schneider's (1987) attraction-selection-attrition (A-S-A) model of behavior in organizations uses an interactionist perspective to discuss how interorganizational differences in group composition arise, how these differences are sustained, and the consequences of group composition. Although Schneider's psychological approach to the topic of composition contrasts with Pfeffer's sociological perspective, the two arguments are not incompatible.

Schneider's model is based on the well-documented principle that people are attracted to similar others (Byrne, 1971). Due to the attraction effect, bias in the selection of new employees occurs. Job applicants who are more similar to current employees have a higher probability of being hired, in comparison to applicants who are dissimilar. In addition, once hired, the more similar one is to others in the organization, the more attracted one will be to them. Attraction to others in the organization, in turn, decreases the probability of subsequent turnover. Conversely, attrition rates are likely to be relatively high for those who feel like misfits because they are dissimilar to others in the organization.

Over time, Schneider argued, the A-S-A cycle results in organizations filled with people who are relatively homogeneous. Although interpersonal relationships are facilitated by this homogeneity, the organization's ability to be creative and to adapt to a changing environment may be hindered.

Taken together, the organizational demography and A-S-A models suggest many hypotheses that lend themselves to being tested in field settings. Two studies that illustrate how these hypotheses can be tested in field settings are described in some detail below. As these studies illustrate, field studies of group composition effects are consistent with much of the laboratory research.

Top Management Team Composition and Organizational Innovation

For several decades, management researchers interested in understanding the determinants of organizational performance focused on the role of the top-most organizational leader, for example, the chief executive officer (CEO) or president of the firm. By the 1980s, several studies had drawn into question the importance of organizational leadership by showing that changes in leadership often had little or no relationship to changes in organizational performance (Pfeffer & Salancik, 1978).

Firm in their belief that organizational leaders were important to the performance of organizations, Hambrick and Mason (1984) pointed out that few large organizations are run by a single person at the top. Instead, top management teams usually were responsible for making critical decisions. Therefore, research that focused on a single person and ignored other members of the top management team could not be expected to capture the impact of organizational leaders. The wisdom of Hambrick and Mason's argument is illustrated by a study of innovation in 199 U.S. banks (Bantel & Jackson, 1989).

The ability of U.S. businesses to innovate has become a topic of national concern. Many observers believe that, to be successful in global competition, U.S. firms will need to continually revise and improve their products, services, and operations. We reasoned that for organizations to be innovative they needed top management teams that were likely to be effective at solving problems—both problems for which there is no known correct answer and problems for which correct answers do exist—and they needed to be creative.

As our review of the literature shows, group heterogeneity should predict whether or not a team performs well on such tasks. Therefore, we predicted that banks with heterogeneous top management teams would be more innovative than their counterparts with more homogeneous top management teams.

Although our hypothesis was straightforward, we could not test it without first deciding how to operationalize heterogeneity. Which attributes would be the important ones to assess? Many of the laboratory studies had operationalized heterogeneity in terms of race and sex, but when members of the teams of interest are executives in large U.S. corporations, very few teams that are heterogeneous with respect to these two variables can be found.

In order to develop hypotheses about how characteristics of top management teams would impact decisions to innovate, we considered the nature of organizational decision processes in general. Numerous models of organizational decision processes exist (e.g., see Daft & Weick, 1984; Hickson, 1987; Simon, 1976). Most share the assumption that three general types of activity are involved: (a) problem identification and formulation; (b) exploration, formalization, and decision making; and (c) decision dissemination and implementation. The abilities and expertise of project or management teams might influence each of these activities in ways that impact the probability of innovation occurring.

During problem identification and formulation, team members are responding to ambiguous and complex stimuli. Each team member may attend to different cues and construct different understandings about a situation (see Moreland & Levine, 1991). Consequently, the composition of the decision-making team can determine what information is available during problem identification and formulation and the meaning it is given. During the problem-solving phase, team composition can influence the number, variety, and quality of the solutions generated and considered, as well as the nature of the discussions about alternative solutions. During the implementation phase, the characteristics of top team members may affect their ability to sell decisions to others and to access and mobilize needed resources.

Attributes Studied

A review of research on innovation and creativity led us to select the following personal attributes for attention in this study: age, organizational tenure, education level, major area of study, and area of functional expertise. Our predictions were as follows:

1. *Younger teams would be more innovative.* Youth is correlated with cognitive resources important to the innovation process (Botwinick, 1977; Burke & Light, 1981) as well as with attitudes toward risk-taking, which are also related to innovation (Vroom & Pahl, 1971).

2. *Teams with shorter average tenure in the organization would be more innovative.* More tenured executives have more psychological commitment to the organizational status quo (Staw & Ross, 1980; Stevens, Beyer, & Trice, 1978). Consequently, change may be resisted. In addition, long tenure within the same organization may result in insulation and a narrowing of one's perspective (Katz, 1981).

3. *Teams with more educated members would be more innovative.* Assuming that education level reflects cognitive ability, higher levels of education should be associated with a team's ability to generate creative solutions to complex problems. Also, people who are more educated have more receptive attitudes toward innovation (Kimberly & Evanisko, 1981; Rogers & Shoemaker, 1971).

4. *Teams that were heterogeneous with respect to educational curriculum would be more innovative.* The educational curriculum choices people make correspond to their personalities, attitudes, and cognitive styles (Holland, 1976). Educational curriculum is also associated with job experiences throughout one's career (National Science Foundation, 1963; Miller, 1968). We expected teams comprised of members who completed

dissimilar types of curricula to benefit from the diversity of perspectives team members bring to the problem solving task.

5. *Teams that were heterogeneous with respect to their functional background would be more innovative.* Functional experiences (e.g., experience in marketing versus accounting) are likely to shape attitudes, knowledge, and perspectives (Dearborn & Simon, 1958; Hambrick & Mason, 1984). These can affect how managers behave at all stages of the innovation process, including the problems one identifies as important, how these problems are formulated, the types of solutions generated, evaluations of alternative solutions, and involvement during implementation.

Study Design

To test these hypotheses, we contacted the CEOs at 199 banks in six midwestern states. We asked the CEO to respond to a questionnaire designed to assess the level of innovation that had occurred in the organization. Innovation was operationalized as the number of innovative "items" (products, programs, and services) firms had adopted and/or developed. Because we were interested in differences among firms, we assumed a field-based frame of reference for judging innovativeness; that is, innovations were identified through reference to the state of the art in the industry. We also asked the CEO to identify up to eight people whom he considered to be key players in his top management team. These names were given to the human resource manager, who then filled out a form designed to provide information about the background characteristics of interest to us.

Results

Regression analyses were conducted to test our hypotheses. In a liberal test of the hypotheses, we regressed innovation on the set of five team composition variables. This analysis revealed a strong association between composition and innovation ($R^2 = .31$, $p < .01$). Significant ($p < .05$) coefficients were found for average age, average education level, and heterogeneity of functional background. The coefficient for heterogeneity of educational specialties was marginally significant.

In a second, more conservative test of our hypothesis, we statistically controlled for several variables that might be confounded with innovation and team composition, including the size (total assets) of the bank, the state in which it was located, the degree of centralization in the decision-making process, and team cohesiveness (as reported by the CEO). After controlling for all of these variables, team composition again predicted innovation (R^2 = .11). In this analysis, significant coefficients were obtained for average education level and heterogeneity of functional background. An additional analysis revealed that the relationship between innovation and top team composition was stronger in banks for which the decision-making responsibilities were centralized within the top team rather than delegated to lower-level managers within the organization. In other words, top management team composition was more predictive of innovation in banks when the top team had more control over the decisions made in the organization.

Conclusions and Implications

This study gives us some confidence in our ability to generalize results from laboratory studies of group composition to field settings, although prudence calls for replicating our findings using other types of teams and different industries. Such replications may find different effects. This would be expected if the teams studied were more heterogeneous. In this study, team members were very homogeneous on a number of dimensions (including age, sex, race, and probably religion). Such homogeneity may serve an important function for teams that spend much of their time together discussing complex and high-stakes problems. If basic attitudes and values are shared, cognitively based conflict may be more tolerable. Alternatively, the substantial level of homogeneity that characterized the teams in this study may represent a restriction in range that decreases the effect size that can be obtained.

The primary outcome of interest in this study was innovation, but we also assessed team cohesiveness. Our expectation was that team cohesiveness would be lower for more heterogeneous teams. Instead, we found essentially no relationship between team heterogeneity and cohesiveness. This result appears to stand in contradiction to much of the evidence reviewed above. But the contradiction is more apparent than real. Our measure of cohesiveness was based on the report of the CEO, a fact that might lead one to question the validity of the measure. Not surprisingly, the average reported level of cohesiveness was quite high, which created a range restriction problem. Thus, we were unwilling to conclude from this study that heterogeneity of top management teams is unrelated to cohesiveness. A second study was needed to deal more specifically with this question.

A Study of Team Composition and Turnover

To explore more fully the implications of team composition for affective reactions, we conducted a second study (Jackson, Brett, Sessa, Cooper, Julin, & Peyronnin, in press). Top management teams in the banking industry were again used. Our central hypotheses were as follows:

1. *Top level executives are not randomly distributed across top management teams. Instead, they are grouped into teams characterized by greater homogeneity than would be expected by chance.* This hypothesis follows directly from Schneider's A-S-A model, which argues that over time our attraction to similar others naturally results in organizations becoming homogeneous.

2. *Demographically heterogeneous teams have higher turnover rates in comparison to demographically homogeneous teams.* This hypothesis follows from the finding that heterogeneity is associated with interpersonal conflict and lack of cohesiveness. These conditions should lead to higher turnover because team members will have few social reasons to stay with the organization. Thus, they may be more likely to seek alternative work settings; and when outside offers are received, they may be more likely to accept them.

3. *Top management teams that exhibit a propensity to fill open positions on the team with people from inside the firm, will be relatively more homogeneous, in comparison to teams that recruit externally.* Relative homogeneity presumably evolves in some teams as a consequence of selection biases that favor hiring new members who are relatively similar to oneself. Hypothesis 3 assumes that a similar bias operates when promotion decisions are made, and that a bias favoring similarity leads to the presence of homogeneous teams.

Hypotheses 1 through 3 are stated with groups as the unit of analysis. Hypotheses 4 and 5 are stated with individuals as the unit of analysis.

4. *Top managers who are demographically dissimilar to their teammates will be more likely to leave the firm, in comparison to top managers who are demographically similar to their teammates.* This hypothesis tests Schneider's assertion that attrition processes are partially responsible for the evolution of homogeneous organizations. According to Schneider, attrition should be more likely for the more dissimilar members.

5. *Top managers who are demographically similar to their teammates will be more likely to be promoted, in comparison to members who are demographically dissimilar.*

Just as Hypothesis 4 is the individual-level analog of Hypothesis 2, Hypothesis 5 is the individual-level analog of Hypothesis 3.

Method

These hypotheses were tested using archival data sources. The target organizations were 93 bank holding companies. Information about the top management teams of these companies was obtained from Dunn & Bradstreet's *Reference Book of Corporate Managements* (1985-1988). Independent checks of the validity of this information indicated that this source is quite accurate (see Jackson et al., in press, for details). The information contained in Dunn & Bradstreet allowed us to assess the following demographic attributes of team members: age, tenure, education level, college attended, military experience, experience in an industry other than financial services, and whether an MBA degree was held. Individual differences on each of these attributes were believed to be associated with individual differences in attitudes and values that could influence interpersonal attraction processes.

Information about organizational characteristics (such as size, age, and rate of growth), which we wished to control statistically in our analyses, was obtained from *Moody's Bank and Finance Manual* (1985). These control variables had no significant consequences, however, so they will not be discussed in detail here.

Results

One-way multiple analysis of variance (MANOVA) was used to test Hypothesis 1. The MANOVA treated individuals ($N = 939$) as the unit of analysis. Employing organization (93 levels) was the independent variable. The dependent variables were age, tenure, education level, MBA degree, experience outside the industry, and military experience. Results for the multivariate test revealed a significant effect of employing organization, and the univariate tests revealed significant effects for all of the dependent variables except experience outside the industry.

To test Hypothesis 2, team turnover rate was regressed on average age, entered first, and the seven indices of demographic heterogeneity (age, tenure, education level, MBA degree, experience outside the banking industry, military experience, and college attended), entered second. Age was controlled for in our analyses because it is known to be a significant predictor of turnover. The set of demographic heterogeneity variables explained 22% of the variance in team turnover, supporting Hypothesis 2. The beta coefficients for the heterogeneity indicators revealed significant unique effects for heterogeneity of ages and heterogeneity of experience outside the industry and a marginally significant effect for MBA heterogeneity.

The independent variable of interest for Hypothesis 3 was the percentage of *all new team members* (i.e., members who joined the team in 1986, 1987, or 1988) whose immediately prior position had been within the firm. The percentage of new members hired from within the firm was significantly correlated with four of the team heterogeneity variables. The teams that were less likely to select new team members from within the firm were more heterogeneous with respect to whether they had MBA degrees, experience outside the industry, military experience, and the colleges they attended. Canonical correlation analysis supported the conclusion that team composition predicts propensity to rely on internal sources for new team members.

Hypothesis 4 predicted that team members who were demographically dissimilar to their teammates would be more likely to leave the team, in comparison to team members who were demographically similar. Multiple regression analyses were used to test Hypothesis 4. Age was entered on the first step and the seven demographic dissimilarity variables were entered on the second step. A significant but small (4%) amount of additional variance in turnover was accounted for by the heterogeneity variables. Beta weights for the full equation indicated that members were significantly more likely to leave if they were older and dissimilar to their teammates in terms of education level, MBA degree, and experience outside the industry.

Our final hypothesis predicted that promotion within the team would be more likely for lower status members who were similar to their teammates, in comparison to members who were dissimilar. This hypothesis was not supported. We conducted several exploratory analyses to determine whether the use of alternative indices of dissimilarity would yield different results. The alternative indices included dissimilarity from one's status subgroup, dissimilarity from an elite subgroup, and dissimilarity from the longer tenured elite members. Regardless of the dissimilarity index used, there were no significant relationships between demographic dissimilarity and promotion from non-elite to elite status.

Discussion

Considered in total, our results support the general proposition that the demographic composition of top management teams predicts group turnover rates, with turnover being higher for more heterogeneous teams. Hiring patterns were also predictive of team composition , with homogeneous teams being more likely to fill vacancies with employees from inside the firm.

Two explanations for these group-level phenomena are possible. The first explanation assumes that the group-level phenomena can be understood by examining patterns of individual behaviors. According to this explanation, the group-level turnover effects would occur as a result of an association between personal dissimilarity and probability of turnover at the individual level of analysis. Dissimilar others might be more likely to leave, either voluntarily or involuntarily, because they have more conflictual interactions with other team members. Heterogeneous groups have higher levels of individual dissimilarity, so the association between group heterogeneity could reflect simply the aggregation of effects that are found at the individual level.

An alternative explanation for the group heterogeneity-turnover effect is that heterogeneity impacts group dynamics, which in turn impact the turnover propensities of *all* members (not only the more dissimilar members). According to this explanation, individual turnover should be associated with group heterogeneity, independent of individual dissimilarity.

To examine the roles played by the two related but distinct constructs of individual dissimilarity and group heterogeneity, we regressed individual turnover on (a) age, (b) the set of individual dissimilarity indices, and (c) the set of group heterogeneity indices. The results of this regression analysis indicated that a person's probability of leaving was associated with both the individual dissimilarity and the group's heterogeneity.

In addition to turnover, we examined staffing patterns. Based on the similarity-attraction effect, we hypothesized that promotions from lower to higher status positions within the team would be less likely for the more dissimilar team members. Contrary to our predictions, we found no evidence that a similarity bias operated to decrease the probability of more dissimilar members being promoted. However, more homogeneous groups were more likely to fill vacant positions with people already employed in their firm. One explanation for the association between group homogeneity and reliance on internal sources when filling vacancies may be that homogeneous teams are more risk-avoiding than heterogeneous teams (cf. Bantel & Jackson, 1989). Because more information would be available for internal recruits, they may simply represent a more certain outcome.

Overall, the results of this study support the argument that demography may be an important determinant of behavioral patterns in organizations. Although this study did not examine the relationship between team composition and actual group processes, the assumption that group composition influences interpersonal dynamics, which in turn determine organizationally relevant outcomes, appears warranted.

The strength of our findings illustrates the potential value of studying group-level behavior patterns in addition to studying behaviors at the individual level. Using comparable variables at the group and individual levels of analysis, we observed notably better prediction at the group level of analysis in comparison to the individual level of analysis.

General Discussion

Assuming high levels of turnover can be disruptive to a top team's functioning, the study just described suggests that top team heterogeneity needs to be carefully managed in order for organizations to realize the benefits that heterogeneity can bring, which include improved performance and innovation (Bantel & Jackson, 1989; Murray, 1989). Our data suggest that adding experts from other industries—a strategy that organizations may adopt when faced with environmental turbulence—may be risky because, as predicted by Schneider's (1987) A-S-A model, a high rate of attrition apparently follows the selection of dissimilar members, who may not be easily assimilated into the extant team. If our results hold for teams at levels below the top executives, they indicate that organizations wishing to intentionally increase the diversity of their work forces may find it necessary to increase the resources they devote to socializing new members. More sophisticated selection procedures might also be tried. For example, Schneider (1987) suggests that new employees who are brought in to turn around a poorly performing organization should have secondary or tertiary characteristics that complement those of the existing group. This implies that selecting for personal characteristics other than task-related skills and expertise may be warranted and that valid, formal systems for doing so should be developed. Additional research on group composition and turnover would facilitate the development of such selection systems.

There is much to be learned about both the determinants and consequences of work-group heterogeneity. Fortunately, the field of social psychology provides a rich theoretical and empirical literature on which organizational researchers can build. However, as various authors have pointed out (e.g., Ilgen, 1986; Goodman, Ravlin, & Schminke, 1987), the generalizability of results reported in the extant social psychological literature is not yet well documented. Perhaps the two most important reasons to question whether findings from laboratory studies of groups hold true in organizational settings are related to differences in the nature of the tasks typically studied in the laboratory versus those performed in organizations, and differences in the nature of groups studied in the laboratory versus organizational groups (see McGrath, 1984). These differences point to a number of issues that field research might address in the future.

Regarding tasks, laboratory groups are typically given defined problems, whereas work teams often find and define the problems they tackle. Thus, the small groups literature in social psychology has little to say about how team composition affects the process by which groups scan for, identify, and choose the problems for their agenda (see Moreland & Levine, Chapter 1). Also, whereas laboratory studies often use tasks with known correct answers, the problems faced by work teams are ambiguous and seldom have answers that can be objectively characterized as correct or incorrect (McCaskey, 1982). Differences in which problems team members perceive as important to their organization may be as significant a source of conflict as disagreement about the best way to solve problems identified as important. If so, the strength of the effects of group composition that is typically found in laboratory studies may underestimate the true impact of group composition.

Groups studied in laboratories and those that exist in organizations differ on many features. For example, laboratory groups are usually composed by the researcher, whereas teams within organizational settings often actively compose themselves; in addition, laboratory groups generally consist of strangers, whereas organizational groups consist of members who become familiar with each other over time.

Finally, it is worth noting that when researchers begin to think about applying the findings of social psychological laboratory research to field settings, they are forced to take into account the fact that group composition effects differ as a function of the outcome of interest. As the two studies described above suggest, heterogeneity can be viewed as a positive or negative attribute of a group. Heterogeneity may be positive when the group's performance requires creative problem solving and innovation, but it may be negative if the organization is concerned about minimizing turnover. This presents a dilemma because both innovation and low turnover rates are likely to be valued outcomes for employers. Thus the challenge is to find ways to compose groups with heterogeneity to facilitate creative problem solving *and* homogeneity to facilitate the development of social cohesiveness. It seems likely that this challenge can only be met by research that simultaneously considers several of the many dimensions of homogeneity-heterogeneity that characterize intact teams. Additional field research examining group composition thus has the potential to contribute substantially to our understanding of group processes; and it may stimulate a resurgence of interest in and research on basic group processes.

Conclusions

Although the United States is often described as a melting pot, in the context of work, a variety of forces have resulted in the segregation of employees of different ages, sexes, religions, and ethnic backgrounds. However, as the demand for labor intensifies and as lifestyles change, it is predictable that work groups in U.S. organizations will become more heterogeneous along a number of dimensions. The available evidence suggests that the increasing diversity of the work force is likely to affect both interpersonal relations among employees and productivity. As employers begin to experience the changes that greater diversity is likely to create, they will (hopefully) turn to psychologists in search of ways to take full advantage of the positive consequences of diversity and to minimize the potential negative consequences. A review of what psychologists know about how group composition affects group processes and group performance reveals that we have much to learn before we will be adequately prepared to assist employers when called upon. Hopefully, the projected changes in the nature of the work force and employers' growing reliance on work teams will stimulate new research in this area.

References

Anderson, L. R., & Blanchard, P. N. (1982). Sex differences in task and social-emotional behavior. *Basic and Applied Social Psychology, 3,* 109-139.

Banas, P. A. (1988). Employee involvement: A sustained labor/management initiative at the Ford Motor Company. In J. P. Campbell, R. J. Campbell, & Assoc., *Productivity in organizations: New perspectives from industrial and organizational psychology* (pp. 388-416). San Francisco: Jossey-Bass.

Bantel, K. A., & Jackson, S. E. (1989). Top management and innovations in banking: Does the composition of the top team make a difference? *Strategic Management Journal, 10,* 107-124.

Bengston, V. L., & Lovejoy, M. C. (1973). Values, personality, and social structure: An intergenerational analysis. *American Behavioral Scientist, 16,* 880-912.

Botwinick, J. (1977). *Aging and behavior.* New York: Springer.

Burke, D. M., & Light, L. L. (1981). Memory and aging: The role of retrieval processes. *Psychological Bulletin, 90,* 513-546.

Byrne, D. (1971). *The attraction paradigm.* New York: Academic Press.

Clement, D. E., & Schiereck, J. J., Jr. (1973). Sex composition and group performance in a visual signal detection task. *Memory and Cognition, 1,* 251-255.

Cosier, R. A. (1981). Dialectical inquiry in strategic planning: A case of premature acceptance? *Academy of Management Review, 6,* 643-648.

Daft, R. L., & Weick, K. E. (1984). Toward a model of organizations as interpretation systems. *Academy of Management Review, 9,* 284-296.

Dearborn, D., & Simon, H. A. (1958). Selective perception: A note on the departmental identification of executives. *Sociometry, 35,* 38-48.

DeLuca, J. R. (1988). Strategic career management in non-growing, volatile business environments. *Human Resource Planning, 11,* 49-62.

Driskell, J. E., Hogan, R., & Salas, E. (1987). Personality and group performance. In C. Hendrick (Ed.), *Group processes and intergroup relations* (pp. 91-112). Newbury Park, CA: Sage.

Dumaine, B. (1989, Feb. 13). How managers can succeed through speed. *Fortune,* pp. 54-59.

Dunn & Bradstreet (1985-1988). *Reference book of corporate managements.* New York: Author.

Eagly, A. H. (1987). *Sex differences in social behavior: A social-role interpretation.* Hillsdale, NJ: Lawrence Erlbaum.

Elder, G. H., Jr. (1974). *Children of the great depression.* Chicago: University of Illinois Press.

Elder, G. H., Jr. (1975). Age differentiation and the life course. *Annual Review of Sociology, 1,* 165-190.

Fenelon, J. R., & Megaree, E. I. (1971). Influence of race on the manifestation of leadership. *Journal of Applied Psychology, 55,* 353-358.

Filley, A. C., House, R. J., & Kerr, S. (1976). *Managerial process and organizational behavior.* Glenview, IL: Scott Foresman.

Goodman, P. S., Devadas, R., Hughson, T.L.G. (1988). Groups and productivity: Analyzing the effectiveness of self-managing teams. In J. P. Campbell, R. J. Campbell, & Assoc., *Productivity in organizations* (pp. 295-327). San Francisco: Jossey-Bass.

Hackman, J. R. (1982). The design of work teams. In J. W. Lorsch (Ed.), *The handbook of organizational behavior* (pp. 315-342). Englewood Cliffs, NJ: Prentice-Hall.

Hambrick, D. C., & Mason, P. A. (1984). Upper echelons: The organization as a reflection of its top managers. *Academy of Management Review, 9,* 193-206.

Haythorn, W. W. (1968). The composition of groups: A review of the literature. *Acta Psychologica, 28,* 97-128.

Heider, F. (1958). *The psychology of interpersonal relations.* New York: John Wiley.

Hickson, D. J. (1987). Decision-making at the top of organizations. *Annual Review of Sociology, 13,* 165-192.

Hill, G. W. (1982). Group versus individual performance: Are $N + 1$ heads better than one? *Psychological Bulletin, 91,* 517-539.

Hoerr, J. (1989, July 10). The payoff from teamwork. *Business Week,* pp. 56-62.

Hoffman, L. R. (1979). Applying experimental research on group problem solving to organizations. *Journal of Applied Behavioral Science, 15,* 375-391.

Hoffman, L. R., Harburg, E., & Maier, N.R.F. (1962). Differences and disagreement as factors in creative group problem solving. *Journal of Abnormal and Social Psychology, 64,* 206-214.

Hoffman, L. R., & Maier, N.R.F. (1961). Quality and acceptance of problem solutions by members of homogeneous and heterogeneous groups. *Journal of Abnormal and Social Psychology, 62,* 401-407.

Holland, J. L. (1976). Vocational preferences. In M. D. Dunnette (Ed.), *Handbook of industrial/organizational psychology* (pp. 521-570). Chicago: Rand McNally.

Ilgen, D. R. (1986). Small groups in an individualistic world. In R. McGlynn & B. George (Eds.), *Interfaces in psychology: Organizational psychology and small group behavior* (pp. 149-169). Lubbock: Texas Tech University Press.

Jackson, S. E., Brett, J. F., Sessa, V. I., Cooper, D. M., Julin, J. A., & Peyronnin, K. (in press). Some differences make a difference: Interpersonal dissimilarity and group heterogeneity as correlates of recruitment, promotion, and turnover. *Journal of Applied Psychology.*

Janis, I. L. (1972). *Victims of groupthink.* Boston: Houghton-Mifflin.

Johnston, W. B., & Packer, A. H. (1987). *Work force 2000.* Indianapolis, IN: Hudson Institute.

Jones, M. B. (1974). Regressing group on individual effectiveness. *Organizational Behavior and Human Performance, 11,* 426-451.

Kanter, R. M. (1988). When a thousand flowers bloom: Structural, collective, and social conditions for innovation in organization. In B. M. Staw & L. L. Cummings (Eds.), *Research in organizational behavior* (Vol. 10, pp. 169-211). Greenwich, CT: JAI.

Kimberly, J. R., & Evanisko, M. J. (1981). Organizational innovation: The influence of individual, organizational, and contextual factors on hospital adoption of technological and administrative innovations. *Academy of Management Journal, 24,* 689-713.

Laughlin, P. R. (1980). Social combination processes of cooperative problem-solving groups on verbal intellective tasks. In M. Fishbein (Ed.), *Progress in social psychology* (Vol. 1, pp. 210-231). Hillsdale, NJ: Lawrence Erlbaum.

Laughlin, P. R., & Bitz, D. S. (1975). Individual versus dyadic performance on a disjunctive task as a function of initial ability level. *Journal of Personality and Social Psychology, 31,* 487-496.

Lott, A. J., & Lott, B. E. (1965). Group cohesiveness and interpersonal attraction: A review of relationships with antecedent and consequent variables. *Psychological Bulletin, 64,* 259-302.

Maier, N.R.F., & Hoffman, L. R. (1960). Quality of first and second solutions in group problem solving. *Journal of Applied Psychology, 44,* 278-283.

McCain, B. R., O'Reilly, C. C., III, & Pfeffer, J. (1983). The effects of departmental demography on turnover. *Academy of Management Journal, 26,* 626-641.

McCaskey, M. B. (1982). *The executive challenge: Managing change and ambiguity.* Boston: Pitman.

McGrath, J. E. (1984). *Groups: Interaction and performance.* Englewood Cliffs, NJ: Prentice-Hall.

Miller, R. A. (1968). *Current occupation and past training of adult workers.* Office of Statistical Standards, Statistical Evaluation Report, Bureau of the Budget. Washington, DC: Government Printing Office.

Moody's Investor Service (1985-1988). *Moody's bank and finance manual.* New York: Author.

Moreland, R. L., & Levine, J. M. (1991). Problem identification by groups. In S. Worchel, W. Wood, & J. Simpson (Eds.), *Group process and productivity.* Newbury Park, CA: Sage.

Murray, A. I. (1989). Top management group heterogeneity and firm performance. *Strategic Management Journal, 10,* 125-142.

Nadler, D. A., Hackman, J. R., & Lawler, E. E., III. (1979). *Managing organizational behavior.* Boston: Little, Brown.

National Science Foundation (1963). *Two years after the college degree.* NSF Report 63-26. Washington, DC: Government Printing Office.

Newcomb, T. E. (1956). The prediction of interpersonal attraction. *American Psychologist, 11,* 575-586.

Newcomb, T. M. (1961). *The acquaintance process.* New York: Holt, Rinehart, & Winston.

O'Reilly, C. A., III, Caldwell, D. F., & Barnett, W. P. (1989). Work group demography, social integration, and turnover. *Administrative Science Quarterly, 34,* 21-37.

Pelz, D. C. (1956). Some social factors related to performance in a research organization. *Administrative Science Quarterly, 1,* 310-325.

Pelz, D., & Andrews, F. (1966). *Scientists in organizations.* New York: John Wiley.

Pfeffer, J. (1983). Organizational demography. In L. L. Cummings & B. M. Staw (Eds.), *Research in organizational behavior* (pp. 299-357). Greenwich, CT: JAI.

Pfeffer, J., & Salancik, G. R. (1978). *The external control of organizations: A resource dependence perspective.* New York: John Wiley.

Piore, M. J., & Sabel, C. F. (1984). *The second industrial divide: Possibilities for prosperity.* New York: Basic Books.

Rogers, E. M., & Shoemaker, F. F. (1971). *Communications and innovations.* New York: Free Press.

Schmidt, W. H. (1974). Conflict: A powerful process for (good and bad) change. *Management Review, 63,* 4-10.

Schneider, B. (1987). The people make the place. *Personnel Psychology, 40,* 437-453.

Schwenk, C. R. (1983). Laboratory research on ill-structured decision aids: The case of dialectical inquiry. *Decision Sciences, 14,* 140-144.

Shaw, M. E. (1976). *Group dynamics: The psychology of small group behavior.* New York: McGraw-Hill.

Shaw, M. E. (1981). *Group dynamics: The psychology of small group behavior.* New York: McGraw-Hill.

Simon, H. A. (1976). *Administrative behavior: A study of decision-making processes in organizations* (3rd ed.). New York: Free Press.

Simon, H. A. (1979). *The sciences of the artificial* (2nd ed.). Cambridge, MA: MIT Press.

Sirota, Alper, & Pfau, Inc. (1989). *Report to respondents: Survey of views towards human resources policies and practices.* New York: Author.

Staw, B. M., & Ross, J. (1980). Commitment in an experimental society: A study of the attribution of leadership from administrative scenarios. *Journal of Applied Psychology, 65,* 249-260.

Steiner, I. D. (1972). *Group process and productivity.* New York: Academic Press.

Stevens, J. M., Beyer, J. M., & Trice, H. M. (1978). Assessing personal, role, and organizational predictors of managerial commitments. *Academy of Management Journal, 21,* 380-396.

Stogdill, R. M. (1972). Group productivity, drive, and cohesiveness. *Organizational behavior and human performance, 8,* 26-43.

Terborg, J. R., Castore, C., & DeNinno, J. A. (1976). A longitudinal field investigation of the impact of group composition on group performance and cohesion. *Journal of Personality and Social Psychology, 34,* 782-790.

Thernstrom, S. (1973). *The other Bostonians: Poverty and progress in the American metropolis. 1880-1970.* Cambridge, MA: Harvard University Press.

Triandis, H. C., Hall, E. R., & Ewen, R. B. (1965). Member heterogeneity and dyadic creativity. *Human Relations, 18,* 33-55.

Turner, J. C. (1987). *Rediscovering the social group: A self-categorization theory.* New York: Basil Blackwell.

Voiers, W. D. (1956). *Bombing accuracy as a function of the ground-school proficiency structure of the B-29 bomb team.* (Research Report AFDTRC-TN-56-4) Lackland Air Force Base, TX: Air Force Personnel and Training Research Center.

Vroom, V., & Pahl, B. (1971). Relationship between age and risk-taking among managers. *Journal of Applied Psychology, 55,* 399-405.

Walton, R. E., & Hackman, J. R. (1986). Groups under contrasting management strategies. In P. S. Goodman (Ed.), *Designing effective work groups.* San Francisco: Jossey-Bass.

Willems, E. P., & Clark, R. D., III. (1971). Shift toward risk and heterogeneity of groups. *Journal of Experimental and Social Psychology, 7,* 304-312.

Wood, W. (1987). Meta-analytic review of sex differences in group performance. *Psychological Bulletin, 102,* 53-71.

Zander, A. (1979). The psychology of group processes. In M. R. Rosenzweig & L. W. Porter (Eds.), *Annual review of psychology* (pp. 417-451). Palo Alto, CA: Annual Reviews.

Zenger, T. R., & Lawrence, B. S. (1989). Organizational demography: The differential effects of age and tenure distributions on technical communications. *Academy of Management Journal, 2,* 353-376.

Ziller, R. C., Behringer, R. D., & Goodchilds, J. E. (1962). Group creativity under conditions of success or failure and variations in group stability. *Journal of Applied Psychology, 46,* 43-49.

PART III

Group Development, Privilege, and Power

Introduction

Katherine A. Hannula

Historically, social psychologists have relied on two different approaches to study group dynamics, one in which the individual serves as the primary unit of analysis and the other in which the group functions as the primary unit. Arguing for the individualistic approach, Allport (1924) suggested that all group behavior could be explained in terms of individuals' actions. In particular, he described group phenomena as the sum total of the actions of each individual taken separately. Some of Allport's own research, however, contradicted this view. When examining the effect of the group on cognitive functioning, he found that individuals in a group produced more arguments than individuals working alone. Nonetheless, the quality of the arguments was better for isolated individuals than for those in the group (Allport, 1920). In contrast to the individualistic approach, the "group-mind" approach suggested that the group had an independent existence apart from the specific individuals who composed it. The work of McDougall (1920) best exemplifies this position.

Nearly four decades later, Bonner (1959) argued that "neither the individual nor the psychological group structure has a separate existence. Each implies and functionally depends upon the other." Lewin's field theory (1951) exemplifies this position in that it attempts to link the individualistic and the "group-mind" approaches.

Nevertheless, as Steiner (1974) has noted, even the Lewinian approach to group dynamics does not fully embody and reflect the mutual interdependence of the individual and the group, given that Lewin sought to reduce group behavior to the level of individuals' thought processes. Instead of arguing the pros and the cons of the various positions, Steiner (1974) has called for a complementary pluralism of approaches, with greater emphasis being placed on the mutual interdependence of individual and group. According to Steiner, the goal of current research should not be to identify one "optimal" approach; rather it should be to integrate various approaches to maximally enhance our understanding of group phenomena.

It is important to recognize that analysis at *both* levels can provide unique contributions to our understanding of group dynamics. In this section, there are chapters dealing with both levels of analysis.

In their chapter on group development, Worchel, Coutant-Sassic, and Grossman argue for the importance of studying groups in their developmental context, as well as in the more traditional "minimal group paradigm" developed by Tajfel (1970). They suggest that the most popular methods currently used for studying groups often leave the true nature of group dynamics hidden. For example, in most empirical laboratory studies, total strangers are brought together for a short period of time as members of a "group." The members of these "groups" have little or no sense of group history, development, and relationship to other groups, all of which are defining features of real-life groups. Results from such studies, therefore, ignore the impact that these features have on individuals' behavior and group functioning. While recognizing some of the valuable findings produced with this "minimal group paradigm," Worchel et al. point out its limited external validity. They propose that, in addition to the "minimal group paradigm," social psychologists should examine long-term groups, whether in naturalistic settings or in the laboratory.

Worchel et al. then offer a model of naturalistic group formation and development that includes six stages. These stages are believed to occur in a specific cyclical order, but movement from stage to stage is not exclusively dependent on temporal factors. The *period of discontent* is the first stage, characterized by individuals feeling alienated and exhibiting a lack of involvement in existing groups. The onset of Stage 2 is marked by a *precipitating event*. This event involves some specific situation in which members in power in an existing group alienate a faction of individuals from those still loyal to the group. The development of a new group begins with Stage 3—*group identification*. During this stage, the new group is concerned with defining its boundaries and internal positions. Intergroup conflict at this point helps to strengthen the individual member's ties to the group, and there are strong pressures on group members to conform to newly established group norms. Attention to *group productivity* marks Stage 4. Once the group has confirmed its independent identity, it sets goals and becomes task-oriented. Although the group starts to establish limited contact with outgroups, it is careful to maintain its own identity and boundaries. During Stage 5—*individuation*—the emphasis is on personal goals and satisfaction rather than group identity. Members begin to weigh the benefits of group membership against those that other groups may offer, and they yearn for extensive interaction with outgroups. *Decay* of the group marks Stage 6. Members try to manipulate the group for their own benefit. If unsuccessful, they may become discontent and alienated, moving once again into the stage of discontent.

The next two chapters in this section focus less on the group as the level of analysis and more on the individual *within* the group. One outcome of group life is that hierarchies develop within groups in which some individuals occupy positions of higher status and power than others. The chapter by Messé, Kerr, and Sattler discusses how high-status positions invoke a sense of privilege. Specifically, occupants of highly valued positions within groups come to believe they are entitled to special treatment simply because of the position they hold. In their empirical studies, Messé et al. demonstrate that (a) privileged behaviors are a central component of peoples' role schema for "supervisor"; (b) due to this sense of privilege, supervisors expend less effort than subordinates on shared tasks; and (c) occupants of high-status positions act in a privileged manner by taking more than an equal share of the rewards offered to the group.

Similar to Messé et al., Kipnis examines the dynamics involved in occupying a certain role within the group. Kipnis describes how persons in a position of power make attributions about subordinates' behaviors that are contingent on the type of influence tactics the powerholder uses. Kipnis proposes that the use of power is closely related to technology in that the goal of both is to reduce uncertainty about a future outcome. When powerholders use strong tactics, such as orders or demands to influence a target person's behavior, uncertainty is reduced because the target person often will comply to such influence attempts. This leads powerholders to attribute the target person's behavior to external factors. Likewise, when technological advances make work more routine and predictable, managers tend to attribute workers' successful performance to new technology rather than to internal motivations or attitudes held by employees. Kipnis uses both the workplace and the clinician's office to demonstrate the relationship between technology, power, and the resulting attributions.

References

Allport, F. H. (1920). The influence of the group upon association and thought. *Journal of Experimental Psychology, 3,* 159-182.

Allport, F. H. (1924). *Social psychology.* Boston: Houghton Mifflin.

Bonner, H. (1959). *Group dynamics: Principals and applications.* New York: Roland.

Lewin, K. (1951). Problems of research in social psychology. In D. Cartwright (Ed.), *Field theory in social science: Selected theoretical papers by Kurt Lewin.* New York: Harper & Row.

McDougall, W. (1920). *The group mind.* New York: G. P. Putnam's Sons. (Revised edition, 1928)

Tajfel, H. (1970). Experiments in intergroup discrimination. *Scientific American, 223*(2), 96-102.

Steiner, I. D. (1974). Whatever happened to the group in social psychology? *Journal of Experimental Social Psychology, 10,* 94-108.

7   A Developmental Approach to Group Dynamics: A Model and Illustrative Research

Stephen Worchel

Dawna Coutant-Sassic

Michele Grossman

One of the more interesting debates in social science has centered on the nature of groups. Arguing that groups were entities different from individuals, Emile Durkheim stated, "If, then, we begin with the individual, we shall be able to understand nothing of what takes place in the group" (1898, p. 104). Floyd Allport (1924) countered this position, arguing that groups do not think, feel, or act—people do. His *coup de grace* was his observation that no one ever tripped over a group, therefore the groups were not real and not deserving of study. Adopting the middle ground that characterizes today's approach, Solomon Asch (1952), compared groups to water. He argued that in order to understand the properties of water, it is important to know the characteristics of its elements, hydrogen and oxygen. However, this knowledge alone will not be sufficient to understand water; the combination of hydrogen and oxygen must be examined as a unique entity. So, too, must

AUTHORS' NOTE: This chapter was prepared with support from a Texas Advanced Research Project from the Texas Coordinating Board of Higher Education. We would like to thank the following people for their help in developing the model and/or comments on the manuscript: Frankie Wong, Janusz Reykowski, Daniel Bar-Tal, Bradley Scott, Diedre Franklin, Robert Agans, and Sharon Lundgren.

individual and group behavior be studied to understand the nature of group dynamics.

Evidence for the importance of understanding group dynamics is the central role groups play in everyday life. We are born into a group; we learn, work, and play in groups. Tajfel and his colleagues (Tajfel & Turner, 1986; Turner, 1987) argue cogently that a significant part of our individual identity is derived from group membership: our social identity. Some of the most important decisions in our society are made in groups; the jury system is the foundation of the United States judicial system. Group therapy for emotional disorders has become increasingly popular since World War II (Sheras & Worchel, 1979). Organizations are also increasingly structured around groups. For example, the quality circle has been introduced in many work settings to improve productivity (Lawler & Mohrman, 1985).

Despite the importance of groups, research on groups has a rather checkered history. Like a recurring fad, research on groups seems to ebb and flow (Jones, 1985; Steiner, 1974). Indeed, group research is more time consuming and involves more subjects than studies of individuals. Group research is also more confounded than individual research because of the uncontrollable interaction among subjects in the group setting. Recent trends toward increasing precision and control have conspired to make group research more difficult to conduct. Recognizing this tendency in research Leon Festinger (1980) cautioned: "Precision of measurement and precision of experimental control are a means to an end—the discovery of new knowledge. Too much emphasis on precision can lead to research which is barren" (p. 252).

We do not wish to suggest that group research has entered a period of deep slumber. There is clearly an active interest in group behavior. In fact, new ground has been turned in such areas as social loafing (Harkins & Szymanski, 1989), minority influence (Moscovici, 1980; Nemeth, 1986; Tanford & Penrod, 1984), and group productivity (Diehl & Stroebe, 1987; Pritchard, Jones, Roth, Steubing, & Ekeberg, 1988). There has, however, been a subtle change in the nature of group research. Turning the dusty pages of group research in the 1940s and 1950s, we find one prototype of "group." Groups in many of these studies had a wide range of interaction opportunities, met together over a period of time, and clearly perceived themselves as a group. Sherif, Harvey, White, Hood, and Sherif (1961) studied camp groups over a period of time. Lewin, Lippitt, and White (1939) examined the effect of leadership styles in groups that met for 18 weeks undergoing different patterns of leadership changes. Festinger, Schachter, and Back (1950) studied interaction patterns among families in a housing project. Tuckman (1965) was able to identify 50 studies that examined groups over an extended time period in his attempt to develop a model of group development.

However, more recent group research has focused on a different type of "group." In most cases, the new group is composed of strangers who meet for a short period of time. Members feel little sense of belonging to a group, and there is little sense of purpose or opportunity for interaction between members. In fact, in some cases, subjects are asked to imagine that they are part of a group. Tajfel (1970) proudly dubbed his model "minimal group paradigm" to indicate that subjects were randomly assigned to a category and never met other group members. Rather than being a collection of people who work, interact, and react together, in modern treatments the group is often a cognitive schema that exists in the mind of subjects.

This approach has proved economical and has offered precision and control. Indeed, a number of new and exciting findings and theories have resulted from this approach. In fact, this conception of the group may be partly responsible for the growing volume of recent research on groups. However, while proving a blessing on one count, the current tendency may be a curse on another.

Groups, like individuals, do not exist in isolation. They have a critical context which includes their history, their expectations for the future, their structure, their purpose, and their relationship with other groups. People do not suddenly find themselves to be a member of a group; they generally make decisions about joining (or not joining) a group. The group does not exist in isolation; rather it has a place in a context that includes the existence of other groups. And the group is not a static unit; it develops and changes over time, and its membership also is often in flux. Paradigms that involve group schema or collections of strangers with little purpose, little interaction, and little longevity ignore these factors. Studying a group in isolation from this context is similar to studying individuals in isolation from their social context. We can learn a great deal from these studies, but much can be obscured if the limited external validity is ignored.

The Lewin et al. (1939) study is a case in point. They examined the influence of leadership style on group behavior. One of the most striking findings was that when a laissez-faire leader followed an autocratic leader, ingroup aggression and scapegoating was much greater than when the laissez-faire leader entered the group on the first session. In other words, the pattern of leadership change was a critical factor in determining group aggression. Similar evidence for the importance of context can be found in studies on group deviants (Schachter, 1951), attitude change (Newcomb, 1943), and interpersonal attraction (Aronson & Linder, 1965).

Despite this and other data on the importance of context, there have been surprisingly few attempts to examine context in a systematic way. One critical issue that has received some attention is group development. It has been recognized that groups develop and change over time in a relatively orderly fashion and that these changes can have dramatic impact on group behavior, productivity, process, and intergroup relations (Bennis & Shepard, 1956; Borgatta & Bales, 1953; Dunphy, 1968).

Interest in development and change crosses disciplinary lines and can be found in psychology, political science, and sociology. The most careful analysis of group development was offered by Tuckman (Tuckman, 1965; Tuckman & Jensen, 1977), who reviewed over 50 studies. Tuckman concluded that groups go through predictable developmental stages, which he labeled "forming," "storming," "norming," "performing," and "adjourning." At each stage groups focus on specific issues and this focus influences members' behaviors. Tuckman's work offered a potential beginning to the investigation of a model of group development, but it stimulated little research. Part of the problem was that most of the studies on which Tuckman based his model employed therapy and training groups or laboratory groups of limited duration.

More recently Moreland and Levine (1982, 1988) revived interest in development and change in groups. Their major concern, however, has been with group member development rather than group development. Their work represents an important and stimulating contribution. Briefly, they suggest that group members go through predictable stages of membership: prospective member, new member, full member, marginal member, and ex-member. At each stage, the member is concerned about a different aspect of group life. For example, the new member attempts to change the group to meet his or her needs while the group attempts to mold the new member to fit group needs. The full member engages in role negotiation in order to find a niche that is most comfortable. This model, however, is relatively recent and still being developed.

Outside the area of group research, in the field of interpersonal relationships Levinger (1980) addressed the importance of temporal variables in predicting phases of close relationships. A five-stage sequence including phases of initial attraction, building a relationship, continuation, deterioration, and ending was developed (Levinger, 1980).

These psychological models have a common starting point in groups that have already been formed; the interest is in groups whose membership has been established. Pushing the concern back one step, some interesting analyses have detailed how groups and social movements begin. One focus has been on the revolutionary process. The prototype of research on revolution involves the formation of a new group whose aim is to overthrow a ruling group and replace the old group's values with a new set of values (Payton & Blakey, 1971). The struggle is one of power in the classic Marxian sense. A revolution generally is aimed at destroying the group in power.

Hopper (1950) argued that revolutions develop through a series of identifiable stages. The first or Preliminary Stage of Revolution is characterized by a general restlessness which manifests itself in an increase in crime, suicide, travel, and emigration. There is recognition that "something" is wrong and the ruling government takes steps to reform. If these efforts are insufficient, the process moves into the Popular Stage, which is characterized by a spread of discontent and the development of propaganda. In this stage there is conflict between the ingroup and outgroup and demand for the abdication of the group in power. Conflict becomes a central theme, supposedly in support of differentiating the ingroup from the outgroup. The third phase is the Formal Phase. A clear identification of attitudes and values is seen in this stage. A struggle between radicals, moderates, and conservatives in the revolutionary group ensues. The moderates typically gain control and there is an attempt at reform despite attacks from radicals and conservatives and the moderates' political inexperience. Norms are formalized and become dogma. The revolution is in full fury at this point; if the reform efforts are unsuccessful, the radicals gain control and the Reign of Terror begins. The destruction of the Reign of Terror and chaos lead to the Institutional Stage 3, in which psychological exhaustion and economic distress signal the need for moderation. The Reign of Terror ends and amnesty is granted to many prisoners. A new government is established, often with dictatorial powers to put an end to the chaos. People accept the changes in lifestyle, reconcile their attitudes appropriately, and the new group is established.

A Preliminary Model of
Group Formation and Development

After questioning the identity of the "group" in much of the recent research and examining some diverse models of small group development and revolution, ultimately the question arises: What can we make of all this?

For our present purposes, two points stand out. First, it does seem that groups develop and change in a rather predictable fashion. Whether our concern is small groups or revolutionary movements, a number of stages can be identified. These stages affect and are affected by individual, group, and intergroup behavior. In drawing this conclusion, we are certain to have offended many social psychologists who blanche and bristle at even the hint of a stage approach. However, we may avoid total rejection by pointing out that these stage models argue only for an order effect to group formation and development; there is no suggestion that each stage occupies a specific amount of time or that movement from one stage to the next is determined by temporal factors. Therefore, these models can be clearly distinguished from such developmental models offered by Freud or Piaget, which not only identify order of stages but also incorporate time as a determining factor. A second conclusion that we wish to draw from our review is that in most cases group research has paid little attention to issues of development and structure; in fact, much group research has taken a rather cavalier approach to the definitive factors that determine whether or not a collection of people (or the cognitive representation of this collection) is a group.

These conclusions represent the starting point for our research efforts. Our aim was to examine how groups develop and whether or not developmental issues affect individual, interpersonal, and intergroup behavior in predictable ways. We began by examining previous models of group formation and development to determine if clear and testable predictions would be possible. Although this was possible in some cases, it sometimes proved difficult. While the models were rich in description and covered a host of situations, they were often vague, incomplete, incompatible, and narrow. For example, Tuckman's work (Tuckman 1965; Tuckman & Jensen, 1977) focused on T groups and small laboratory groups which existed in isolation and whose membership was predetermined and stable. Moreland and Levine (Moreland,

1987; Moreland & Levine, 1982) dealt with group development only as it interacted with group member development. Specific predictions about a variety of group behaviors can be developed only by stretching these models far beyond their intentions and level of description.

Therefore, we decided to develop our own model by incorporating the earlier observations with additional research. We insisted that our model deal with the influence of group development on individual, group, and intergroup behaviors. We wanted to address issues of group formation in addition to group development. And, unlike studies of revolution, we wanted to include cases in which groups gained independence by breaking away from a parent group. Studies of revolution are mainly concerned with the overthrow and/or elimination of the group in power. In many cases, however, the aim of a group is to develop an identity and recognition *and* to co-exist with other groups. In these cases, the existence of the outgroups is necessary to define the boundaries of the ingroup.

As an initial step in developing a model, the decision was made to cast the widest possible net rather than to immediately focus on a few carefully controlled laboratory groups. This procedure would sacrifice precision and control to obtain a rich and generalizable data set. In addition to reviewing previous scholarly work on group development (e.g., Bailis, Lambert, & Bernstein, 1978; Baker, 1983; Bales & Strodtbeck, 1951; Dunphy, 1968; Goodman, 1981; Tuckman, 1965), newspaper, magazine, and popular book accounts detailing the development of groups were examined. The groups included large unions such as the civil rights movement and the women's movement, professional organizations such as divisions within the American Psychological Association, labor unions at specific factories, community political action and environmental groups, a variety of small work groups that functioned during crisis situations or difficult environments (Kon Tiki crew, exploring expeditions in the Arctic, rescue teams, disaster reaction teams), and a variety of small social and religious groups. Individual researchers trained in social psychological theory and method identified groups and described their formation and development. The researchers then met to compare notes and identify commonalities in group process. The only limitation in choosing groups was that group membership had to be a matter of individual choice rather than assignment. This factor was specified because of our interest in group formation as well as group development.

In addition to these accounts, two collaborative opportunities to study group development presented themselves. Together with Dr. Maria Jarymowicz data, including interviews, were collected on newly forming political groups in Poland. The second opportunity involved Dr. Daniel Bar-Tal at the University of Tel Aviv. This study examined the development of two small political parties in Israel before and after the elections of 1989. An interesting characteristic of this study was that one of the parties succeeded in electing a member to the Knesset while the other party failed to achieve this goal.

The aim of this work was to identify the commonalities in the development of these groups and to examine the impact of this development on individual, interpersonal, and intergroup behavior. The broad sample of groups we obtained also allows us to examine the influence of a variety of factors (size, structure, task, and situation) on group development.

Despite the diversity of the groups studied, a surprising degree of uniformity in their formation and development was identified. Based on these observations we were able to develop a preliminary model of these processes. We emphasize the preliminary nature of the model because it is still being developed. One of the more interesting findings from this work is that group development is an ongoing and circular process. Groups exist in a state of constant change, no matter how successful the group is at achieving its goals. Like a star that periodically ejects meteors, as a group grows it spins off new groups. The conditions that created the group are also responsible for destroying the group and ensuring the formation of a new group. This circular nature of formation and change can be seen in Figure 7.1, which represents the stages of group development.

A point of interest is the role that crisis and external threat play in group development. Crisis and threat often interrupt the development process and can throw the group back into an earlier stage. Let us briefly examine the model. Remember, however, that in presenting stages, we are concerned not with temporal factors but with order in development. Note also that we are dealing with probabilities and likelihoods, not inevitabilities. As Payton and Blakey (1971) argue, "Nothing in the course of revolution is inevitable, but much is likely" (p. 235).

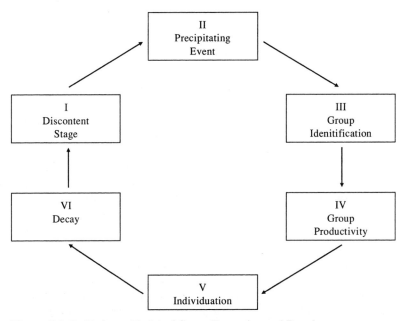

Figure 7.1. Preliminary Model of Group Formation and Development

Stage 1: Period of Discontent

This is the initial stage in group formation. Like Hopper's Preliminary Stage of Revolution, this stage is characterized by individuals who feel that their present group (or groups) are not meeting their needs. These individuals feel alienated and experience a sense of not belonging to or fitting into any group. Estrangement from the group threatens the individual's social identity. These people may feel helpless and hopeless. At the group level, this stage is characterized by "drop out" behavior. Participation in group activities declines and becomes very unequal; a few members are active participants while the majority cease group involvement. The lack of involvement is seen in low voter turnout for elections and an unwillingness by members to take leadership roles. Although passivity is the prevalent behavior, there may also be incidents of senseless violence, such as vandalism, aimed at expressing frustration or seeking attention.

This period can last a relatively short time or it can extend for a long time. Its life will be determined in part by the reaction of group members in power. Given that opposition has not mounted against the power structure, reduction of tension is possible if the reasons for discontent are identified and addressed with a problem-solving approach. All too often, however, the members in power choose to ignore these seeds of discontent, or react to them with attempts to further consolidate their power. The first approach tends to prolong this stage, whereas the latter approach hastens the Precipitating Event. Two other common reactions by group members in power are also nonproductive, but may prolong this period. The first is to appeal to the loyalty and patriotism of the discontented members by outlining what the group has done for them in the past or evoking an almost religious quality of the sanctity of the group. The second approach is to identify an outside threat. Both approaches may temporarily dampen dissent, but if the larger group is to survive intact, they must be followed by attention to the discontent.

Stage 2: Precipitating Event

Unlike the Stage of Discontent, the Precipitating Event has a clear onset. It is difficult to predict exactly what event will be seized upon to bring the members together. In some cases, it may be a dramatic situation such as the violent and public punishment of a dissenter (or dissenters). One relevant example is the shooting of four student protesters at Kent State University in 1970. These four deaths instigated the anti-Vietnam War movement. Another example is the demonstration at the Gdansk Shipyard in Poland in August of 1980. This incident became the force that galvanized Solidarity Union members. In other cases, it may be less dramatic such as the elimination of freedoms or opportunities previously available to the members. In still other cases, it may be rumors about an action that is forthcoming. The Attica prison riot in 1971 was sparked by a rumor that prison officials had beaten an inmate and that they planned to restrict inmate privileges. Whatever the event, it seems to have certain characteristics. First, it is clear and distinctive. Second, it symbolizes issues that lead to dissatisfaction with the group. Third, by members' reaction to the event it separates those who are loyal to the original group from those who are alienated from the group. In doing this, the event helps identify those members and leaders who will make up the new group. Fourth, although the event may involve repression, it also gives alienated individuals hope that the situation can change. It galvanizes activity because it reduces general feelings of helplessness.

Stage 3: Group Identification

This stage begins the development of the new group. Groups without prescribed membership may progress through the first two formation stages. In groups in which membership is prescribed and the group boundaries are identified, identification will be the first issue faced by the group. The process of identification has broad effects on personal, group, and intergroup behaviors (Linville & Jones, 1980).

The group becomes very concerned with drawing clear ingroup-outgroup boundaries. This desire leads the group to adopt clear, extreme, and uncompromising positions on issues central to the group. A central dogma or theme for the group may be established. Group norms and structure are identified, and leadership is centralized. Group members are unwilling to accept new members, boundaries are closed to penetration. Group members are discouraged from interacting with outgroup members. When such interaction occurs, it generally takes place between groups and in public; individual members are punished for interacting one-on-one with outgroup members. Competition and conflict with outgroups is invited, and the group avoids opportunities to cooperate or reduce intergroup conflict. Intergroup conflict is the meat that nourishes the distinction between ingroup and outgroup. Relevant outgroups are portrayed as dangerous, corrupt, and immoral.

Within the group conformity is demanded and dissent is punished. The group may adopt a uniform, group symbol, name, and even a unique language. In an effort to demonstrate legitimacy, group members become interested in identifying the group's history and its roots. There is interest in other groups who have developed under similar circumstances in the past. The group may demand that members demonstrate their commitment to the group through personal sacrifices or initiation rites. The group develops the perception that it is powerful, legitimate, and moral. This feeling sets the stage for the groupthink process, in which premature consensus seeking possibly leads to poor decision making (Janis, 1972, 1982). The group members perceive an ingroup homogeneity in which they see themselves as belonging together and as being similar to each other (Simon & Brown, 1987).

At the individual level, members make public demonstrations of their loyalty to the group. The group becomes an important part of the individual's personal identity. Individuals feel a sense of power and security, and personal activity level increases. They view the future with optimism.

Although this stage naturally occurs at the beginning of the group, the existence of an external threat or a significant change in group membership may move more mature groups to re-examine the issues of this stage of development. In fact, skillful leaders often "manufacture" crises for the purpose of focusing member's attention on group identity issues and away from individual concerns.

Stage 4: Group Productivity

As the group establishes its independent identity, attention is turned toward group productivity. The first agenda is to identify group goals and tasks. During the early phases of this stage, the goals are often modest, ensuring group success. Distinctions are made between members based on the ability to help the group achieve goals. Leaders become task oriented and less attention is paid to the socio-emotional climate of the group. The group begins to selectively recruit new members based on their ability to perform specific tasks. When possible, the group will seek out "temporary members" who will help the group with specific tasks and then exit the group. Interaction with the out-group becomes less antagonistic. Members realize that the group cannot exist in isolation, nor can group doctrine remain so extreme. Cautious compromise results at a number of levels. Failure is attributed to factors external to the group and success is attributed to internal group factors. Equality as opposed to equity is the norm of the group. All group members are expected to contribute and rewards are shared equally among members.

This stage is similar to the final Institutional Stage of Revolution identified by Hopper (1950), but with a few important differences. A successful revolution destroys the old group and the new group must continue to protect and establish its identity. However, in the case in which the new group has won its independence from an existing group, the old group remains and the new group has a constant standard by which it can define its boundaries. This is both an advantage and a disadvantage. To some degree, conflict must be nurtured between the two groups. An overture to dissolve this remaining conflict could pose a threat to either group's identity and may be met with resistance. The position adopted by the new group is that they will work together with the old group only as long as their independence is recognized and acknowledged. This cautiousness also lends the new group to limit its contact with the outgroup to task-related activities. The process of cooperation may be punctuated by incidents of conflict and isolation.

An interesting prediction derived from this view is that the more similar the members of the old and new group are, the more difficult it may be for the two groups to work together. In the similarity (physical, attitudinal, and background) is the implicit threat to the separate identity of the two groups. Furthermore, it may be predicted here that the more similar these groups are, the more likely there will be periodic incidents of conflict aimed at reminding all parties of the independent identity of the two groups. These periodic conflicts are especially likely to occur when the groups originate from the same pool of members. If the groups see themselves as separate and independent initially, then, as research suggests (Taylor & Moriarity, 1987; Worchel, Axsom, Ferris, Samaha, & Schweitzer, 1978), this conflict is not necessary, and an ingroup bias, in which there is a tendency to evaluate the ingroup more favorably than the outgroup, is more likely to be directly related to group differences. The groups can acknowledge their similarity only so long as this acknowledgment does not threaten group identity. Once again, the point should be raised that intergroup conflict maintains an important role in maintaining group identity and boundaries.

Stage 5: Individuation

During the previous two stages, the focus has been on the group. During the Individuation stage, attention shifts to the individual group member. Individuals begin to negotiate with the group to expand task efforts to meet personal goals. Subgroups may form to work on new or different tasks. Individuals demand personal recognition; equity norms are pushed. Group members base their satisfaction with the group on their personal views of what they deserve from the group. Here the standard against which a member evaluates the attractiveness of the group, or the comparison level (CL), in Thibaut and Kelley's (1959) terms, becomes very salient. In response to these demands, the group may develop a system of awards to recognize individual members. Individuals, rather than the group, may recruit new members who will help the individual achieve personal goals. Greater personal freedom is demanded. Individual members may alter their uniform to become more distinctive. Group structure may be altered and relaxed. Cooperative interaction with outgroups is desired. Individuals begin to compare themselves with other ingroup members and with outgroup members. Members begin to explore the opportunities for membership in other groups and develop a standard to decide whether to leave or remain in the group, also described as the comparison level for alternatives, or CLalt (Thibaut & Kelley, 1959). Individual members may use the threat of defection to achieve concessions from the group. Leadership becomes more diffuse and less centralized.

Stage 6: Decay

During this stage the group begins to disintegrate. Members begin to question the value of the group. They focus on the personal sacrifices involved in group membership rather than the advantages of group membership. Competition among individual members and among subgroups escalates. The honesty and ability of the leaders is questioned. Leaders are viewed as taking too much and giving too little. Failure is blamed on the group and its leaders and success is attributed to personal effort and/or external factors. New members are invited into the group and contact with outgroups is greatly increased. Distrust among members increases and there is a demand to recruit new leaders from the outside. Subgroups struggle for power and those subgroups in power become repressive. Groups often try to increase group loyalty by inventing a threat from the outside. Members begin to hoard resources. This stage creates the conditions for the subsequent Stage of Discontent. An important difference between these stages is that during Decay, group members focus on the group. Their desire is to take control of the group and/or take as many resources from the group as possible. Their efforts are aimed at manipulating the group for their own end. Discontent and alienation set in when these efforts are unsuccessful and individuals begin to perceive the situation as hopeless.

There is research to support specific issues within the stages. O'Reilly and Chatman (1986) lend support to the Period of Discontent. They adopted Kelman's (1958) theory of compliance, identification, and internalization for a basis of prediction of psychological attachment to an organization. Their results suggest that Internalization and Identification could predict prosocial behavior, whereas compliance was significantly related only to an intent not to stay with the organization. Pertaining to the Identification stage, Linville and Jones (1980) had subjects evaluate either ingroup or outgroup applicants with the same credentials. Outgroup members were appraised more extreme or polarized than ingroup members.

In support of the Group Productivity stage, Gersick (1988) followed the lifespan of eight naturally occurring groups with lifespans varying from seven days to six months. Each of the groups underwent a great change at the midpoint of its lifespan, and became extremely task-oriented.

The Next Step: Developing and Testing Hypotheses

We began work on the model with two goals in mind. The first was to craft a heuristic device that would describe group development and demonstrate the importance of development as a legitimate factor to be considered in theories of group dynamics. The second goal was to create a model from which testable hypotheses could be drawn. These hypotheses would not only stimulate research, but the results of the research could be used to further develop and refine the model.

Several studies to test this model are, in fact, currently in progress and one has been completed. In order to demonstrate the predictive value of the model, let us briefly consider the completed study. An intriguing and important finding in the intergroup area is that group members tend to perceive ingroup membership as being more heterogeneous than outgroup membership (Jones, Wood, & Quattrone, 1981; Park & Rothbart, 1982). This pattern of results has been found when participants are asked to describe a variety of different types of groups.

For instance, when asked to describe members of their own and other eating clubs at Princeton University, subjects attributed a significantly greater variability of traits to the members in their own eating club than to members of a different club (Jones et al., 1981). Similarly, subjects have demonstrated a stronger tendency to generalize from a single outgroup member's behavior in order to describe the entire group, than to generalize from a single ingroup member (Jones et al., 1981). These researchers asked subjects from two rival universities to view a confederate's decision-making behavior. If the confederate was supposedly from the rival school, subjects were inclined to estimate that a higher number of people from that university would be likely to make the same decision. On the other hand, if the confederate was from the same university, subjects tended to estimate that a lower number of people from their own university would decide in a similar fashion. Park and Rothbart (1982) have demonstrated similar effects.

This effect is potentially important because it can help explain stereotypes. If one believes that the outgroup members are "all the same," one need merely interact with a single representative of the outgroup to know what "they" think, feel, and believe.

Several explanations have been given for the tendency to perceive the outgroup as more homogeneous than the ingroup. One explanation refers to the fact that we have more exposure to members of our own group in contrast to members of other groups. This increased exposure allows more variability to be observed within the ingroup (Quattrone, 1986).

A second explanation for an outgroup's perceived homogeneity deals with the quality of group contact (Quattrone, 1986). Ingroup contact is more likely to be cross-situational, whereas outgroup contact is prone to be restricted to a very limited number of situations. Due to this limited interaction with the outgroup, observations of variability within the outgroup are likely to be discounted, or ignored.

The literature thus reveals a strong and theoretically interpretable tendency for people to perceive their own group as more heterogeneous than the outgroup. However, a nagging contradiction occurred in many of the accounts of groups we examined in developing the present model. We found numerous examples of people describing their own groups as being very homogeneous. Members of ingroups often described their group by saying "We think as one," or "We belong together."

According to the model, during the early stages of development groups are concerned with identity and unity. A strong emphasis is placed on conformity. We suggest that during these stages members are motivated to see similarity within the group and to view themselves as representing the norm of the group. Likewise, they are motivated to perceive the outgroup as being disorganized and lacking unity. This effect should be particularly pronounced when the ingroup and outgroup were once part of the same larger group. The more the ingroup and outgroup have in common, the greater the threat to the independent identity of the ingroup.

However, as the group matures and concerns shift to task productivity and individual goals, it becomes beneficial to perceive heterogeneity within the ingroup. Members with different perspectives and skills can help the group succeed on complex tasks. Further, acknowledging diversity within the group implies a certain degree of personal freedom to be and act idiosyncratically.

We are, therefore, suggesting that perceptions of the ingroup and outgroup should be influenced by the stage of group development. Early in the developmental process, group members should perceive the ingroup as more homogeneous than during later developmental stages. The reverse should hold true for perceptions of the outgroup. That is, early tendencies will be toward perceiving outgroup heterogeneity and later stages will show perceptions of homogeneity. Further, the effect will be accentuated if the two groups were initially part of the same large group.

In order to examine this hypothesis, an experiment was designed so that in some conditions groups of eight subjects cooperated on a series of tasks. The subjects were then randomly divided into two equal-sized groups that were to compete against each other. In one condition the subjects were questioned about their perceptions and desires for interaction immediately after the division and before the competitive endeavor. In a second condition, the questionnaire was administered after the two groups engaged in one competitive encounter. In a third condition, the questionnaire was administered after the two competitive encounters had occurred between the two groups. A fourth condition was run in which subjects never worked together in the large group; instead they were divided into two four-person groups on arrival. After completing one task, they completed the questionnaire.

Members were asked to rate how similar ingroup and outgroup members were on a number of traits including intelligence, friendliness, personal appearance, and talkativeness. The mean ratings were combined to yield a mean similarity for ingroup and a mean similarity for the outgroup. The difference between ingroup and outgroup similarity ratings was then examined. The results indicated that groups that represented subgroups of the larger group perceived significantly more ingroup than outgroup similarity when questioned immediately after formation or after completing one task (see Table 7.1). However, greater outgroup than ingroup homogeneity was seen when subjects were questioned after the second competitive task or when the two groups had never been together as a single unit. In addition, splinter groups

Table 7.1
Perceived Differences in Ingroup and Outgroup Similarity

Condition	Traits			
	Intelligence[a]	Friendliness	Appearance	Talkativeness
Combined-questioned immediately	3.78[b,c]	3.84	1.24	2.47
Combined-questioned after one task	2.97	4.03	.97	1.33
Combined-questioned after two tasks	−3.11	−1.66	−.67	−.12
Never combined	−2.69	−2.07	−2.00	−1.25

NOTES: a. Subjects were asked: How similar were the members of your group (outgroup) on the following dimensions: intelligence, friendliness, personal appearance, and talkativeness. 1 = very dissimilar, 10 = very similar.
b. Scores were determined by ingroup-outgroup. Positive score indicates ingroup more similar; negative score indicates outgroup perceived as being more similar.
c. $N = 6$ groups in each condition.

questioned either immediately after separation or after one competitive episode showed greatest ingroup attraction ($F(1,22) = 8.92, p < .01$) and desire to continue competition ($F(1,22) = 10.60, p < .01$) as opposed to cooperation with the other group.

These results not only support the hypothesis based on the group independence process, but are revealing in light of recent research on the effects of group membership on people's cognitions. As previously mentioned, Quattrone and Jones (1980) found that individuals perceive more homogeneity in outgroups than in their own group. In the present study, this pattern was found in groups that were either separate from the beginning or were formed from a combined group and then competed on two tasks. However, the opposite pattern of results was found when the groups were formed from a larger group and either had no time to work together or competed with the outgroup on only one task.

Given the present analysis, we might view these latter two groups as being in the stage of separation, in which their primary concern is with breaking away from the outgroup. They have been part of the outgroup and now must develop their own identity. According to previous discussion, they should be motivated to see themselves as very similar. When groups have competed for a longer time (e.g., two tasks), they have established their identity and should not be as concerned with ingroup homogeneity. Interestingly enough, the lowest ratings of attraction for the outgroup members occurred in the break-away groups that had not yet competed or had competed only on one task, and these were the two groups that desired to continue competing. Finally, groups that were assigned to compete from the outset should not be as concerned with differentiating themselves from the outgroup and, therefore, should not have an overriding need to see themselves as similar.

Concluding Comments

This study represents only one example of ways in which group development may impact group behavior. In other research we are testing hypotheses that social loafing should be found late in group development, but not during the early stages of group identification. Another study is focused on the prediction that conformity (especially public compliance) will be more likely in newly formed groups than in more mature groups.

It is clear, even as we conduct the research, that the model needs revision and fine tuning. However, it is equally clear that group development factors have a significant impact on a host of individual, group, and intergroup behaviors. Including the developmental factor greatly enhances an understanding of and the ability to predict group behavior. Because of this, we feel that it is important to include this factor in group dynamics. If groups cannot be studied at different stages of development, a clear description of the group, its history, and member expectations about future interactions can help place results in the development context.

There is a great deal of work to be done, both in developing the model and identifying hypotheses. One issue that must be dealt with involves separating familiarity from group development. For example, it could be argued that our group perception effects were the result of the fact that members in the more mature groups interacted over a longer period of time (and were more familiar with each other) than members in the newer groups. The differences in the results in the "combined" and "never combined" groups argue against this interpretation. However, the issue demands greater attention. One interesting way to deal with the question is to examine group member development within the group development context by integrating the work by Moreland and Levine

(1982, 1987) with the present work. But this will have to wait for a later date.

We close, therefore, with hope that we have presented a convincing case for the need to consider group process within a group development context and that the present model will serve as a canopy under which group process and development can meet.

References

Allport, F. H. (1924). *Social psychology.* Cambridge, MA: Riverside Press.

Aronson, E., & Linder, D. E. (1965). Gain and loss of esteem as determinants of interpersonal attractiveness. *Journal of Experimental Social Psychology, 1,* 156-171.

Asch, S. (1952). *Social psychology.* New York: Prentice-Hall.

Bailis, S. S., Lambert, S. R., & Bernstein, S. B. (1978). The legacy of the group: A study of group therapy with a transient membership. *Social Work in Health Care, 3,* 405-418.

Baker, P. M. (1983). The development of mutuality in natural small groups. *Small Group Behavior, 14,* 301-311.

Bales, R. F., & Strodtbeck, F. L. (1951). Phases in group problem solving. *Journal of Abnormal and Social Psychology, 46,* 485-495.

Bennis, W. G., & Shepard, H. A. (1956). A theory of group development. *Human Relations, 9,* 415-437.

Borgatta, E. F., & Bales, R. F. (1953). Task and accumulation of experience as factors in the interacting of small groups. *Sociometry, 26,* 239-252.

Diehl, M., & Stroebe, W. (1987). Productivity loss in brainstorming groups: Toward the solution of a riddle. *Journal of Personality and Social Psychology, 53,* 497-509.

Dunphy, D. C. (1968). Phases, roles, and myths in self-analytic groups. *Applied Behavioral Science, 4,* 195-224.

Durkheim, E. (1898). *The rules of sociological method.* New York: Free Press.

Festinger, L. (1980). *Retrospection on social psychology.* New York: Oxford University Press.

Festinger, L., Schacter, S., & Back, K. (1950). *Social pressures in informal groups: A study of a housing community.* Stanford, CA: Stanford University Press.

Gersick, C. J. (1988). Time and transition in work teams: Toward a new model of group development. *Academy of Management Journal, 31,* 9-41.

Goodman, M. (1981). Group phases and induced countertransference. *Psychotherapy: Theory, Research, and Practice, 18,* 478-486.

Harkins, S. G., & Szymanski, K. (1989). Social loafing and group evaluation. *Journal of Personality and Social Psychology, 56,* 934-941.

Hopper, R. (1950). The revolutionary process. *Social Forces, 28,* 270-279.

Janis, I. L. (1972). *Victims of groupthink: A psychological study of foreign policy decisions and fiascos.* Boston: Houghton Mifflin.

Janis, I. (1982). *Groupthink* (2nd ed.). Boston: Houghton Mifflin.

Jones, E. E. (1985). Major developments in social psychology during the past five decades. In G. Lindzey & E. Aronson (Eds.) *Handbook of social psychology,* (Vol. 1, 3rd. ed., pp. 1-46). New York: Random House.

Jones, E. E., Wood, G. C., & Quattrone, G. A. (1981). Perceived variability of personal characteristics in in-groups and out-groups: The role of knowledge and evaluation. *Personality and Social Psychology Bulletin, 7*, 523-528.

Kelman, H. C. (1958). Compliance, identification, and internalization: Three processes of attitude change. *Journal of Conflict Resolution, 2*, 51-60.

Lawler, E. E., & Mohrman, S. A. (1985, January). Quality circles: After the fad. *Harvard Business Review,* pp. 65-71.

Levinger, G. (1980). Toward the analysis of close relationships. *Journal of Experimental Social Psychology, 16*, 510-544.

Lewin, K., Lippitt, R., & White, R. (1939). Patterns of aggressive behavior in experimentally created social climates. *Journal of Social Psychology, 10*, 271-299.

Linville, P. W., & Jones, E. E. (1980). Polarized appraisals of out-group members. *Journal of Personality and Social Psychology, 38*, 689-703.

Moreland, R. L. (1987). The formation of small groups. In C. Hendrick (Ed.), *Group processes* (pp. 80-110). Newbury Park, CA: Sage.

Moreland, R. L., & Levine, J. M. (1982). Socialization in small groups: Temporal changes in individual group relations. In L. Berkowitz (Ed.), *Advances in experimental social psychology* (Vol. 15). New York: Academic Press.

Moreland, R. L., & Levine, J. M. (1988). Group dynamics over time: Development and socialization in small groups. In J. E. McGrath (Ed.), *The social psychology of time* (pp. 151-181). Newbury Park, CA: Sage.

Moscovici, S. (1980). Toward a theory of conversion behavior. *Advances in Experimental Social Psychology, 13*, 209-239.

Nemeth, C. J. (1986). Differential contributions of majority and minority influence. *Psychological Review, 93*, 23-32.

Newcomb, T. (1943). *Personality and social change.* Hinsdale, IL: Dryden.

O'Reilly, C., III, & Chatman, J. (1986). Organizational commitment and psychological attachment: The effects of compliance, identification, and internalization on prosocial behavior. *Journal of Applied Psychology, 71*, 492-499.

Payton, C., & Blakey, R. (1971). *Why revolution? Theories and analysis.* Cambridge, MA: Schenkman.

Park, B., & Rothbart, M. (1982). Perception of out-group homogeneity and levels of social categorization: Memory for the subordinate attributes of in-group and outgroup members. *Journal of Personality and Social Psychology, 12*, 1051-1068.

Pritchard, R. D., Jones, S. D., Roth, P. L., Stuebing, K. K., & Ekeberg, S. E. (1988). Effects of group feedback, goal-setting, and incentives on organizational productivity. *Journal of Applied Psychology, 73*, 337-358.

Quattrone, G. A. (1986). On the perception of a group's variability. In S. Worchel & W. G. Austin (Eds.), *Psychology of intergroup relations* (pp. 25-48). Chicago: Nelson-Hall.

Quattrone, G. A. & Jones, E. E. (1980). The perception of a variability with in-groups and out-groups: Implications for the law of small numbers. *Journal of Personality and Social Psychology, 36*, 247-256.

Schacter, S. (1951). Deviation, rejection, and communication. *Journal of Abnormal and Social Psychology, 46*, 190-207.

Sheras, P. L., & Worchel, S. (1979). *Clinical psychology: A social psychological approach.* New York: Van Nostrand Reinhold.

Sherif, M., Harvey, O., White, B., Hood, W., & Sherif, C. (1961). *Intergroup conflict and cooperation: The robber's cave experiment*. Norman: University of Oklahoma, Institute of Group Relations.

Simon, B., & Brown, R. (1987). Perceived intragroup homogeneity in minority majority contexts. *Journal of Personality and Social Psychology, 53,* 703-711.

Steiner, I. D. (1974). Whatever happened to the group in social psychology? *Journal of Experimental Social Psychology, 10,* 94-108.

Tajfel, H. (1970). Experiments in intergroup discrimination. *Scientific American, 223*(2), 96-102.

Tajfel, H., & Turner, J. C. (1986). The social identity theory of intergroup behavior. In S. Worchel & W. G. Austin (Eds.), *The psychology of intergroup relations*. Chicago: Nelson-Hall.

Tanford, S., & Penrod, S. (1984). Social influence model: A formal integration of research on majority and minority influence processes. *Psychological Bulletin, 95,* 189-225.

Taylor, D. A., & Moriarity, B. F. (1987). Ingroup bias as a function of competition and race. *Journal of Conflict Resolution, 1,* 192-199.

Thibaut, J. W., & Kelley, H. H. (1959). *The social psychology of groups*. New York: John Wiley.

Tuckman, B. W. (1965). Developmental sequences in small groups. *Psychological Bulletin, 63,* 384-399.

Tuckman, B. W., & Jensen, M.A.C. (1977). Stages of small-group development revisited. *Group and Organization Studies, 2,* 419-427.

Turner, J. C. (1987). *Rediscovering the social group: A self-categorization theory*. Oxford: Basil Blackwell.

Worchel, S., Axsom, D., Ferris, F., Samaha, G., & Schweitzer, S. (1978). Determinants of the effects of intergroup cooperation on intergroup attraction. *Journal of Conflict Resolution, 22,* 429-439.

8   "But Some Animals Are More Equal Than Others": The Supervisor as a Privileged Status in Group Contexts

Lawrence A. Messé

Norbert L. Kerr

David N. Sattler

The quote from *Animal Farm* that is the main title of this chapter is a part of the credo of the bucolic society that Orwell (1946) created to parody the Soviet revolution and its aftermath. In Orwell's fable, the livestock of a farm overthrow their human masters and form an egalitarian cooperative system. At first, the ideology of the new order is summarized in seven simple, but high-toned maxims, including the pronouncement: "All animals are equal." However, as the story unfolds, the pigs—who assume the managerial positions on the farm—soon take advantage of their new status and power to bestow all kinds of special treatment on themselves. For instance, they take no part in performing the many arduous chores that are the essence of farm work; and they lay claim to what little creature comforts the farm has to offer (e.g., use of the farmhouse). Moreover, these swine legitimize their behaviors by formally changing the farm's ideology. They delete six of the seven maxims, retaining only the equality principle, which they qualify with the addendum: "But some animals are more equal than others." In Orwell's world, the pigs, by assuming a superior status on the farm, come to see themselves as meriting favorable treatment—that is, as privileged.

We speculated that expectations of favorable treatment (often self-administered), which stem from a sense that one has a special place in the order of things, are not limited to the pigs of *Animal Farm*—nor to the power elite of the Soviet Union, for that matter. Rather, we thought it likely that such feelings are a generic psychological phenomenon, that they tend to exist in almost every person who occupies a superior status in a group or social system. Consider the following examples as at least anecdotal support for our position.

For many years, the parking and traffic congestion in Manhattan was exacerbated by the behavior of delegates to the United Nations, who, by virtue of their diplomatic immunity (and license plates), could park their cars nearly anywhere they wanted without fear of legal sanctions. Their status gave them leave to disregard the traffic laws that constrained the ordinary citizen, and many of them took advantage of their favored position to park wherever they pleased. Moreover, from quotes in news stories, television interviews, and so forth, it was obvious that the delegates who did take liberties with New York City's parking regulations thought that such privileged behavior was very much in keeping with the importance of their mission—persons who must worry about problems of the magnitude of world peace should not have to be bothered with such trifling matters as finding a legal parking space.

Manhattan is not the only place in the world with parking problems that some people solve by invoking status-based privilege. Believe it or not, Michigan State University has parking problems of its own. Many more people want to park on campus at locations that are convenient for them than there are suitable spaces available. Most of the spaces that do exist are designated as legal parking for university staff (i.e., paid employees such as secretaries, faculty, administrators, and so on), which anyone with an appropriate car sticker can use on a first-come-first-serve basis. However, regulations permit some staff members—those with appropriately high status (meaning administrators)—to "rent" a particular space for their exclusive use. Such specially-marked spaces are particularly noticeable (and annoying) in a parking lot that happens to abut the administration building, the main library, and a building that houses both the psychological clinic and some offices of the College of Business. A large (and increasing) number of spaces in this lot are designated as rented, leaving the many faculty who wish to park near the library to fight over the few spaces that remain unmarked. We have heard advantaged administrators (e.g., the director of a nearby facility) justify this self-favoring situation by claiming that their jobs are so critical to the operation of the university that they should not have to waste their time searching for parking spaces.

One might argue that the egoistic contentions of privileged diplomats and university administrators have some validity, that their special competencies, vital missions, the "dues" that they had to pay to get where they are, and so on, entitle them to favorable treatment. We might begrudge the administrator her or his special parking space, but a part of us accepts and understands that such "perks" go with the job. Similarly, there are favors bestowed on university faculty (e.g., at Michigan State, professors do not get fined for keeping library books past their due date) that we accept as facilitative, appropriate, and right for our role.

It is this general acceptance of privilege as an integral part of certain high-status roles that might lead people to expect and feel comfortable with favorable treatment. And given that privileged treatment often is rewarding in a multitude of ways—economically advantageous, time saving, ego-enhancing, and so forth—we speculated that the acceptance of privilege as one's due is likely to be evoked rather easily, even by rather trivial symbols of superior status.

An event in the life of the first author provides a compelling example of how even the external trappings of superior status can lead one to accept (and come to expect) favorable treatment. By a confluence of fortuitous circumstances, he obtained "VIP" badges to a world's fair that he and his wife were attending. These badges were very official and distinctive—of a specific color, signed by both the bearer and the director of the fair, and with the letters VIP actually emblazoned across them—and they really provided those persons lucky enough to have them with some very favorable treatment. For instance, while regular attendees had to endure long waiting lines to see exhibits, VIPs were entitled to use special entrances that kept access times to a minimum.

At first, the author felt a little guilty and embarrassed about exercising the privileges that came with the VIP badge. However, before very long, he began to accept the favorable treatment that he and his wife were receiving as their due; and he even began to relish his privileged situation, for example, noting with pleasure how long the regular lines were at exhibits to which he, as a VIP, had immediate entry.

These examples illustrate two interesting and potentially valid premises about human social behavior:

1. Certain superordinate statuses (i.e., positions in a social system) can carry with them the sense of privilege—a self-favoring perspective that assumes entitlement to special treatment.
2. When the association between a status and privilege is well established, the sense of entitlement to special treatment can be evoked in people merely by investing them with the superficial symbols of that position.

Over the past few years, we have been systematically exploring some implications for group performance and cooperation of investing persons with superior status. Before presenting this work, however, we thought it would be useful to summarize the theoretical and empirical literature in social psychology that has guided our efforts.

Theoretical Bases

Two theoretical perspectives—role theory[1] and schema theory—are particularly relevant to understanding the potential for feeling privileged as a consequence of superior status. In the framework of *role theory* (e.g., Biddle, 1979; Biddle & Thomas, 1966; Cottrell, 1966; Stryker, 1980; Turner, 1979-1980), the actions that individuals express in a social encounter are viewed as moderated by the expectations that each person has about both her or his own behaviors *and* those of the other participants; and these expectations in large measure are a function of the positions (or statuses) that these people occupy in their social system. In other words, social expectations are the *roles* that are associated with particular statuses. As such, the regularity in behavior patterns that typifies many social encounters is a consequence of beliefs, which the participants share, about what is going to happen. As Stryker (1980) notes:

> When entering interactive situations, persons define the situation by applying names to it, to the other participants in the interaction, to themselves, and to particular features of the situation, and use the resulting definitions to organize their own behavior in the situation. (p. 53)

These "names," or role expectations, are products of past experiences, either direct (i.e., actually participating in an encounter) or vicarious (e.g., reading about a situation, watching an encounter on television, and so on). One category of role expectations, involving supervisory activities, is especially relevant to the present work, because we speculated that the generic supervisor role tends to be associated—in reality and in people's minds—with privilege. For example, the pigs in *Animal Farm* started treating themselves favorably because, after all, they were running the farm.

We assumed that college students, being typical of young adults in this regard, have learned to associate certain behaviors with the role of supervisor. Obviously, this role encompasses a complex set of beliefs and expectations. We hypothesized that the sense of privilege was prominent among these beliefs, since the "name" *supervisor* connotes a high, superordinate status of the type associated with expectations of entitlement. If so, then to the extent that participants in a work group encounter could be induced to name one of their number as supervisor (boss, manager, etc.), we would expect that person to feel privileged. As such, she or he would be less inclined to perform "low-level" work (a task best left to subordinates) and more inclined to reap a greater share of the benefits and rewards that are available to the group.

Similar ideas about the generic supervisor role and the sense of privilege can be derived from *schema theory* (e.g., Hastie, 1981; Rumelhart & Ortony, 1977; Taylor & Crocker, 1981). Basically, schemas are cognitive structures that represent distilled, organized knowledge about entitles (i.e., persons, events, and so on) that individuals derive from their experiences. When the entities in question are positions in a social system or are behaviors associated with those positions, the relevant schemas conceptually are very similar to statuses and roles as defined within the perspective of role theory.

Schemas have a number of important psychological properties, including their capacity to give meaning to the new events that persons experience. Within this perspective, well-established beliefs about roles—what Abelson (1981) refers to as *role schemas*[2]—can have a major impact on the actions that persons in a social encounter express, to the extent that they process the situation in a rather automated, mindless fashion (Langer, 1989). Schematic processing of situations often leads to scripted (i.e., automated, non-self-conscious) enactment of behavior sequences. As such, providing someone with the external trappings of a superior status—for example, a badge that proclaims "VIP"—can evoke a script that contains elements of privileged, self-favoring behaviors. Similarly, giving a participant in a work group situation the title of "Supervisor," even without providing her or him with any real supervisory duties or authority, might trigger a script in which this person acts to reap the benefit of this privileged position.

Role theory and schema theory provide a conceptual basis for linking people's expectations and beliefs to their overt actions in general. However, no component of either perspective postulates that egoism and the sense of privilege are specific elements of the supervisor, or any similar superior role schema. Fortunately, support for this contention can be found in the empirical literature summarized below.

Empirical Bases

Past studies have demonstrated, sometimes in a highly dramatic fashion (Haney, Banks, & Zimbardo, 1981; Johnson & Downing, 1979), that role schemas can strongly influence behavior (e.g., Callero, Howard, & Piliavin, 1987; Eskilson & Wiley, 1976; Kerr & MacCoun, 1984, 1985; Kerr & Sullaway, 1983; Langer & Benevento, 1978; Wagenaar & Keren, 1986). Kerr and his colleagues (Kerr & MacCoun, 1984, 1985; Kerr & Sullaway, 1983; Vancouver, Rubin, & Kerr, in press), for instance, have demonstrated that sex role schemas can affect the amount of effort that persons expend in a collective work situation.

Moreover, research, such as Johnson and Downing (1979), Langer and Benevento (1978), and Wagenaar and Keren (1986), has shown that merely providing persons with some external symbol of a status can evoke role-consistent behaviors in them. For example, Langer and Benevento (1978, Study 2) were able to manipulate people's task performance by previously investing them (or not) with a high- or low-status label for an earlier work experience. In this experiment, pairs of subjects first solved a set of math problems as individuals. Next, they were given an anagram task in which one member of the pair timed the other's work on these word puzzles. Control subjects were merely given descriptive work labels ("timer" or "solver") for their respective jobs, whereas subjects in the other pairs were randomly assigned status-relevant titles ("boss" or "assistant") for these same tasks. Finally, all subjects again were asked to individually solve a set of math problems. Results showed that the performance of persons who had been "bosses" improved significantly. In contrast, the performance of "assistants" actually decreased, whereas that of control subjects did not change.

In a study that was a direct predecessor of our research on status and privilege, Weathers, Messé, and Aronoff (1984) also found that a prior experience in a group situation with different status levels can affect subsequent behaviors—in this case people's willingness to be helpful. In this experiment, pairs of subjects first worked together to compose a public relations communique. In one condition, participants worked on this task as peers; in another, they were assigned to work together as supervisor and assistant. Soon after this work experience was over, a fellow undergraduate asked the subjects for help. He explained that he needed people to complete an extensive questionnaire for a class project being conducted in his methods course.

Results indicated that the position that the subjects had occupied during the previous group task influenced their willingness to help. Congruent with the notion that experience with superior status promotes egoism and a sense of privilege—"people do things for me, I don't do things for people," Weathers et al. (1984) found that persons who just recently had been supervisors were significantly less likely to agree to help. Moreover, this finding is consistent with the conclusions of Kipnis (1974) and others (e.g., Sorokin & Lunden, 1959), based mainly on data from field research, that in organizations persons with superior status both have an inflated view of their own worth and undervalue the needs and contributions of their subordinates. It is understandable, then, how these individuals, who have such an egoistic sense of themselves, could see privileged treatment as their rightful due.

The studies that we have cited here, although very compelling in many ways, clearly are only suggestive of the possibility that certain high status positions (VIP, boss, supervisor) foster a sense of privilege in their occupants and, as such, promote egoistic, self-favoring behaviors. For this reason, our recent research efforts, which are summarized below, were an attempt to examine more directly the relationships between status, privilege, and egoistic behaviors in group settings.

The Supervisor as a Privileged Status

A major issue that we wanted to explore was the extent to which a higher order status, such as "supervisor," was associated in people's minds with privileged, egoistic behavior, that is, the extent to which privileged behaviors were a prominent component of people's role schema of "supervisor." To this end, we developed a simple depiction of a work group situation—a six-person road repair crew that included a person named Taylor. The scenario noted that such crews are charged with performing minor road repairs and that it is the job of all members to carry out the repair work that needs to be done.

Three different versions of this scenario were devised. In one, Taylor is described as "the supervisor, who is the person in charge of the work group." In a second version, Taylor is given a low status, that of "record keeper, who is the person who has to keep track of the crew's activities," a job that is given to the "newest member" of the group. In a third version, Taylor is given no special status. We distributed the three versions of the work crew scenario to 40 undergraduates and asked them: "Compared to the other members of the work crew, how hard do you think Taylor actually works at doing road repairs?"

Results were consistent with the proposition that privilege is a salient feature of the supervisor role schema. When Taylor was depicted as just another road crew member, about 85% of the respondents estimated that he (or she, Taylor's sex was left unspecified) works as hard as the others; however, only about 7.5% thought this was the case when Taylor was described as having a special status (supervisor or record keeper). Moreover, a majority (65%) of the subjects who read about the supervisor guessed that Taylor works less hard than the others, whereas most (70%) who had read about the record keeper estimated that this person works harder than the others.[3]

Of course, there could be a number of reasons why the respondents estimated Taylor's work behaviors as they did. Of most importance, there is no direct evidence from this data set that subjects tended to believe that Taylor, the supervisor, works less hard because of a privileged status in the group. To examine this issue directly, we again used the work crew scenario, but in a modified form. Now, Taylor (as supervisor, record keeper, or crew member) was always depicted as at first "working quite capably at the job." Not much later, however, Taylor is noted as "working much less hard at doing the actual repair work than are the other five members of the crew."

Three versions of this scenario (varying with regard to Taylor's status) were distributed among 124 undergraduates. After reading the description of the work crew, these respondents were asked to rank, in order of likelihood, eight possible reasons for Taylor's behavior: fatigue, lack of experience, role beliefs, laziness, lack of interest, other responsibilities, lack of ability, and sense of privilege.

Results strongly supported the idea that privilege is a prominent part of the supervisor role schema. The two highest ranking reasons for Taylor, the supervisor's behavior were role beliefs and privilege. In contrast, privilege ranked a lowly (and significantly lower) eighth as a likely reason why Taylor, the record keeper, worked less hard, and only fifth (again significantly lower) when Taylor was just identified as a crew member. Moreover, the rankings of reasons for Taylor, the supervisor's behavior were very similar across respondents (coefficient of concordance = .46). Such agreement suggests that there exists a reasonable consensus that role beliefs and privilege are the reasons why a supervisor does not work at "menial" tasks, while other explanations (e.g., lack of ability or interest) are much less likely.

Supervisor Status and Actual Work Behavior

That persons believe supervisors feel privileged, of course, does not mean that they will tend to act in a self-favoring manner if invested with this status, particularly in group settings in which *all* participants, in fact, share responsibility for task completion. Thus, we needed to examine this possibility in another study.

To do so, we assembled aggregates of four male undergraduates to participate in an "industrial simulation." The subjects were placed in separate cubicles, each equipped with a computer terminal, where they were shown a simple, but effortful motor task: a spring-resistant hand-grip exerciser that they had to squeeze as hard and as fast as they could for a series of 25-second trials. They first were allowed to familiarize themselves with this task via a series of four practice trials.

After the practice trials, subjects were informed that for efficiency in data collection, they had been randomly divided into two independent, two-person work teams for the actual work trials. On a trial, subjects were told, the pair would earn a small monetary bonus for each member if at least one teammate's performance on the task exceeded a predetermined criterion of success.

It was at this point in the session that we invested some subjects with special status, using a procedure similar to that of Langer and Benevento (1978). We wanted to grant people superior status without investing them with any real power or responsibility. To this end, some pairs—those in the supervisor condition—were told:

Real work crews have a leader or supervisor—someone who is in charge of the group. And, in many actual work situations—a highway repair crew or the work shift at a fast-food restaurant—the crew supervisor works along with his men, but, in addition, has other responsibilities as well. As in these situations, in the present industrial study, one of you will be appointed team supervisor.

Instructions went on to explain that a different code letter would appear on the supervisor's computer screen at the end of each work trial. Since all performance scores were supposedly stored in the computer using a special code (to maintain confidentiality), the displayed letter was needed as a key for decoding the data. The crew supervisor, thus, was in charge of writing these code letters down on a special sheet so that the performance data could be deciphered later. The team then was informed which of them the computer had randomly chosen to be the crew supervisor.

Other pairs—those in the log keeper condition—were given the same basic information about the necessity for having and recording the code letters, but now the job was a low-status assignment. These teams were told that their situation was designed to simulate actual work conditions in which:

> besides working on the task, someone—usually the newest person on the crew—keeps a record of the group's progress. For example, a clerk on a shipping dock not only loads cargo himself, but also keeps an account of all the items that he and his fellow workers load and ship.

In a third (control) condition, subjects were not given any titles nor assigned any special jobs.

By this procedure, we were able to have the crew supervisors and the log keepers engage in exactly the same activities, but they did so thinking that their tasks were associated with very different status levels—superior or subordinate. It is this difference in status that we expected to be related to the effort that subjects expended during their performance of the hand-exercise task. Based on our reasoning about superior status and privilege, we predicted that so-called supervisors would work less hard than either the low-status log keepers or the subjects who were not invested with any special status.

We examined 131 subjects in the three status conditions. Analysis of the performance data—basically the number of times a subject pulled the exerciser, weighted by the distance of the pull, in each of 17 trials—yielded a significant effect of status. As expected, supervisors worked significantly less hard than did either log keepers or control subjects. Moreover, subjects assigned to the inferior status of log keeper worked significantly harder than did control subjects, results that are consistent with the findings from the road crew questionnaire study.

The performance difference between supervisors and log keepers is especially important, because the subjects assigned to these two conditions had very equivalent experiences. Both groups were given the same additional job: recording trial codes. Thus, it had to be the status label attached to this job, and not the job itself, that affected how hard supervisors and log keepers worked at the exercise task. High-status supervisors could use their "other duties" as a rationale for expending less effort at the actual task, whereas low-status log keepers could not. In our view, such license, which the supervisors accorded themselves, is the essence of privilege.

We should note that, in addition to manipulating nominal status, we also systematically varied the feedback subjects received about their teammate's performance. In one condition, subjects consistently were given information that their teammate had done enough work on the trial to earn the group the bonus money; in a second condition, subjects were always informed that their teammate failed to reach criterion; and in a third condition, no performance feedback was given, so individual contributions to the group product were thought to be unidentifiable.

We included this feedback manipulation in the study to examine a possible limiting condition for the impact of status differences on task effort. It might have been the case, for instance, that supervisors would temper their sense of privilege and actually work harder when faced with evidence that the group they nominally headed would fail if they did not compensate for the poor showing of their subordinate. As it turned out, however, no such limiting conditions occurred. Data analysis indicated that feedback did not mediate the effect of status differences on work performed ($F < 1$); there were no performance difference across feedback conditions for supervisors ($F < 1$), or for the other two status categories.

Taken together, the results of the work performance and road crew studies suggest that in group settings the sense of privilege associated with supervisor status tends to decrease effort expended at tasks shared with subordinates. Persons expect supervisors to work less hard at such "menial" (but essential) jobs and accept that it is their privilege to do so. As such, when persons become invested with supervisor status, their role schema about this position prompts them to act in self-favoring ways.

Working less hard at collective tasks involving subordinates is only one of many possible consequences of privilege that supervisors could express in keeping with their status. For instance, it is likely that supervisor status prompts persons to accept as their due a large share of the rewards that are available as a product of collective activity, for example, the reserved parking space, the executive washroom, lucrative stock options, and so forth—a possibility that we also have examined empirically.

There Is Profit in Privilege

News stories about the astronomical bonuses that top-level executives sometimes receive by now are commonplace enough that the very sizable numbers involved appear to have lost much of their shock value. Readers and viewers—to say nothing of the fortunate recipients of such largess—seem to have come to accept these occurrences as a matter of course. We speculated that million-dollar executive bonuses are but one example of a more general phenomenon: Superior status, no matter what its basis, raises the expectation of and sense of entitlement to greater rewards. Privilege entitles one to take a bigger share of collective resources.

To examine this premise, we conducted research on profit-taking in a group context that to a great extent, parallels our studies of superior status, privilege, and lower effort. For one investigation, we developed a scenario of a computer-based investment club. In this depiction, readers are told that for a small initial fee, a national company forms about 15 to 25 persons from different parts of the country into an investment club chapter. The chapter members conduct all club transactions via their home computers. At first, all members buy a specified number of "chapter shares," of the same value for all. Then, the company invests this capital in some short-term venture, for example, trading in commodities futures. Once such investments are made, the value of the shares for a chapter's members is determined by two factors: (a) how well a chapter's investments are doing (which in actuality is difficult to determine on a day-to-day basis) and (b) the extent to which the shares are in demand among the members.

The scenario goes on to note the social dilemma aspect of selling shares (e.g., Orbell & Dawes, 1981). Members would like to sell lots of their shares when the price is high; however, if too many participants try to sell too many shares, the worth of the shares drops precipitously and the chapter could easily go bankrupt. Thus, for everyone to do well, most members have to restrain their inclinations to sell many shares when the price is high—but it is always better for an individual to sell her or his shares.

Readers learn about the activities of one particular chapter of 16 members, including a person named Taylor. Information reveals that Taylor is selling many more shares than is any other chapter member. As such, Taylor is portrayed as reaping a larger profit than the rest of the chapter members and doing so at their collective expense.

We constructed three versions of this scenario. In one, Taylor is described as the "Chapter Manager." Managers are depicted as the people in charge of the operation of their particular units. In another version, Taylor is described as the "Chapter Clerk," which is depicted as a low-status appointment (e.g., the person who sends out mailings). In a third version, Taylor is merely described as a club member (with no special status).

For each version, respondents were asked to rank in order of likelihood nine possible reasons for Taylor's behavior, that is, why Taylor took more profit from the chapter's resources than did the other members: greed, privilege, experience (or lack thereof), thought (or lack thereof), lack of concern for other members, other responsibilities, role beliefs, competence (or lack thereof), and self-interest.

We had 129 undergraduates respond to the investment club scenario. Results indicated that, irrespective of Taylor's status, self-interest and greed always were seen as the two most likely explanations for his or her behavior. However, privilege was ranked as the third most likely reason for Taylor, the Club Manager, whereas it ranked significantly lower for both Taylor, the Clerk (sixth), and Taylor, the club member (eighth). Similarly, role beliefs were seen as a significantly more likely explanation when Taylor was depicted as the club manager than as the clerk or a club member. These findings once again suggest privilege is a prominent feature of role schemas associated with superior status.

We also examined the extent to which investing persons with superior (or inferior) status affected their actual profit-taking in a real social dilemma.[4] In this study, 45 undergraduates were examined in small aggregates of three or four persons, but with each housed in a separate cubicle. In a session, subjects were told that they constituted a stock investment group of four persons that had access to a pool of financial resources (i.e., a mutual stock fund) from which any member could draw money. The fund initially contained 200 units, with each unit worth an amount of money—ranging from 1 to 25 cents—to be determined later. Subjects individually had to decide how many chips (up to a maximum of 20), if any, to take in a series of trials. They were informed that after each trial the amount remaining in the fund would be replenished by 10%, and that trials would continue until the session ended, or sooner if no chips remained in the fund.

Some subjects were invested with a superior status, the title of Managing Director. In this condition, subjects were informed:

> Real investment groups usually have a managing director—someone with authority who is in charge of the group. In these actual investment groups, the managing director is a participant in the group, but he or she has additional duties as well. As such, the managing director invests and withdraws his or her money along with the other group members, but, in addition, has other management responsibilities.

The experimenter went on to say that they had been chosen at random to be the managing director of their group. In this capacity, they were to make individual chip-taking decisions, just as the other members were, but they also had a job to do: to select and record a code letter for each trial so that the researchers could keep responses confidential, yet be able to recover what the group members did.

Subjects in a second condition were invested with an inferior status by giving them the title of Clerk. Clerks were given exactly the same coding task to perform, but now this job was couched in terms of menial work. In a third (control) condition, subjects were also given the coding task to perform, but they were not invested with any title for doing so.

Note that in this procedure, all participants engaged in exactly the same tasks and activities. As such, in actuality, all had the same responsibilities, power, and so forth. They differed only with regard to the status implied by the titles given to them. Thus, any systematic differences in profit-taking that occurred would likely be due to the role schemas associated with the positions of Manager, Clerk, and member.

All subjects were led to believe that they had been chosen by chance to be the first person on each trial to take chips. Moreover, everyone was always given the same feedback about how many chips were taken each trial (cf. Messick, Wilke, Brewer, Kramer, Zemke, & Lui, 1983). This information led subjects to believe that the resource pool was rapidly being depleted, for example, that it had diminished to less than half (88 chips) in just four trials and that there were only 15 chips left in the pool after six trials.

Because the diminished pool placed severe restrictions on subjects' choices in the later trials, we analyzed their chip-taking in two blocks. These analyses revealed a significant status effect for the first block, but not the second (although the pattern of means was the same in both blocks). As expected, relative to their fellow club members, subjects invested with the superior status of Club Manager took significantly more chips than did either Clerks or members given no special status. Moreover, consistent with the findings of our other studies, subjects invested with the inferior status of Clerk tended (marginally) to take relatively less than did members with no special status. Once again, occupants of a superior status acted in a self-favoring, privileged manner, and occupants of an inferior status acted in a self-sacrificing manner, even though objectively there was no actual difference in the tasks that anyone had performed.

Implications and Conclusions

We believe that our work demonstrates in a reasonably compelling fashion that in group settings privilege is associated with superior status. We showed that persons will work less hard and take more rewards when their participation in a collective enterprise is couched in terms of some higher order status. And they will do so even though their "other responsibilities" are, in fact, rather trivial and certainly no different from what other, ostensibly inferior-status group members are doing.

It is likely that the self-favoring decrease in effort that we found in the work group study was moderated to some extent by the actual task that we had asked subjects to perform. Pulling on a hand-exerciser is tiring and tedious, a job that most persons would choose to avoid if they could; and subjects invested with supervisor status did put less effort into this rather onerous work. It could be, then, that the privilege associated with superior status involves a sense of freedom to choose the particular activities, if any, to which one will devote one's energy. The pigs of *Animal Farm* chose not to do any of the difficult, labor-intensive farm work; our supervisors put less effort into the boring and strenuous exercise task. Our sense is that both would have been more enthusiastic participants—perhaps to the exclusion of their subordinates—if the tasks in question had been more intrinsically rewarding.

It is important to note that the subjects who were given superior status in our studies engaged in self-favoring behaviors even in the face of collective failure. The work team supervisors worked no harder when they knew their subordinate was failing than they did when they thought he was succeeding. Similarly, the investment club managing directors consistently took a greater share of the resource pool, even though they received feedback that their group was quickly heading toward bankruptcy.[5] Thus, it appears that the exercise of privilege is a difficult pleasure to forego—as the actions of many (former) executives of failed savings banks dramatically attest.

We do not believe our results are unconditionally applicable, however. No doubt there are factors present in many group and organizational settings that can temper the potentially destructive consequences of privilege-based actions or even inhibit their expression altogether.

For example, it is likely that the structural properties of the task (or tasks) confronting the group moderate what happens when a member has privileged status (Steiner, 1972). Our research employed rather simple task situations in which every participant did the same work; and, as such, group performance simply and directly was a product of the combined efforts of all group members. Although there are tasks at which reduced effort can actually enhance group performance (cf. Jackson & Williams, 1985), the reverse is more likely to hold for simple unitary tasks of the type that we have examined. In these circumstances, as we have demonstrated, the group's overall performance can be compromised by a member whose sense of privilege is expressed as diminished task effort.

On the other hand, not all collective tasks are unitary; often the nature of the work to be performed permits division and specialization of labor. It is possible that in such situations privilege-based diminution of effort in one domain may actually improve group members' contributions in other domains by facilitating coordination, by providing incentives to aspirants to superior status, and so forth. Such trade-offs may be favorable enough for the group that overall performance is enhanced. Unfortunately, our research suggests that group members who are favored with superior status, in fact, do not readily consider issues such as the nature of the group task, because they still tend to act in a privileged manner even when they are well aware that their actions are harming group performance.

It is also likely that not every status associated with influence or authority carries with it the sense of privilege. For instance, we would speculate that the term *leader*—the person who most directs a group's activities—does not connote the sort of superior status and social hierarchy that a title such as *supervisor* or *manager* does.

It seems probable that, to most people, a leader tends to emerge from group process, whereas a supervisor has a more formal status designation (cf. Gibb, 1969). As such, a group member can become a leader precisely because she or he is recognized as the best, most active, or hardest working performer (Marak, 1964; Zdep & Oakes, 1967) or because she or he is viewed as personifying consensus values (Homans, 1950). In contrast, someone typically becomes a supervisor because she or he is appointed to a formal position. Sometimes—as was the case for the pigs of *Animal Farm*—leaders appoint themselves to such superior statuses, but we contend that the assumption of status per se, independent of the capacity to influence group activities, can promote a sense of privilege in managers, supervisors, and their ilk.

Research by Samuelson and Allison (1991, Study 3) provides compelling evidence that not all positions of influence carry with them expectations of privilege. In this investigation, subjects, who were given the title of supervisor, leader, or guide, had the opportunity to be the first person in a group of six to take a reward from a common resource pool. Results showed that only nominal supervisors took more than an equal share of the available reward. Clearly, then, the role schema associated with leader status does not contain the same element of privilege that the role schema for supervisor does. As such, leaders would not be expected to act in the same self-favoring manner as supervisors (managers, directors, etc.) would.

Of course, we are not suggesting that occupants of a superior status always take advantage of their privileged positions. Examples abound of persons in superior statuses who work harder and sacrifice their individual welfare to promote the success of their group. We would speculate that these instances occur primarily because strong situational forces are present to militate against (at least temporarily) the expression of privilege.

We believe that privilege is more likely to be foregone when the person with superior status perceives his or her own personal welfare as being closely tied to collective success. For example, organizations often explicitly link supervisory employees' personal welfare—salaries, bonuses, opportunities for advancement, and so forth—to the collective performance of their subordinates. Knowing that one is being judged (and rewarded) on the basis of the group's ability to perform is probably a powerful motivator against the expression of privilege when such behaviors impede collective success. It is likely that the small monetary prizes that we offered were not sufficient inducement for those subjects whom we had invested with superior status to forego the privileges to which their positions entitled them. In the world outside of the social psychological laboratory, however, groups and organizations often have much more potent incentives available for this purpose.

Persons with superior status are also likely to be more concerned about collective outcomes when they perceive their psychological welfare to be strongly linked to the fate of the group. For example, social identity concerns (cf. Tajfel & Turner, 1985) might induce a supervisor to view her or his sense of competence, self-worth, and so forth as tied to the performance of the collective: The group is *his* (or *her*) group. If so, then to the extent that collective failures are construed as personal failures, the supervisor might forego the rewards of privilege if she or he believed that such a sacrifice would benefit the group. Clearly, the temporary (and tenuous) social links that were established in our laboratory studies did not generate much cohesiveness or social identity. However, many group settings do promote such feelings and probably create conditions that can moderate the inclinations of high-status members to act in a self-favoring manner.

Somewhat paradoxically, the role schema associated with superior status might also contain elements that could work to moderate the expression of privilege. It is probable that, in addition to the expectation of privilege, persons also perceive that responsibility (for group performance) is part of the supervisor's role. Such beliefs that the person in charge is responsible for what happens could raise supervisors' concerns about collective failure. It may be the case, however—and our data support this contention—that for persons with superior status, beliefs about responsibility to the group tend to be less salient than beliefs about privilege. If so, then the sense of privilege would be more likely to influence supervisors' thoughts and actions than would the sense of responsibility (Taylor & Fiske, 1978). Even so, certain conditions (e.g., clear and explicit indications that group members are counting on the supervisor to "pull them through") might raise the relative salience of the responsibility component of the supervisor role schema so that concerns with collective welfare would overcome the sense of privilege.

Note that our discussion assumes that privilege tends to be a salient and potent component of the role schema associated with superior status. Although there probably are many mechanisms that potentially can dampen the self-favoring expression of privilege by supervisors, the inclination in these persons to be egoistic is likely to have an enduring and pervasive influence on their judgment and actions. After all, the opportunity to be "more equal than others" is a very seductive prospect—for both humans and pigs.

Notes

1. For the purposes of this discussion, we are not distinguishing between *role theory* and *symbolic interactionism,* the perspective from which it was derived. Although there are some differences between the two formulations, these distinctions are not germane to the points that we are addressing in this chapter.

2. Although Abelson (1981) distinguishes between the related categories of *role* and *event schemas,* for convenience and consistency with role theory, we employ the term *role schema* as a more comprehensive concept that encompasses both types of knowledge structures.

3. All of these differences were statistically significant. For a more detailed presentation of these and other results, see Kerr, Messé, and Sattler (1991).

4. Such a situation is a social dilemma because participants have a choice between acting in their individual interest or in the interest of the collective to which they belong. The dilemma occurs because widespread self-interested action results in poorer outcomes than acting in the collective interest would have yielded. In this sense, as Kerr (1983, 1986) noted, both the investment club and the work team situations that we studied confronted participants with social dilemmas, since in both cases individual self-interest (working less hard, taking more profit), when commonplace, results in poor outcomes (team failure, bankruptcy).

5. Data indicated that managing directors consistently tried to take more chips than their fellow participants across all seven trials. In contrast, the actions of subjects in the other conditions only became significantly more self-interested as they realized the resource pool was quickly evaporating.

References

Abelson, R. P. (1981). The psychological status of the script concept. *American Psychologist, 36,* 715-729.

Biddle, B. J. (1979). *Role theory: Expectations, identities and behaviors.* New York: Academic Press.

Biddle, B. J., & Thomas, E. J. (Eds.). (1966). *Role theory: Concepts and research.* New York: John Wiley.

Callero, P. L., Howard, J. A., & Piliavin, J. A. (1987). Helping behavior as role behavior: Disclosing social structure and history in the analysis of prosocial action. *Social Psychology Quarterly, 50,* 247-256.

Cottrell, L. S., Jr. (1966). The analysis of situational fields in social psychology. In A. P. Hare, E. F. Borgatta, & R. F. Bales (Eds.), *Small groups: Studies in social interaction* (rev. ed., pp. 57-70). New York: Knopf.

Eskilson, A., & Wiley, M. G. (1976). Sex composition and leadership in small groups. *Sociometry, 39,* 183-194.

Gibb, C. A. (1969). Leadership. In G. Lindzey & E. Aronson (Eds.), *The handbook of social psychology* (Vol. 4, 2nd ed., pp. 205-282). Reading, MA: Addison Wesley.

Haney, C., Banks, C., & Zimbardo, P. G. (1981). A study of prisoners and guards in a simulated prison. In E. Aronson (Ed.), *Readings about the social animal* (3rd. ed.). San Francisco: Freeman.

Hastie, R. (1981). Schematic principles in human memory. In T. E. Higgens, C. P. Herman, & M. P. Zanna (Eds.), *Social cognition: The Ontario Symposium* (Vol. 1). Hillsdale, NJ: Lawrence Erlbaum.

Homans, G. C. (1950). *The human group.* New York: Harcourt Brace.

Jackson, J. M., & Williams, K. D. (1985). Social loafing on difficult tasks. *Journal of Personality and Social Psychology, 49,* 937-942.

Johnson, R. D., & Downing, L. L. (1979). Deindividuation and valence of cues: Effects on prosocial and antisocial behavior. *Journal of Personality and Social Psychology, 37,* 1532-1538.

Kerr, N. L. (1983). Motivation losses in task-performing groups: A social dilemma analysis. *Journal of Personality and Social Psychology, 45,* 819-828.

Kerr. N. L. (1986). Motivational choices in task groups: A paradigm for social dilemma research. In H.A.M. Wilke, D. M. Messick, & C. G. Rutte (Eds.), *Experimental social dilemmas.* Frankfurt am Main, FRG: Verlag Peter Lang.

Kerr, N. L., & MacCoun, R. J. (1984). Sex composition of groups and member motivation II: Effects of relative member ability. *Basic and Applied Social Psychology, 5,* 255-271.

Kerr, N. L., & MacCoun, R. J. (1985). Role expectations and social dilemmas: Sex roles and task motivation in groups. *Journal of Personality and Social Psychology, 49,* 1547-1556.

Kerr. N. L., Messé, L. A., & Sattler, D. N. (1991). *Egoism as a privilege of rank: Superior status and self-favoring behaviors in social dilemmas.* Manuscript submitted for publication.

Kerr. N. L., & Sullaway, M. (1983). Group sex composition and member motivation. *Sex Roles, 9,* 403-417.

Kipnis, D. (1974). The powerholder. In J. T. Tedeschi (Ed.), *Perspectives on social power.* Chicago: Aldine.

Langer, E. J. (1989). *Mindfulness.* Reading, MA: Addison-Wesley.

Langer, E. J., & Benevento, A. (1978). Self-induced dependence. *Journal of Personality and Social Psychology, 36,* 886-893.

Marak, G. E. (1964). The evolution of leadership structure. *Sociometry, 27,* 174-182.

Messick, D. M., Wilke, H.A.M., Brewer, M. B., Kramer, R. M., Zemke, P. E., & Lui, L. (1983). Individual adaptations and structural change as solutions to social dilemmas. *Journal of Personality and Social Psychology, 44,* 294-309.

Orbell, J., & Dawes, R. (1981). Social dilemmas. In G. Stephenson & J. H. Davis (Eds.), *Progress in applied social psychology* (Vol. 1, pp. 37-65). Chichester, UK: John Wiley.

Orwell, G. (1946). *Animal farm.* New York: Harcourt Brace.

Rumelhart, D. E., & Ortony, A. (1977). The representation of knowledge in memory. In R. C. Anderson, R. J. Spiro, & W. E. Montague (Eds.), *Schooling and the acquisition of knowledge.* Hillsdale, NJ: Lawrence Erlbaum.

Samuelson, C. D., & Allison, S. T. (1991). *Decision making in resource dilemmas: A social decision heuristic approach.* Manuscript submitted for publication.

Sorokin, P. A., & Lunden, W. A. (1959). *Power and morality: Who shall guard the guardians?* Boston: Sargent.

Steiner, I. D. (1972). *Group process and productivity.* New York: Academic Press.

Stryker, S. (1980). *Symbolic interactionism: A social structural version.* Menlo Park, CA: Benjamin/Cummings.

Tajfel, H., & Turner, J. C. (1985). The social identity theory of intergroup behaviour. In S. Worchel & W. G. Austin (Eds.), *The psychology of intergroup relations.* Chicago: Nelson-Hall.

Taylor, S. E., & Crocker, J. (1981). Schematic bases of social information processing. In E. T. Higgens, C. P. Herman, & M. P. Zanna (Eds.), *Social cognition: The Ontario symposium* (Vol. 1). Hillsdale, NJ: Lawrence Erlbaum.

Taylor, S. E., & Fiske, S. T. (1978). Salience, attention, and attribution: Top of the head phenomena. In L. Berkowitz (Ed.), *Advances in experimental social psychology* (Vol. 11). New York: Academic Press.

Turner, R. H. (1979-1980). Strategy for developing an integrated role theory. *Humbolt Journal of Social Relations, 7,* 123-139.

Vancouver, J., Rubin, B., & Kerr, N. L. (in press). Sex composition of groups and member motivation III: Motivation losses at a feminine task. *Basic and Applied Social Psychology.*

Wagenaar, W. A., & Keren, G. B. (1986). The seat belt paradox: Effect of adopted roles on information seeking. *Organizational Behavior and Human Performance, 38,* 1-6.

Weathers, J. E., Jr., Messé, L. A., & Aronoff, J. (1984). The effects of task-group experiences on subsequent prosocial behavior. *Social Psychology Quarterly, 47,* 287-292.

Zdep, S. M., & Oakes, W. F. (1967). Reinforcement of leadership behavior in group discussion. *Journal of Experimental Social Psychology, 3,* 310-320.

9 Does Behavior Technology Change Practitioners' Behavior as Well as the Behavior of People They Are Trying to Help?

David Kipnis

Technology is the use of systematic procedures to produce intended effects. Thus technology is not synonymous with engineering hardware, but includes techniques found in the social sciences and in everyday culture (Ellul, 1964). Its goal is to produce outcomes with less effort and outcomes that are more uniform and predictable than can be produced by unassisted human effort. The use of technology, then, reduces the amount of uncertainty in attempts to solve practical problems. Reducing uncertainty means increasing the probability that events will occur as wanted by an influencing agent.

Just as there are technologies to transform physical materials, there are technologies to transform behaviors. Behavior technologies have similar goals to those that I have just described. They seek to produce behaviors that are predictable and controllable from the point of view of an influencing agent (for example, an advertiser, a supervisor, a psychotherapist, or a parent, people who have to influence others to achieve practical outcomes). Attempts to reduce behavior uncertainty in the target person most often involve reducing the amount of control and free choice available to that person. That is, behavior techniques guide people so that they behave in some ways, but not in others, or think and feel in some ways, but not in others.

Because of the requirement that outcomes be controlled, technology and power are closely related (Kipnis, 1990). The purpose of this chapter is to describe one consequence of this relationship: how people who use technology to control behavior perceive and evaluate persons who are the targets of such control.

The Metamorphic Effects of Power

In an earlier article, I speculated that the use of behavior technology by social science practitioners might inadvertently change the values and attitudes of these practitioners, as well as the behavior of persons who were the planned targets of the technology (Kipnis, 1987). This speculation was based on earlier research which had found that husbands, wives, and business managers who used controlling tactics of influence to get their way viewed persons they influenced as less worthy than themselves and moved away from them socially and psychologically. These changes were labeled the metamorphic effects of power, to suggest that the successful use of power transforms the influencing agent's view of self and others as a result of causing behavior in others (Kipnis, 1976). I should mention that earlier studies of the metamorphic effects of power were based on verbal influence tactics of the agent's own devising, rather than on the use of systematic techniques of influence, developed by social scientists and validated through research.

Metamorphic effects involve two sets of variables: (a) the strength of the influence tactics that are used to cause change in the person being influenced and (b) the subsequent attributions (Weiner, 1981) of the influencing agent concerning who controls the target person's behavior—the target person or external forces, including the powerholder.

Tactics of influence refer to the actual means used by influencing agents to change the behavior of other people. Tactics can be verbal, nonverbal, or ecological (i.e., tactics that change peoples' environment and so change their behavior). Regardless of the particular modality used, however, tactics can be described in terms of the amount of pressure they exert on target persons. Research in industry, and among dating and married couples, has described stronger tactics as those in which the influencing agent, for example, insists, demands, or orders the target person to comply. Weaker tactics, on the other hand, have been described as those in which the agent, for example, pleads, requests, discusses, or uses other gentle measures to gain compliance (Kipnis, 1984a; Kipnis, Schmidt, & Wilkinson, 1980).

When the use of influence is successful, we have found that strong and weak tactics have quite different effects on the influencing agent. When agents use strong tactics that are successful, they believe, not surprisingly, that it was their tactics that caused the target person to change. When agents use weak tactics that are successful, they believe that the target person was responsible for the change. Stated in terms of Weiner's formulation, the successful use of strong tactics produces the belief that the target person's behavior is externally controlled.

This relation has been demonstrated in both experimental (Kipnis, Schmidt, Price, & Stitt, 1981) and field (Kipnis, 1984a) studies. In all instances, the successful use of strong tactics was found to create the belief among influencing agents that the person being influenced no longer controlled his or her own behavior, but was controlled by outside forces.

The successful use of strong tactics also causes powerholders' evaluations of target persons to change for the worse. That is, persons who are perceived to be externally controlled are evaluated more unfavorably than those who are perceived to be internally controlled (Kipnis, 1976, 1984a). One explanation for these less favorable evaluations is that the behavior of the target person, no matter how excellent, is seen as guided by the powerholder's orders rather than by the abilities and motivations of the target person. Hence the target person is not given full credit for anything he or she does. Social relations also suffer under these circumstances, because we seldom treat as equals or actively seek the company of persons who are not in control of their own behavior.

In summary, metamorphic effects describe a process through which the use of power alters the social relations between influencing agents and targets of influence. This process is contingent on the strength of the influence tactics that are used. To the extent that powerholders use influence tactics that allow the target person autonomy, relations remain positive. When the tactics that are used to gain compliance restrict the target person's freedom to choose and to act autonomously, relations deteriorate, that is, powerholders denigrate the worth of target persons and believe them to be less worthy than themselves. Thus the exercise of influence, per se, is not problematic for social relations. Rather problems arise when strong and controlling tactics are chosen to get one's way.

Within the context of these views, I suggest that behavior technology provides influencing agents with strong tactics of influence. With few exceptions, technologies are designed to reduce uncertainty by controlling the behavior of the target person. For example, attitude change technology is concerned with controlling the alternatives that are available for people to consider when forming opinions (programmed instructions control the number of incorrect responses that trainees can make); and leadership technology teaches leaders how to choose the influence tactics most likely to control subordinates. To the extent that these procedures appear successful, it is reasonable to believe that the technology will be seen as the cause of the target person's behavior. Hence the target person will be given little credit for what he or she does.

In short, I suggest that the more controlling the behavior technology used by practitioners, the less favorable their evaluations will be of persons they are influencing. With this reasoning as background, I would now like to describe research that has sought to empirically test these ideas.

The Routinization of Work

An important use of technology in organizations is to simplify and routinize the work done by employees. The benefits to management of routinization are many, including increased managerial control of the work flow (Pfeffer, 1978), increased ability to make long-range plans (Galbraith, 1967), increases in the consistency and quantity of work, decreased reliance upon specialized employee talents and skills, and consequently reduced labor costs (Braverman, 1974). Routinization is accomplished through the use of automation, robots, improved machinery, and scientific management techniques that rationalize the process of work.

One consequence of routinization is that employees lose bargaining power in their relationship with management. This is because the skills needed by employees are reduced with the introduction of routinized technology. The planning and skill components of work are taken over by management, or by machines, leaving the less skilled functions to employees. As a result, management's dependence on labor is reduced. In terms of French and Raven's theory of power (1959), we can say that knowledge and expertise provide labor with a major base of power, whereas technology that routinizes work provides management with the means to deprive labor of this power base.

Findings from systematic social science research that has examined individual work units at the first line of production provide strong evidence that the more simplified the operations required to transform raw material, the less power employees in that work unit possess (James, Gent, Hater, & Coray, 1979; Reiman & Inzerilli, 1978; Rousseau, 1978). For example, James et al. found that employees engaged in routinized production work reported that they had significantly less influence over their work, or over their supervisor's decisions, than employees engaged in nonroutinized work. Their supervisors also independently reported that they consulted less with employees engaged in routinized work.

Empirical Studies[1]

Evaluations of Employee Performance

The above literature provides a reasonable amount of information about the impact of work routinization at the individual level. The evidence indicates that routinization reduces the amount of self-control and influence that employees can exercise. Less is known, however, about the impact of routinized technology on the managers who control the means of production.

From the perspective of the metamorphic model, it can be argued that technology, as it routinizes work, provides managers with strong means of influence, that is, the direct control of employees through routinization provides an environment that limits, almost without notice once it is established, the number of free choices available to employees. This is because the pace of employee work is regulated by machine, or takes place in a setting where employee performance can be monitored and immediately evaluated, where the discretionary powers of the employee to plan and make decisions are slight, and where minimal cognitive skills are needed to do the work. Under these circumstances, employees should be seen by managers as externally controlled, that is, not in control of their work-related behaviors. It is far more reasonable for managers to attribute satisfactory work to the effects of such external causes as machinery, the system of work, and the manager's direct orders. Based on what has been said about the relation between perceived autonomy and evaluations, we predict that managers of routinized work units will evaluate their employees' performances less favorably than managers of nonroutinized work units.

Three field studies were carried out to test this prediction. In each study, first line supervisors (*n*s of 34, 22, and 73) were first asked to describe the technology of their work unit. Items included questions about the predictability of work outcomes, frequency of encountering nonroutine work problems, the use of repetitive work procedures, and the amount of training and/or job experience required to do satisfactory work. Answers to these questions were combined into an Index of Work Routinization (α = .77), with high scores indicating that the manager's work unit was highly routinized.

Supervisors also evaluated the nontechnical aspects of their employees' work in terms of accepting responsibility for their work, the need to continually supervise employees, the amount of employees' pride in their work, and the quality of work that they performed. Answers to these questions were combined into an Index of Employee Evaluation with high scores reflecting favorable evaluations (α = .67).

In support of our prediction, the correlations between the Indices of Work Routinization and Employee Evaluation were $-.34$ ($p < .05$), $-.39$ ($p < .05$), and $-.40$ ($p < .01$), respectively, in the three samples. In all samples, employees who worked in routinized units were described by their supervisors as avoiding responsibility, requiring close supervision, and taking little pride in their work. The reader should bear in mind that we did not ask managers to evaluate the technical skills of their employees, but the attitudinal and motivational aspects of their work. In practice, it is possible to find lazy craftsmen and diligent production line workers. These evaluations make sense only if we assume that, for most people, a negative relation exists between the extent they see people as autonomous and the extent they think well of them.

Evaluation of Poor Performance

The above findings were based on the assumption that managers of routinized work settings attributed satisfactory employee performance to the technological system, rather than to the employees' own efforts. What happens, however, when unsatisfactory work is done in routinized work units?

I suggest that under these circumstances there may be three sources that managers can blame: (a) breakdowns in the technology, (b) the employee's lack of ability, or (c) the employee's deliberate efforts. Of the two causes attributing fault to the employee, I believe that we can discount the likelihood of managers attributing poor performance to a lack of employee ability. This is because technology has simplified work to the point where few skills are needed.

To examine this question empirically, the first-line supervisors in our last sample ($n = 73$) were asked the following two questions:

1. About what percentage of your subordinates, if any, have a basic weakness in their work because they lack the ability to do the work? Answered on a 7-point scale: None, Less than 5%, 10%, 15%, 20%, 25%, 30% or more.

2. About what percentage of your employees, if any, have a basic weakness in their work because of poor attitudes and/or a lack of motivation? Answered using the same alternatives as (1) above.

What we found was that when the work that employees did was complex, that is, when the work was challenging, nonroutine, involved varied components, and required planning, then supervisors described employees with "basic weaknesses" in their work as lacking in ability. The correlation between the Index of Work Routinization and estimates by the supervisor of the number of employees who did poor work because they lacked skill was −.40 ($p < .01$).

Fewer supervisors attributed poor work to this reason as the work became routinized. These latter supervisors had a different explanation for the poor work done by their employees. When the work that employees did was routinized and paced by machines and machine systems, employee weaknesses were attributed by supervisors to the employee's lack of motivation and poor attitudes. The corresponding correlation between the measure of routinization of work and the explanations that this poor work was due to poor attitudes was +.22 ($p < .05$).

Similar results were found in an experimental simulation of routinization. In this study, student managers supervised workers who assembled model airplanes. Construction of the airplanes was done either by means of an assembly line process in which the model airplane was built by units in a rote manner or by working directly from a complex set of plans. In each condition, one of the workers, who was a confederate, consistently did poor work. In an evaluation of their workers' performances, 77% of the managers in the routine condition and 27% in the nonroutine condition attributed the unsatisfactory worker's performance to poor attitudes or a lack of motivation. The remaining managers in each condition attributed the poor work to either a lack of ability or the difficulty of the work ($p < .01$). These latter explanations are certainly less harsh.

Thus, if work is so simplified that even a child can do it, and still errors occur, it seems logical for managers to assume that employees deliberately made mistakes.

Technology, Managerial Power, and Influence Tactics

I have suggested that employees doing routinized work are relatively powerless in their dealings with management. We can also expect that the supervisors of employees doing routinized work will have little organizational power. As organizational theorists, such as Salancik and Pfeffer (1977) have pointed, power in organizations is contingent on the management of uncertainty. That is, in the same organization, the supervisor of a group of clerk-typists has less influence than the supervisor of a group of design engineers. This is because the work of the clerk-typists presents fewer problems of importance to the organization than does the work of engineers. We found confirmation of this view, when we asked supervisors in the third sample ($n = 73$) how much influence they had in such matters as setting their unit's budget, influencing their own superiors, and influencing organizational policy. Managers of routine units reported significantly less influence in these areas than their counterparts who managed skilled units.

If people are powerless and we want them to do something, the metamorphic model suggests that we don't waste time explaining what we want. We simply tell people what to do. By the same token, people who are powerless should confront authority in a passive and meek way, so as not to give offense.

To test this view, managers in the third sample studied ($n = 73$) completed two managerial influence scales. The first measured the strategies they used to influence their subordinates and the second the strategies they used to influence their own bosses (Kipnis, Schmidt, & Wilkinson, 1980). The subordinate influence scale measured the frequency with which supervisors used each of the following seven dimensions of influence: (a) Assertiveness (e.g., demanding, ordering); (b) Reason (e.g., explains, writes detailed plan); (c) Ingratiation (e.g., acts humble, makes the other person feels important); (d) Sanctions (e.g., threatens job security, promises raises); (e) Exchange of Benefits (e.g., offers to help in exchange for compliance); (f) Appeal to Higher Authority (e.g., obtain the informal support of higher ups); and (g) Coalition (e.g., obtain the support of co-workers). The second influence scale asked how frequently supervisors used each of the above dimensions (with the exception of Sanctions) to influence their own bosses.

What we expected to find was that the supervisors of employees doing complex work would rely on logic and reason when influencing both their subordinates and their bosses. On the contrary, we expected supervisors of employees doing routinized work to use strong tactics (i.e., assertiveness and sanctions) when influencing subordinates, but to avoid such tactics and be relatively passive when trying to influence their bosses. These different patterns of using influence should emerge if technology alters the balance of power in ways that I have suggested.

Table 9.1 shows the correlations between the Index of Work Routinization and the frequency with which supervisors used the various strategies to influence both subordinates and superiors.

The findings about face-to-face influence support, if not fully, the belief that technology is implicated in the kinds of social relations that emerge between management and labor. Supervisors of nonroutine units used reason more often with their employees and a variety of different tactics, including reason and assertiveness, with their bosses. Originally, I had thought that supervisors of routinized work units would use strong and controlling tactics with their subordinates. We did not find this to be true, although the sign of the correlations for assertive tactics and the use of sanctions were in the predicted direction. Instead, supervisors of routinized units were relatively passive in their attempts to influence both their employees and their superiors. The best explanation I have for their passiveness in exercising influence is that supervisors of routinized work felt powerless to intervene, either with their employees or with their bosses.

In summary, then, the findings of the above research lead me to conclude that technology, as it routinizes work, enmeshes individuals in a system where they do not appear to be in control of their own behavior, where they are not given credit for acceptable performances, where they run the risk of being assigned responsibility for poor performances, and where people are relatively powerless to exercise influence.

Table 9.1
Correlations Between Influence Strategies and the Routinization of Work Index
($n = 73$)

Strategy	Used to Influence Employees (*r*)	Used to Influence Superior (*r*)
Ingratiation	−.06	+.05
Reason	−.24*	−.29**
Assertiveness	+.14	−.25*
Sanctions	+.11	—
Exchange of benefits	−.06	−.18
Appeal to higher authority	−.02	−.45**
Coalition	−.26*	−.13

NOTE: High scores on the Routinization of Work Index mean the supervision of units doing routine work.
*$p < .05$; **$p < .01$

Psychotherapy and Behavior Technology

Recent developments in the field of behavior therapy have provided psychotherapists with a wide range of technologies for correcting patients' thoughts, feelings, and behavior. Such techniques as "flooding," desensitization, hypnosis, homework, and cognitive restructuring are but a few of the many behavioral technologies that have been developed to change client behavior and feelings. I believe it is fair to say that these techniques do not rely on patient insights about the cognitive-affective causes of their neurotic behavior. Rather, behavior changes as a consequence of the patient following the prescriptions of the therapist (London, 1976; Sweet, 1984).

In contrast, the task of humanistic and psychodynamic therapists is to provide patients with an understanding of the sources of stress and distress in their lives (Rogers, Gendlin, Keisler, & Truax, 1967). Insight is achieved through such techniques as reflective listening, encouraging the patient to connect what is happening within the therapy session to his or her life's stress, occasionally providing explanations about the patient's behavior that differ from the patients own explanation, and sometimes even frustrating the patient so that he or she learns about how they cope with their frustrations and hostility. It is generally agreed that dynamic therapy is a long and uncertain process, the success of which depends on the ability of the patient to understand and eventually to change his or her own behavior (London, 1976).

Stages in Technology

Let me digress for a moment to talk about the evolutionary stages of technology. Most technologies follow a uniform path of development from human control to machine or system control. The industrial sociologist, William Faunce (1981) describes this evolution as proceeding from craft production in which management's dependence on the skills of labor is almost complete, to mechanized production in which dependence on labor is reduced, to automated production in which most employees are eliminated. Each stage increases the efficiency of productive activity, and at the same time changes the relation between workers and machines. In their initial development technologies are labor intensive. However, skilled operators are costly, and even the best make mistakes from time to time. To solve these problems, technologies evolve in predictable ways by transferring the skill components to machines and machine systems. This transfer reduces costs of operations, increases the efficiency of operations, and improves the quality of the products that are produced. The research that I described in the preceding pages, in fact, contrasted the ways managers evaluated employees at the craft and mechanized stages of technological development.

There are several ways in which psychodynamic therapy resembles the first stage in the development of technology, aside from the obvious fact that it was the first workable form of therapy. Psychodynamic techniques are labor intensive, that is, they depend on both the skills of the therapist and the capacity of the patient for insight. It is no accident that psychoanalysts write books about the art of therapy and the ability to listen with a third ear. Therapeutic outcomes appear to depend upon only partially understood therapist skills. As a consequence there is a fair amount of uncertainty in predicting the outcomes of psychoanalytic therapy. Another resemblance to the early stages of technological development is in terms of costs. Psychoanalytic forms of therapy require two or three years to effect patient change. As a result, the costs of treatment are high in terms of money and in terms of therapist and patient time.

In contrast, cognitive-behavior therapies represent the beginnings of the second stage in the development of a technology of psychotherapy. We hear less about the art of therapy and more about *techniques* when cognitive behavior therapies are discussed. There is a presumption that if the therapist uses the methods of this approach to therapy, there is a high probability that patient distress will be reduced. Thus the art of psychodynamic therapy has been transferred to the techniques of cognitive behavior therapy. Benefits of this process of de-skilling the therapist's work include a reduction in time to complete treatment, reduced costs of treatment, claims of greater frequency of treatment success, and the fact that the techniques themselves can be taught in a relatively short period of time. Like the Luddites of the early 19th century, traditional psychoanalysts have bitterly attacked what they perceive as overly simplistic approaches to therapy.

The Strength of Psychotherapeutic Interventions

The simultaneous use of different technologies of psychotherapy allows us to test ideas about the ways in which the use of behavior control technology may affect practitioners. In terms of the metamorphic model of power, I would describe cognitive-behavior techniques such as homework assignment, systematic desensitization, flooding, exposure, and hypnosis as directive and high in control, that is, as strong tactics. On the other hand, I would describe such techniques as interpretation, challenging, reflective listening, and unconditional positive regard as weaker tactics. Based on what I've said so far, one could expect the use of behavioral-based therapeutic techniques to alter the behavior of psychotherapists, as well as the behavior of their patients. That is, one might expect that any gains by patients in therapy would be seen by cognitive-behavioral therapists as caused by their therapeutic techniques rather than by the motivations and understandings and insights of the patient. Further, to the extent that the patient was seen as not responsible for his or her own therapeutic gains, the metamorphic model predicts that therapists would devalue their patients.

In short, we could expect differences in therapists' evaluations of their patients as a function of the therapeutic technologies they used. Those who used the more controlling technologies should see patients as less autonomous, and consequently evaluate them less favorably, than therapists who use dynamically oriented techniques of therapy.

Empirical Research

To test these ideas, two clinical colleagues, Finy Hansen and April Fallon, of the Medical College of Pennsylvania and I mailed a questionnaire to slightly over 500 randomly selected members of the Pennsylvania Psychological Association (PPA), and 100 randomly selected members of the American Association of Behavioral Therapists (AABT).[2] Ninety-four (19%) members of the PPA and 19 (19%) members of AABT returned the completed questionnaire. All respondents had doctoral degrees, and had been in practice for an average of 14 years. Twenty-nine percent of the respondents were female, and 71% were male. Of the 113 patients described, 72% were female and 28% were male. Their average age was 37 years, and they had an average of 14 years of education.[3]

The questionnaire asked each therapist to describe a recent episode in which an adult patient in individual psychotherapy showed progress in therapy. This represents an instance in which the use of therapeutic techniques achieved their intended effects of patient progress.

Specifically, the therapist was asked: (a) to describe the interventions that were most helpful in bringing about this change, (b) to rate the importance of several possible explanations, or reasons, for their patient's progress, and (c) to evaluate their patient following his or her progress. In addition to this information, therapists were asked to describe the nature of their patient's progress, provide demographic information about the patient including education, gender, prior hospitalization for psychiatric disorders, a DSM III-R diagnosis, and length of time that the patient had been seen when the progress occurred. Therapists were also asked to describe their own training, years of experience, and theoretical orientation.

To limit the extent of severity of mental illness, the therapist was asked to exclude patients diagnosed as schizophrenic, mentally retarded, organically impaired, or those who were currently hospitalized or institutionalized.

We classified the therapeutic techniques used by the therapists into four types of interventions. The proportion of therapists using each intervention is shown in the following list; since most therapists reported using several types of interventions, these add to more than 100%.

1. Cognitive-behavior techniques (e.g., homework, desensitization, breathing exercises, flooding): 50%
2. Empathic responses (e.g., reflective listening, validate patient feelings, unconditional positive regard): 49%.
3. Teaching and guidance (e.g., teaching assertive behaviors, suggestions for change, listing options, giving information): 44%.
4. Dynamic interventions (e.g., interpretation and clarification): 32%.

Based on these classifications, four dummy variables were then created by assigning a score of 1 if the intervention was used and a score of 0 if it was not.

We next asked therapists to indicate the extent to which they believed their patients were responsible for their gains in therapy by rating the following two reasons for gains in therapy: (a) the patient's capacity for insight and (b) the patient's inner strength and drive toward health. The rating scale ranged from *of little importance* (rated 1) to *most important* (rated 7).

The scores on these two reasons were added to form an Index of Patient Responsibility (split half reliability = .61). High scores meant that patients were seen by their therapists as responsible for their own "progress" in therapy; low scores meant they were not.

Finally we asked therapists to rate their impressions of their patients following progress. Nine patient attributes were rated using a 7-point scale, ranging from *poor* (1) to *outstanding* (7). The patient attributes were: (a) Flexibility; (b) Intelligence; (c) Capacity for Insight; (d) Ability to Experience Empathy; (e) Competence; (f) Interpersonal Skills; (g) Ability to Function Autonomously; (h) Ability to Maintain Therapeutic Gains; and (i) Overall Functioning. These nine items were summed to provide a Patient Evaluation Scale (α = .81).

Since the severity of patient problems could affect the therapists' descriptions, patients were divided into two groups: mild and severe. Patients were rated as presenting severe problems if the patient had a previous hospitalization and if the DSM III-R diagnosis included one of these categories: major affective disorder, severe personality disorder, substance abuse not in remission, or impulse disorder. Seventy-three patients were classified as presenting mild symptoms and 40 as presenting severe symptoms.

Techniques of Therapy and Attribution of Control

We predicted that therapists who used cognitive-behavior techniques would be less likely than therapists who use dynamic techniques to attribute gains in therapy to the patients' own efforts. To test this prediction, correlations were computed between the Index of Patient Responsibility and the interventions therapists used in therapy.

The findings supported our prediction. The use of cognitive-behavioral techniques was negatively related ($r = -.36$, $p < .01$) and the use of dynamic techniques was positively related ($r = .30$, $p < .01$) to the Index of Patient Responsibility. Empathic and teaching techniques were also correlated with the Index, but the correlations were lower ($r = .21$, $p < .05$ and $r = .20$, $p < .05$, respectively).

Because the severity of patient symptoms could affect therapists' attributions, we also analyzed the data using only the 73 patients whose symptoms were rated as mild. The findings indicate that the results cannot be explained by assuming that one group of therapists was treating patients with more severe symptoms than the remaining therapists. If anything, the predicted relations were slightly stronger when patients with severe symptoms were excluded from the analysis (cognitive-behavior $r = -.41$; dynamic $r = .34$).

Here then we have support for the belief that the use of behavioral technologies is related to social science practitioners' perceptions of patients; that is, as behavioral control of the patient increases, self-direction on the part of the patient is perceived to decrease.

Attributions and Evaluation

The metamorphic model predicts that we think less of people who are seen as not responsible for their own behavior. In terms of the present study, we would expect that therapists who described their patients as not responsible for their own therapeutic gains would evaluate their patients less favorably than patients who were seen as responsible for these gains. In support of our prediction, we found that the Index of Patient Responsibility correlated with the Patient Evaluation Scale for all patients ($r = .46$, $p < .01$), and for patients with mild symptoms ($r = .41$, $p < .01$).

It was also found that the interventions used by therapists predicted these evaluations, but the magnitude of the correlations was lower than those found for the Index of Patient Responsibility. For the total sample, dynamic interventions were positively correlated ($r = .25$, $p < .01$) and cognitive-behavior techniques were negatively correlated ($r = -.20$,

$p < .05$) with patient evaluations. These correlations were slightly higher when only patients with "mild" symptoms were included.

Conclusion

The thesis of this chapter is that the use of technology to solve the practical problems of society raises issues of some importance to psychologists. In two very different settings, we have described how the use of technology is related to the values and attitudes of persons who control and use the technology. We find that, as technology assumes control of individual behavior, the perception that people are the autonomous source of their own actions lessens, and evaluations of them become less favorable.

Within therapeutic settings, while not being able to demonstrate causality,[4] we would like to suggest the following as a possible sequence of events. First, the therapist's theoretical orientation influenced his or her choice of therapeutic interventions.[5] The use of these interventions, in turn, affected therapists' attributions about whether the patient was internally or externally controlled (patient responsibility). And, finally, attributions about control influenced therapists' evaluations of their patients.

Of course, it may be argued that the link between the techniques used by therapists and their attributions of control is obvious because the goal of dynamic techniques depends on patient autonomy and those of cognitive-behavior techniques do not. However, the consequences of these beliefs about patient autonomy are far from obvious. I do not know of any theoretical writings about psychotherapy that describe how the techniques of therapy will affect therapists' evaluations of their patients for better or worse.

More generally, the suggestion is that as more and more precise means of influencing behavior are developed by psychologists, social relations between users of psychological techniques and those being influenced by them may suffer. This outcome is paradoxical, since the goal of most psychologists is to help people. Yet as psychology develops technologies that increase the certainty that help can be given, psychologists' own attitudes toward their constituencies may sour. This is because behavior technologies promote the belief that those being helped are not responsible for the improvements that result. And as has been reported in the studies described in this chapter, and in other settings in which technology, inadvertently or deliberately, reduces the autonomy of people subject to its use (Kipnis, 1990), devaluation follows loss of autonomy.

It remains to be determined whether the findings reported here can be found in other areas of psychology in which validated behavior techniques are applied to solve practical problems. If such findings are obtained, then I would argue that the utility to control people through technology may lead to unanticipated, but predictable, changes in practitioners' conscious goals of doing good and helping people.

Notes

1. Full details of this research are given in Kipnis (1984b).

2. I wish to thank Willis Overton and Philip Kendall for their help in designing the questionnaire used in this study.

3. The purpose of this survey was to examine the relationship among the kinds of therapeutic techniques that were used, therapists attributions, and their evaluations of patients. Our generalizations, then, concern the relationship among the above variables. The low return rate and the sampling procedures that were used do not permit reliable statements about the beliefs of all therapists.

4. Although no causal explanations can be offered in this study, we have attempted to rule out several obvious alternate explanations of the findings. The reported findings were controlled for the severity of patients' psychological problems. The length of time patients were in therapy did not correlate significantly with the Index of Patient Responsibility or the Patient Evaluation Scale. Although not shown in this chapter, the findings were also controlled for patient educational level and therapists' experience, because both of these variables correlated with the Patient Evaluation Scale.

5. It has been found that the actual practice of therapy differs from the therapist's stated theoretical orientation (e.g., Fiedler, 1950; Luborsky, Woody, McLellan, O'Brien, & Rosenzweig, 1982). We found a modest relationship between the therapist's stated clinical orientation and the therapeutic interventions that he or she used. That is, a directive theoretical orientation correlated $r = .43$ ($p < .01$) with the use of cognitive-behavior interventions and $r = -.43$ ($p < .01$) with the use of dynamic interventions. Similarly, a nondirective theoretical orientation correlated positively with the use of dynamic interventions ($r = .26, p < .01$) and negatively ($r = -.37, p < .01$) with the use of cognitive-behavior techniques. An eclectic orientation also correlated positively with the use of dynamic interventions ($r = .24, p < .05$).

References

Braverman, H. (1974). *Labor and monopoly capital.* New York: Monthly Review Press.

Ellul, J. (1964). *The technological society.* New York: Knopf.

Faunce, W. A. (1981). *Problems of an industrial society.* New York: McGraw-Hill.

Fiedler, F. F. (1950). A comparison of therapists' relationships in psychoanalytic, non-directive, and Adlerian therapy. *Journal of Consulting Psychology, 14,* 436-445.

French, J.R.P., & Raven, B. (1959). The bases of social power. In D. Cartwright (Ed.), *Studies in social power* (pp. 150-157). Ann Arbor, MI: Institute of Social Research.

Galbraith, J. K. (1967). *The new industrial state.* Boston: Houghton Mifflin.

James, L. R., Gent, M. J., Hater, J. H., & Coray, K. (1979). Correlates of psychological influence. *Personnel Psychology, 32,* 563-587.

Kipnis, D. (1976). *The powerholders* (2nd ed.). Chicago: University of Chicago Press.

Kipnis, D. (1984a). The use of power in organizations and in interpersonal settings. In S. Oskamp (Ed.), *Applied social psychology annual, 5* (pp. 172-210). Beverly Hills, CA: Sage.

Kipnis, D. (1984b). Technology as a strategy of control. In S. B. Bacharach & E. J. Lawler (Eds.), *Sociology of organizations* (pp. 125-156). Greenwich, CT: JAI.

Kipnis, D. (1987). Psychology and behavioral technology. *American Psychologist, 42,* 30-36.

Kipnis, D. (1990). *Technology and power.* New York: Springer-Verlag.

Kipnis, D., Schmidt, S., & Wilkinson, I. (1980). Intraorganizational influence tactics. *Journal of Applied Psychology, 65,* 440-452.

Kipnis, D., Schmidt, S., Price, K., & Stitt, C. (1981). Why do I like thee? *Journal of Applied Psychology, 66,* 324-328.

London, P. (1976). *Behavior control.* New York: Harper & Row.

Luborsky, L., Woody, G., McLellan, A. T., O'Brien, C. P., & Rosenzweig, K. (1975). Can independent judges recognize different psychotherapies? *Journal of Clinical and Consulting Psychology, 50,* 49-62.

Pfeffer, J. (1978). *Organizational design.* Arlington Heights, IL: AHM Publishing.

Reiman, B. C., & Inzerilli, G. (1978). *Technology and organization: A review of major research findings.* West Berlin: West Germany.

Rogers, C. R., Gendlin, E. T., Kiesler, D. J., & Truax, C. R. (1967). *The therapeutic relation and its impact.* Madison, WI: University of Wisconsin Press.

Rousseau, D. M. (1978). Measures of technology as predictors of employee attitude. *Journal of Applied Psychology, 63,* 213-218.

Salancik, G. R., & Pfeffer, J. (1977, Winter). Who gets power and how they hold it: A strategic contingency model of power. *Organizational Dynamics,* pp. 22-35.

Sweet, A. A. (1984). The therapeutic relation in behavior therapy. *Clinical Psychology Review, 4,* 253-272.

Weiner, B. (1981). An attributionally based theory of motivation. In N. T. Feather (Ed.), *Expectations and emotions.* (pp. 163-204). Hillsdale, NJ: Lawrence Erlbaum.

PART IV

Work Group Norms and Outcomes

Introduction

John E. Sawyer

The work group holds immense influence over the behavior and productivity of individuals in most work settings. Indeed Hackman (1983) reviewed a number of studies which suggested that: group norms may have a greater influence on the individual's performance than the knowledge, skills, and abilities the individual brings to the work setting; participation in planning change facilitates acceptance of new procedures as group goals; and group identity can have a greater influence on productivity than working conditions. In order to understand the influences of groups on the behaviors and performance of individuals, and on the productivity of the group, we need to investigate the major organizing forces of the work group.

Behavior of individuals occurs within three conceptually independent subsystems (McGrath, 1983): the physical and technical environment; the social medium, or patterns of interpersonal relations; and the person or self system. The physical or technical environment is the stable conditions of the environment that place limitations and requirements on behavior. Much of the physical and technical environment makes up a portion of the ambient stimuli available to the group. Hackman (1983) defined ambient stimuli as "stimuli which potentially are available to all group members . . . whose availability is contingent only on group membership per se" (p. 1457). Much of the behavior of individuals and the group is controlled by the ambient stimuli. A new arrival to the group can infer much of what behaviors are appropriate from the ambient stimuli. Thus the physical and technical environment specify the task contents and the process demands of the task. As such the ambient stimuli make up aspects of the coin of the social exchange within the group (Hackman, 1983).

Discretionary stimuli, defined by Hackman (1983) as "stimulus which can be transmitted selectively to individual group members at the discretion of their peers" (p. 1458). Groups use discretionary stimuli to enforce norms and establish roles. Norms are patterns of interactive behavior which become mutually established within a group. Once established norms dictate how individuals should behave, and thus become rules for appropriate behavior in a given situation. Violations of norms are negatively sanctioned by members of the group. Some norms are general and apply to all members of a group in a wide variety of situations. Frequently these norms, while applying generally to all people and situations, control certain features of social behavior, such as resource allocation norms (McGrath, 1984). McGrath (1984) defined other norms as interactional norms, which define appropriate behavior for specific dyads in a class of situations, and situational norms, which define appropriate behavior specific to a class of situations.

A specific subset of norms are role expectations, which are rules for appropriate behavior of incumbents of specific roles within the group (McGrath, 1984). These roles are thus norms that define the functional differentiation of behavior among members of the group. They define who is responsible for doing what, when, and how (division of labor). Additionally, as McGrath (1984) pointed out, groups tend to develop expectations about patterns of roles so that it is clear who should and should not perform various kinds of behaviors. This functional differentiation afforded by clear role expectations allows for coordination and interdependent activity.

Although many approaches and variants on the development of roles have been proposed, much of the theoretical work on role differentiation is built on the concepts of the role episode model defined by Kahn, Wolfe, Quinn, and Snoek (1964) and elaborated by Katz and Kahn (1978). To summarize their role theory, members of an individual's social environment (role set) hold various expectations (role expectations). The communicated expectations of this role set constitute a sent role. In a work context Naylor, Pritchard, and Ilgen (1980) redefined role behavior as a set of products. Behaviors and acts result in products. It is those products that are evaluated by the person's role set. Thus for Naylor et al. (1980) products are the basic unit of measured behavior. Products become relevant aspects of a given role "if the product of a focal person is evaluated by either the focal person or some specified other" (p. 121). The relevance of a product is thus defined by an evaluation process. A contingency can be viewed as the weight that reflects the degree of relevance of the individual product to the evaluation of the observer (either self or other) (Naylor et al., 1980).

It is the dynamic combination of ambient stimuli, discretionary stimuli, norms, and roles that inform the individual of the particular behaviors or products required in a given context. In addition to informing the individual of expected behaviors, these stimuli and norms allow for the coordination of group members on tasks that require interdependent activity. Established norms define for each group member what he or she should and should not do vis a vis other group members. They also allow co-workers to know what behaviors others will carry out with respect to task activities.

Although it is true that these aspects of group life control and direct individual behavior, individual behavior cannot be aggregated to describe the outcomes of the group. More often than not the outcomes and products of the group are not completely reflected in any aggregate of individual behavior. McGrath (1986) argued that we need to study groups at the group level of analysis. Because of the influence on the coordinative capacity and interdependence characteristic of most work groups, we must deal with the group as an intact social system which exists within a larger system (e.g., the organization) and interacts with other social systems (e.g., other work groups). Steiner (1972) argued that the group is a system, noting that individuals are often quite different when interacting in a group than when alone. Actions of individuals are shaped by the interdependencies within the group. When we look at groups we often see only individuals and their behaviors. However, collective action involves systematic patterning of member behavior. It is this patterning that makes the outcome of group action a very different construct than the aggregation of the action of individual members of the group. The group process insures that, except in the most rudimentary of groups, working on the simplest of tasks, that the gestalt of the group function cannot be described by the aggregate of the individuals in the group.

Both of the chapters in this section recognize the basic principle of group output. For both of these approaches the level of analysis is truly the group. Although role theory tends to be interpreted as an individual level impact of group norm setting, these approaches suggest that the interactions within the group are best measured by the outputs of the group rather than the outputs of individual group members.

Chapter 10, by Pritchard and Watson, embraces the need for group research and intervention to be directed at the group level of analysis. Pritchard's procedure for measuring group productivity is based on the Naylor et al. (1980) conceptualization of roles as contingencies relating products to evaluations. However, Pritchard and Watson explicitly recognize that the output of the group is not a simple aggregate of the outcomes of group members. In their discussion of the definition of productivity, they note that psychologists have previously confused individual performance with group productivity and tried to talk about productivity as though it were performance. Their procedure provides a method of scaling the outputs of the group in terms of group effectiveness. The Productivity Measurement and Enhancement System (ProMES) discussed in Chapter 10 has the advantages that: (a) it is truly a group level measurement, (b) it incorporates efficiency in that indicators can be scaled in terms of input/output ratios, (c) all indicators are scaled in a common metric of effectiveness, (d) the procedure allows for the inclusion of non-linearities in the importance of indicators for group effectiveness, and (e) the procedure allows both comparisons across groups in a common single metric as well as feedback on group achievement on each of the indicators.

Pritchard and Watson report productivity increases up to 75% when ProMES was used to provide feedback and guide goal setting and incentives. They also offer some compelling suggestions for the use of the ProMES system for the investigation of group productivity, including an example of how it might be used in laboratory research with groups performing complex tasks. In this setting one valuable strength is the ability to compare groups with a common metric that is conceptually and operationally at the group level of analysis.

The chapter that follows, by Goodman and Shah, also focuses on the group as the level of analysis. Group outcomes considered in the two studies they report include the frequency of accidents in the group and group productivity. The focus of Goodman and Shah's analysis is familiarity as an independent variable in group functioning. They define *familiarity* as specific knowledge a group member holds about the configuration of work in a particular group or setting.

Familiarity as a construct embraces all aspects of work group norms. First, familiarity includes contextual variables such as the technology and task demands and constraints. These were considered earlier in this introduction as ambient stimuli in Hackman's formulation. In the mining examples that Goodman and Shah discuss, the ambient stimuli include the physical characteristics of the mine section in which the work is being conducted and the machinery involved in the specific mining task. Familiarity also embraces the specific roles of the miners, whether they are operating the miner, the roof bolter, or the shuttle car system. Also included are the work norms and habits of the fellow work crew members. Goodman and Shah document dramatic effects of lack of familiarity resulting from absences, job, mine section, and crew assignment on the number of accidents and on crew output in terms of tons of coal mined.

In addition to reporting two exemplary studies relating familiarity to group outcomes, Goodman and Shah explore the domains and properties of familiarity as well as the processes that create familiarity. They place the concept of familiarity in the context of the literature on work group development which covers such concepts as group longevity, member seniority and job experience, expertise, managerial succession, and newcomer socialization. They then discuss the development of familiarity and practical implications. They conclude by raising a number of questions for further research such as the intersection of domains, properties and processes of familiarity, and concerns about the links between familiarity and group outcomes.

In combination, these two chapters provide conceptual and methodological contributions to the study of group norms, outputs, and productivity. Goodman and Shah elucidate an important group-level phenomena, familiarity, and relate it to several aspects of group norms and processes. Pritchard and Watson provide a useful tool in the study of group outputs as well as a feedback tool to help groups function more effectively. These approaches should prove useful for enhancing future research on work groups.

References

Hackman, J. R. (1983). Group influences on individuals. In M. D. Dunnette (Ed.), *Handbook of industrial and organizational psychology* (pp. 1455-1526). New York: John Wiley.

Kahn, R. L., Wolfe, D. M., Quinn, R. P., & Snoek, J. D. (1964). *Organizational stress: Studies in role conflict and ambiguity.* New York: John Wiley.

Katz, D., & Kahn, R. L. (1978). *The social psychology of organizations* (2nd ed.). New York: John Wiley.

McGrath, J. E. (1983). Stress and behavior in organizations. In M. D. Dunnette (Ed.), *Handbook of industrial and organizational psychology* (pp. 1351-1396). New York: John Wiley.

McGrath, J. E. (1984). *Groups: Interaction and performance.* Englewood Cliffs, NJ: Prentice-Hall.

McGrath, J. E. (1986). Studying groups at work: Ten critical needs for theory and practice. In P. S. Goodman & Assoc. (Eds.), *Designing effective work groups* (pp. 362-391). San Francisco: Jossey-Bass.

Naylor, J. C., Pritchard, R. D., & Ilgen, D. R. (1980). *A theory of behavior in organizations.* New York: Academic Press.

Steiner, I. D. (1972). *Group process and productivity.* New York: Academic Press.

10 Understanding and Measuring Group Productivity

Robert D. Pritchard
Margaret D. Watson

Productivity is a topic that has received a great deal of national attention lately. NBC produced a White Paper on productivity in 1980. A White House Conference on Productivity was conducted in 1984. In addition, productivity was formally identified as a national priority in 1985 when President Reagan asked for congressional support for a government-wide program to improve productivity in the federal government.

Although there are probably many reasons for this pervasive concern, the primary reason appears to be that productivity directly impacts our lives at the national level, the industry or firm level, and at a personal level. At the national level, productivity influences both economic and non-economic outcomes (Fleishman, 1982; Kendrick, 1984; Kopelman, 1986; Mahoney, 1988; Mali, 1978; Riggs & Felix, 1983; Tuttle, 1983). For example, improving productivity affects inflation by offsetting increases in the costs of producing goods. In addition, it allows us to move toward becoming a world of plenty while using fewer of our societal resources. At the industry or individual firm level, increased productivity leads to reduced prices, which in turn lead to an improved market position relative to the competition (Craig & Harris, 1973; Kendrick, 1984; Tuttle, 1983). At the individual level, increased productivity can lead to a higher quality of life. Equally important, people want to be productive. It is a central component of self-fulfillment and self-respect.

The importance of productivity can also be seen by the amount of psychological research done on the topic. Over the eight-year period from 1974 to 1982 an average of 70 studies on the topic of productivity were published each year. In the six-year period from 1983 to 1989 the number of studies on productivity doubled. This represents a substantial investment in productivity research.

Although much of this research focuses on individuals, there is considerable interest in group performance and productivity as well (e.g., Ingham, Levinger, Graves, & Peckham, 1972; Kerr, 1983; Kerr & Bruun, 1983; Latané, Williams, & Harkins, 1979; Locke, Shaw, Saari, & Latham, 1981; Nadler, 1979; Rowe, 1981; Steiner, 1972; Williams, Harkins, & Latané, 1981; Woodman & Sherwood, 1980; Worchel, Hart, & Butemeyer, 1989; Zaccaro, 1984). This is certainly appropriate because so much of the work done in our organizations is done by groups. The focus of this chapter is on group productivity. We first will discuss the conceptualization of group productivity, some issues in the literature, and then present an approach to its measurement.

Understanding Group Productivity

To the casual observer, the concept of productivity seems quite straightforward. However, productivity is not an easy concept to define (Pritchard, 1990a). It has been defined by terms as diverse as output, performance, motivation, efficiency, effectiveness, production, profitability, cost/effectiveness, competitiveness, work quality, and what a new product will enable you to increase if you buy it. To add to the confusion, each of these terms has been applied to every possible level of analysis, ranging from individuals to countries. This means that measures as conceptually distinct as number of components inspected by a given employee and the adjusted gross national product of France divided by total employee labor hours have been used as measures of the same concept, productivity.

When we deal with *group* productivity, the same confusion exists. What we mean by "group" is fairly clear, but we still need to deal with what productivity for the group means. It turns out that we in psychology have been quite casual in how we use the term. In fact, psychologists have been criticized (Tuttle, 1983) for simply taking our usual dependent variables (output or performance) and substituting the word "productivity." The problem with this practice is that productivity is *not* the same thing as output or performance.

When psychologists have developed a precise conceptualization of the term, they most often define productivity as efficiency or a combination of efficiency and effectiveness (Balk, 1975; Craig & Harris, 1973; Ilgen & Klein, 1988; Mali, 1978; Muckler, 1982; Pritchard, 1990b; Tuttle, 1981). An *efficiency measure* is a ratio of inputs to outputs. The number of computers a group assembles divided by the number of personnel hours used to assemble them is an efficiency measure. The dollar value of these computers divided by the cost of the labor to assemble them would also be an efficiency measure. *Effectiveness measures* are ratios of output relative to goal or expectation. The number of computers assembled divided by the number expected to be completed would be an effectiveness measure.

Thus, when applied to the group level of analysis, productivity is an index of the output of the group relative to inputs (efficiency), relative to goals (effectiveness), or relative to both. In other words, a clear conceptualization of group productivity includes the use of group-based measures of both efficiency and effectiveness.

In addition, the concept of group productivity more explicitly acknowledges that the functioning of a group typically requires interdependence between individuals to achieve its objectives. Because of this interdependence, the productivity of the group is not the simple sum of the performances of the individuals involved. Productivity also includes factors such as how well they cooperate with each other, how well the personnel are coordinated and managed, the availability of needed resources, and how well priorities are set so that objectives are reached.

Research on Group Productivity

With this conceptualization of group productivity in mind, we now turn to the psychological research on group productivity. When this literature on group productivity is examined, several things stand out. First, there is very little psychological research on *productivity*. Most of the work deals with output in terms of number of units produced or performance as measured by ratings (Guzzo, 1988). Productivity as measured by efficiency or effectiveness is rarely used.

A second striking feature of the literature is the lack of work with groups. Much of this research has focused on the productivity of individuals. For example, feedback, goal setting, incentives, and performance measurement are topics that are often investigated with some measure of productivity as the dependent variable. A review of the literature on these topics indicates that they are usually evaluated at the individual level (Pritchard, Jones, Roth, Stuebing, & Ekeberg, 1988). Further confirmation of this focus on the individual is provided by examining the list of operational definitions of productivity provided in Katzell and Guzzo (1983). In that review of the psychological literature on productivity, productivity was defined as (a) worker output, such as quality of work, quantity of work, and cost-effectiveness; (b) worker withdrawal behaviors, such as turnover and absenteeism; and (c) disruptions, such as accidents on the job. Most of these indicators were measured at the individual level of analysis.

A third aspect of the literature is that the tasks used in laboratory and field studies, whether individual or group, are frequently very simple ones. The majority of studies use tasks or jobs where everyone does only one thing, everyone does the same thing, there is little or no interdependence, and a measure of output is readily available.

The problem with using such simple jobs and tasks in our research is that most people in actual organizations do work that is more complex than this. In the majority of jobs, each person does many things, different individuals in a group do very different things, the members of the group work closely with each other in an interdependent fashion, and there are no ready measures of performance.

The use of such simple jobs/tasks in the literature has very important implications. First, much of the research in our field has limited applicability when it comes to its impact on productivity in ongoing organizations. It is not done on the types of jobs that are typical of such organizations. The generalizability of our findings based on such simple jobs to the more prevalent complex jobs is unclear.

Another implication is that the interdependence between members of the work group in the typical job means that measures of productivity must be group-based measures. From a practical standpoint, it is impossible to separate out the contributions of each individual when the members must work interdependently to do the work. Furthermore, if one takes the point of view that the output of the whole is greater than the sum of the parts, we would not want to try to separate out individual contributions, even if we could (Steiner, 1972).

The question that comes to mind is why has the literature evolved to this state. Why have we (a) used output or performance as a synonym for productivity, (b) focused on individuals, and (c) used simple tasks? The answers are not hard to find. The conceptualization of productivity as output or performance was a natural extension of psychological research. When declining U.S. productivity became such an important issue in the 1970s, psychologists, like many other disciplines, felt they had something to contribute to improving productivity. Their approach was to apply what they knew to the area of productivity. What they knew was primarily things that influenced output or performance. Thus, they simply renamed their variables in a good-faith attempt to make an impact on an important national priority.

The focus on simple tasks and on individuals rather than groups results from a more pragmatic factor. It is easier to use measures of individuals than groups, it is easier to use simple tasks than complex ones, and it is easier to use situations where simple measures are readily available than to develop new, more complex ones. This is not meant to imply that we only do easy research. Possibly a better way to put it is that our conceptualization of productivity had not yet matured to the point where we thought of it as complexly as we do now. In addition, ways of measuring productivity in complex groups had not been fully developed, so using such groups was not a viable option.

To improve this state of affairs in productivity research we need a way of measuring it in complex groups. The remainder of this chapter describes one method for measuring productivity in such groups. We will first describe how the system works and then summarize empirical evaluations of it. Next, we will discuss possible contributions to the group productivity literature that could be made using such a methodology.

The Productivity Measurement and Enhancement System (ProMES)

There are a number of methods that have been proposed to measure productivity (Craig & Harris, 1973; Kendrick, 1984; Mali, 1978; Riggs & Felix, 1983; Tuttle & Weaver, 1986). The method to be presented here is termed the Productivity Measurement and Enhancement System, or ProMES (Pritchard, 1990a; Pritchard, Jones, Roth, Stuebing, & Ekeberg, 1989). Its major conceptual base is the view of behavior in organizations developed by Naylor, Pritchard, and Ilgen (1980). Using an expectancy theory approach, the basic premise of this theory (referred to hereafter as N-P-I) is that behavior produces specific products and that individuals will be motivated to the extent they are able to perceive a connection between their behavior, the resulting consequences of their behavior, how these consequences are evaluated by the organization, and ultimately the valued outcomes that result from this evaluation. In addition, N-P-I states that it is possible to determine the relationship between the amount of the product produced and how that amount is evaluated. These functional relationships are called product to evaluation contingencies in the theory. The individual's role in the organization is conceptualized as the set of these product to evaluation contingencies.

When Pritchard and his colleagues (Pritchard et al., 1988, 1989) applied N-P-I theory to the problems of measuring productivity, a new approach was developed. This new method not only allowed for the measurement of productivity, it suggested ways that productivity information could be optimally fed back to employees to help improve performance.

Developing ProMES

The development of ProMES is done in a series of steps that start with identifying the primary objectives and end with providing productivity information to the group in the form of a written feedback report that they use to improve their productivity. In order to illustrate these steps, an example will be presented. This example involves a field setting, using a team that is responsible for the final steps in manufacturing electronic printed circuit boards for aircraft. A more detailed description of the ProMES development process can be found in Pritchard (1990a).

Step 1. Develop Products

First, the organization's *products* must be identified. Products are the important objectives that the group is expected to accomplish. Products may consist of services, tangible items, or a combination of the two. This identification of the group's products is done by a team typically composed of supervisors, representative incumbents, and a facilitator. This design team meets and, through a process of group discussion and consensus, develops the list of products. Assume that the design team identified the following products for the assembly group:

1. Maintain high production.
2. Make high-quality boards.
3. Maintain high attendance.

Step 2. Develop Indicators

The next step is to determine a method for measuring how well each product is being accomplished. These measures are called *indicators.* They are typically quantitative, objective measures, but can also be other types of measures such as customer attitude measures. Although products must have at least one indicator, they are not limited to one. The same design team identifies the indicators through group discussion and consensus. Assume that the design team developed the following list of indicators for the three products.

1. Maintain high production
   a. Percentage of boards completed. Number of boards completed, divided by the number of boards received.
   b. Meeting production priorities. Number of high-priority boards completed, divided by the number needed.
2. Make highest quality boards possible
   a. Inspections passed. Percentage of boards passing inspection.
3. Maintain high attendance
   a. Attendance. Total hours worked out of the maximum hours possible.

At this stage, the design team presents the list of products and indicators to upper management for review and approval. Once approval is obtained, the design team can begin the next step.

Step 3. Develop Contingencies

The next step is to determine the *contingencies,* or the relationships between the amount of the indicator and how that amount will be evaluated. Figure 10.1 shows the general form of a contingency. The horizontal axis represents the amount of the indicator ranging from the worst possible level to the best possible level. The vertical axis depicts the different levels of effectiveness for the indicator. This scale ranges

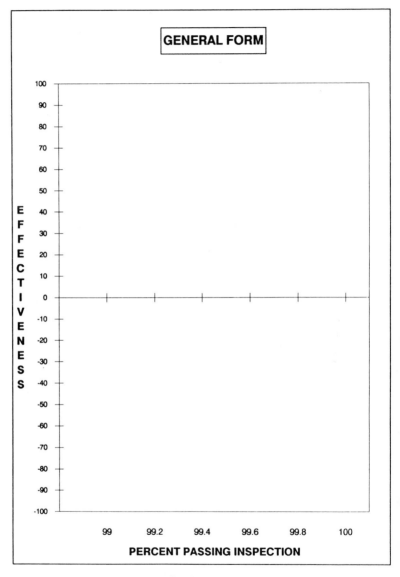

Figure 10.1. General Form of a Contingency

from +100 (maximum effectiveness) to −100 (minimum effectiveness). The zero point represents the expected level of effectiveness. It is defined as the level of the indicator that is neither good nor bad. The basic idea is to identify the function that defines what level of the indicator it takes to achieve what level of effectiveness.

An example of a completed contingency for the quality indicator, percentage of boards passing inspection, is shown in Figure 10.2. A series of specific steps are used to develop these contingencies. The first step is for the design team to identify the best and worst level of the indicator that is realistically possible. In the example, the design team has identified the best possible percentage of boards passing inspection as 100%. This indicates that the team believes it is realistically possible for all the boards to pass inspection. The minimum, or worst feasible level of the indicator, was seen as 99% of the boards passing inspection. Performance at or near this level would be seen by the design team as a major production problem.

Once the team has identified the maximum and minimum possible levels of output for each indicator, their next task is to identify how different levels of the indicator will correspond to different levels of effectiveness. In essence, the group is asked to scale the amounts of the indicators in terms of what level of effectiveness each level represents. This is accomplished by breaking down the scaling task into discrete steps. The design team first determines the zero point, the expected level of the indicator. In the example, this is an inspection passing rate of 99.4%. Next, the design team determines the effectiveness values that correspond to the maximum and minimum indicator levels. In the example these are +70 and −80. Finally, the effectiveness values for the rest of the indicator levels are identified. These steps are explained fully in Pritchard (1990b).

This scaling process is done with all of the indicators so that each indicator has a contingency. Contingencies for all the indicators in the example are shown in Figure 10.3. Once all the indicators are scaled and reviewed for accuracy by higher management, the contingency set is complete.

There are two very important aspects to notice about contingencies. First, the overall slope of the contingency expresses the relative importance of the indicator. Steep slopes are produced for indicators that are very important to the functioning of the unit. This is reflected in the fact that a steep slope implies that small variations in the amount of the indicator will result in large variations in effectiveness. Indicators with

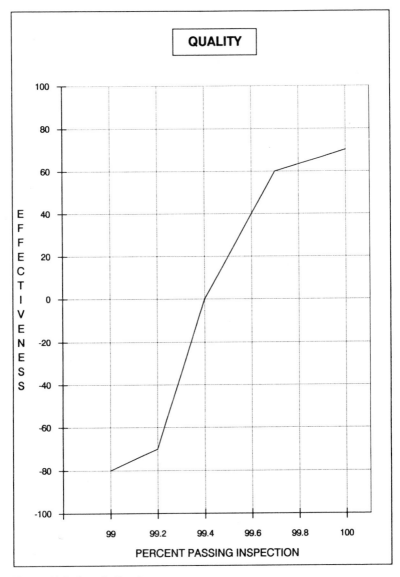

Figure 10.2. Sample Contingency

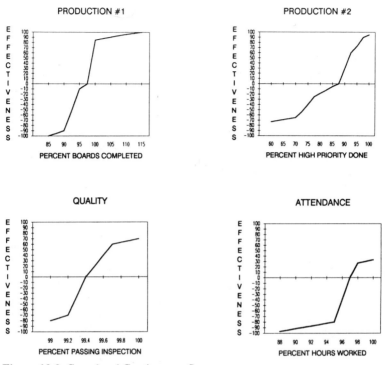

Figure 10.3. Completed Contingency Set

flatter slopes are less important to the functioning of the unit in that variations in these indicators will have a smaller impact on total effectiveness. Thus, the differential importance of the indicators is captured by the contingencies.

The second important aspect of contingencies is their nonlinearity. This is reflected in the contingency in Figure 10.2. It shows that when the number of boards passing inspection is above the neutral point of 99.4% there is a large increase in effectiveness. However, once the passing rate reaches 99.7% further increases do not represent as great a change. This nonlinearity is important because a given amount of improvement at the low end of the measure may not have the same effect at the high end of the measure. It is quite common for improvements in the middle range of the indicator to result in large improvements in effectiveness, whereas improvements at the high end of the indicator result in smaller improvement in effectiveness. In other words, a point of diminishing returns is reached. Once a certain level of productivity is reached, it may be more beneficial to focus on another area rather than to continue to work on an area that is already very good. For instance, if our example unit has completed a very high percentage of boards, it may be better to work on attendance, even though attendance is not as important overall.

Step 4. Create the Feedback Report

The fourth step in developing ProMES is to create a formal feedback report. Once indicator data are collected, effectiveness scores can be determined based on the contingencies for each indicator. As can be seen in Figure 10.3, if 99.8% of the group's boards pass inspection, they would achieve an effectiveness score of +62.

Continuing this process would result in an effectiveness value for each indicator. Once effectiveness values for each indicator are determined, they can be summed to determine the overall effectiveness score for that particular work group. This score represents the group's level of overall productivity. A score of zero means the group is meeting expectations; the higher the score is above zero, the greater they are exceeding expectations. This information is presented to the unit in a formal written feedback report that is presented to them on a regular basis.

Another overall measure that can be derived from the system is the group's percentage of maximum effectiveness. Maximum effectiveness is defined as the overall effectiveness score the group would receive if they were at the highest possible level on every indicator. The unit's actual overall effectiveness score for that period can be expressed as a percentage of this maximum.

For example, when we sum the maximum values for each of the indicators in our example we arrive at the total possible score of 310. Our example unit received a monthly score of +92. Thus, their percent of maximum score was 92/310, or 29.7%. The closer the unit is to 100%, the closer they are to performing at their maximum productivity level.

The advantage of the percent of maximum index is that it allows for the productivity of groups doing very different things to be compared. The group with the highest percentage of maximum score is the most productive work group. This comparison is valid even if the groups have different indicators, because the contingency process scales all indicators on a common metric, overall effectiveness. The comparison between different groups is then based on this common metric.

Advantages of ProMES

ProMES has certain unique features that allow it to address issues that are sometimes missed by other productivity measurement systems. First, ProMES can provide two very important measures of productivity, a *single index* of productivity as well as *subindices* of the important indicators of productivity. Subindices are necessary to allow personnel to see which aspects of productivity are good versus those that need improving. The single index, on the other hand, allows the effectiveness of a complex unit to be summed into one easily communicable number. This number helps management, supervisors, and job incumbents gain an overall sense of how the unit is doing (Felix & Riggs, 1983; Rowe, 1981; Tuttle & Weaver, 1986). Thus, ProMES allows for an evaluation to be made at the level of subindices or at the level of overall effectiveness.

This *feedback* aspect of ProMES is important in improving productivity because it increases the amount and quality of the feedback, and because it changes the focus of that feedback. There is a great deal of evidence to suggest that more frequent, specific, and accurate feedback enhances performance (Annett, 1969; Ilgen, Fisher, & Taylor, 1979; Ivancevich, Donnelly, & Lyon, 1970; Pritchard, Montagno, & Moore, 1978). Such feedback is possible with the use of the formal ProMES feedback system. This is seen as much more effective than just providing descriptive information on how much was done (Dockstader, Nebeker, & Shumate, 1977; Hammond & Summers, 1972). Research also indicates that the focus of feedback needs to be on positive aspects of performance (Feather, 1968; Ilgen & Hamstra, 1972). Many personnel have reported that before ProMES was implemented, they received feedback only when there were problems. Focusing on positive feedback should lead to improved motivation because it helps employees increase their sense of competence.

The feedback in ProMES seems to have other effects as well. The information allows group members to be more accountable for their work, enables them to set production goals, and encourages them to take a proactive approach to managing their own performance. These benefits arise from the specificity and the frequency of the feedback (Dockstader et al., 1977; Ivancevich et al., 1970; Pritchard & Montagno, 1978; Simpson, 1972). With ProMES, the connection between the actions of the unit and their level of productivity is improved. This allows personnel to see how their efforts have increased productivity. In addition, the unit cannot ignore the concrete performance history that is provided by the regular measurement of productivity and the public nature of the data. This fact increases their accountability and encourages personnel to find positive solutions to production problems while reducing their tendency to make excuses.

The existence of this information also encourages the group to set goals, a practice that in and of itself should increase motivation (e.g., Latham & Yukl, 1975; Locke et al., 1981; Tubbs, 1986). A system like ProMES makes it easier to have a formal goal-setting program. This is the result of having a single index of productivity upon which to set goals. In addition, the feedback is presented in a manner that helps personnel to know which areas to focus on as they set their goals. The system indicates which activities are the most important and provides the basis for the early identification and diagnosis of problems. With the feedback reports, personnel are able to see when productivity is starting to deteriorate. Problems can therefore be dealt with before they become serious.

Another advantage of the system is its *validity*. Validity is an essential aspect of any successful productivity measurement system (Campbell, 1977; Craig & Harris, 1973; Duerr, 1974; Muckler, 1982; Schmidt & Kaplan, 1971). It is quite a challenging task, however, to determine the validity of productivity systems. The main problem is that there is no criterion against which to compare the productivity measure. If the unit has a good criterion for productivity, it would be pointless to develop another. Even if a second criterion was developed, which of the two should be the ultimate criterion is not clear. If the new system does not correlate with the old, is that because the new system has considerable error or because the old one does? Or, does the difference result from the inclusion of some important functions of the unit in one system but not in the other?

Part of the problem is that productivity measurement is an operational definition of organizational policy. Thus, a key validity issue is how well the measurement system captures the policy for that unit. Assessing this is not an easy task.

Because of these problems, the validity of a productivity measurement system typically is limited to including the concepts of completeness, accuracy, differential importance, and nonlinearity. ProMES is able to address more of these aspects of validity than many other productivity measurement systems.

Completeness is the first component of validity. A measurement system must include all important aspects of a unit's work in order to be effective (Campbell, 1977; Craig & Harris, 1973; Duerr, 1974; Muckler, 1982; Tuttle, Wilkinson, & Matthews, 1985). In ProMES, these aspects become the products and indicators. The products are determined through careful examination by a subgroup of personnel, who are encouraged to cover all pertinent job tasks. To ensure completeness, products are also reviewed by organizational management.

Another important part of the validity of a system is its *accuracy* (Ghiselli, Campbell, & Zedeck, 1981; Nunnally, 1978; Thorndike, 1982; Wiggins, 1980). ProMES utilizes different methods to ensure accuracy. First, the selection of products and indicators is the result of the extensive involvement of organizational personnel in the system development. In addition, the management review helps to ensure accuracy.

Maintaining the *relative importance* of the different functions in the unit is another aspect of validity (Schmidt & Kaplan, 1971). The contingencies provide the ability to do this. Relative importance is reflected in their overall slopes, and this is carried through in the effectiveness calculations.

In order for a system to be valid it must also allow measures to be either *linear* or *nonlinear* (Campbell, 1977; Seashore, 1972). Forcing measures to be linear when this does not reflect policy is a serious problem. Contrary to most measurement systems, ProMES allows for the development of nonlinear contingencies.

The next unique feature of ProMES is its *flexibility*. A system needs to be flexible enough to respond to changes in organizational priorities (Pritchard et al., 1988, 1989). A change in either the external or the internal environment could cause such changes to arise. ProMES is capable of dealing with such changes. Most often, a change in contingencies is all that is necessary. In the example used above of the printed circuit boards, if attendance increased in importance, the contingency for that indicator could simply be changed to reflect this. If required, products and indicators could also be modified to deal with more extensive changes.

Another unique feature of ProMES as a measurement system is its ability to directly *compare different units* even though they do different things. One effect of this direct comparison is that it allows for competition across units based on each unit's percent of maximum productivity (Pritchard et al., 1988, 1989). In situations where such comparisons have been made (e.g., Pritchard et al., 1989), this competition was clearly present between units.

Finally, in the development of ProMES the process of *roles clarification* takes place. This is done through the process of developing, refining, and obtaining approval for the system. This developmental process helps personnel to more fully understand their roles (e.g., Rizzo, House, & Lirtzman, 1970). Through the discussions to develop the system, unit personnel determine what their objectives should be. Disagreements surface and are then resolved. Expected output levels are discussed and consensus is achieved. The final step is the review of these decisions by higher management. They are debated and a formally approved system results. At the completion of this process, the units have a much clearer picture of what their objectives are, what they should be focusing on to achieve these objectives, what is expected of them in each area, and what is good and bad productivity. This process of role clarification should have positive motivational effects in and of itself.

Research with ProMES

The original evaluation of ProMES was conducted in a multi-year study at an Air Force base (Pritchard et al., 1989). That study included five units, four of which were sections of a large warehouse; the fifth was a unit that repaired electronic equipment. Each of the five units developed their own ProMES system.

Baseline data were collected on the new measures for a total of nine months. Following the baseline period, each unit received monthly feedback from the system for five months. Group goal setting was then added for five months and incentives, in the form of time off from work, for five months.

Increases in productivity were considerable while overtime was substantially decreased. Productivity increased by 50% over baseline during feedback, 74% over baseline during goal setting, and 75% over baseline during incentives. Control groups showed no change or only a small increase over the same time period. The strength and pattern of results was consistent for the five individual units. In addition, surveys indicated that both the incumbents and managers were pleased with the system and the information provided by it and that work attitudes either improved or stayed the same.

Although these results sound quite impressive, one might wonder how they compare with other productivity improvement systems. No research has been done that directly compares ProMES to other systems. However, effect sizes can be calculated to determine how these results compare to the results of other productivity interventions. Effect sizes were calculated using the same procedure used in the Guzzo, Jette, and Katzell (1985) meta-analysis of productivity interventions.

To accomplish this, effect sizes were calculated relative to baseline. That is, for the feedback condition, values calculated were the mean difference in overall effectiveness between baseline and feedback divided by the pooled within-group standard deviation of baseline and feedback. This produced an effect size for each of the five sections for feedback. The mean effect size was 2.44. The effect sizes reported by Guzzo et al. for different studies using feedback to enhance productivity ranged from .08 to .62, with a mean of .35. Thus, the mean effect size using ProMES was 3.9 times greater than the largest effect size for feedback reported by Guzzo et al. More detail on the effect sizes can be found in Pritchard et al. (1988).

Since the original research using ProMES, the system has been successfully implemented in a variety of civilian settings in the U.S. and Europe. These include the assembly line production of batteries, the manufacturing of cardboard boxes, the manufacturing of consumer products, electronics manufacturing, a chemical processing facility, a unit of life insurance agents and their managers, a group that specializes in the sales and repair of office machinery, a photocopier maintenance unit, an in-house corporate library research unit, and a bar in a restaurant.

The Implications for Using ProMES to Investigate Group Productivity

ProMES has been successful in identifying and measuring productivity in a variety of organizational settings. In addition, ProMES provides an approach for addressing the problems that have interfered with efforts to investigate group productivity that were identified at the beginning of this chapter.

First, ProMES uses a definition of productivity that is more consistent with the literature. In the example above, productivity is output relative to standard, that is, effectiveness. However, it is also easy to incorporate efficiency by using indicators that are efficiency measures, such as printed circuit boards produced per labor hour. In this way, both efficiency and effectiveness concepts are incorporated into the final productivity measure, overall effectiveness.

In addition, ProMES can readily be used with groups doing complex tasks. Through the use of multiple indicators combined in a way that preserves differential importance and nonlinearities, the system can be used with the more complex tasks typical of most work. In addition, because the products and indicators are group based, they can capture the interdependencies that exist between members of the group.

ProMES in Laboratory Settings

The example used above was a field setting. However, ProMES can also be used in laboratory studies. The only difficulty is that the design of the system requires significant knowledge of the task. Developing products and indicators require knowledge of what the group needs to do and what would be good measures of these objectives. Developing contingencies requires knowledge of the levels of performance on each indicator that correspond to different levels of effectiveness. This level of task knowledge will not be known by subjects in the typical laboratory experiment.

There are ways to overcome this problem. The first is for the researcher to develop ProMES for the task. This is quite feasible for the researcher to do since he or she has developed the task. With this task expertise, he or she develops the products and indicators. Contingencies can then be developed, either from expectations of productivity or from pilot data with the task. Another alternative is for the subjects to develop the system. They could work on the task for a period of time, then develop the system themselves. This would require more subject time than the typical laboratory study, but would be feasible in some situations. Another possibility is to use some combination where, for example, the experimenter develops products and indicators and the subjects develop contingencies. Finally, one group of subjects could develop the system to be used as the measurement and feedback system for other groups.

A Laboratory Example

Using ProMES in the laboratory allows for tasks with features not often seen in productivity research to be included. This will be demonstrated using a laboratory study conducted by Worchel et al. (1989).

Worchel et al. (1989) conducted a study to determine the effect of group interdependence on social loafing. They argued that social loafing was much more likely to occur in situations where the subjects were merely co-actors as opposed to a true group. The task used in this study was the construction of paper chains. Each person worked individually; although they were in the same room, partitions prevented them from viewing each other's work. Interdependence was manipulated through the instructions given the subjects. The dependent variable, productivity, was defined as aggregated output.

This task fits the questions being asked in the research, especially since individual performance must be identified in this study. However, suppose one wanted to use this task as a basis for a more complex one. Groups could be given some "orders" for chains that were higher priority, and the quality of the chains could be considered. To use ProMES, products, indicators, and contingencies would have to be developed. Based on the experimenters' ideas of the task or by using subjects as part of the design team, the following products and indicators might emerge.

1. Maintain high production
   a. Total number of chain links produced divided by the number of labor hours
   b. Percentage of high priority "orders" filled per work period
2. Maintain high quality
   a. Percentage of chains passing weight inspection. (Inspection involves suspending a weight from each 1-foot section of chain. If it breaks, it fails inspection.)
   b. Percentage of chains passing joint inspection. (Edges of the strips of paper used to make the chains must be aligned evenly. If any sections have links misaligned by more than 1/16 inch, that section does not pass inspection.)

Other work tasks could be included in addition to making chains. For example, the group could include the packaging of the chains. This could be accomplished by having the group pack "orders" of differing amounts of chains. They could assemble the cardboard boxes needed, pack the chains, and seal the boxes. Products and indicators for this activity might include the following.

3. Package material properly
   a. Number of "orders" packaged
   b. Number of boxes incorrectly assembled or sealed

This example demonstrates several features of actual work settings that could be included in the experimental task. First, the research could be designed to investigate the quality of production in addition to the quantity of production. Because most work settings require that employees maintain high levels of both quantity and quality, the inclusion of quality would increase the realism of the work task and therefore increase the generalizability of the research.

In addition, different people in the group are doing different tasks. Although there are many settings in which all employees complete the very same tasks, there are many more settings in which individuals perform different functions. Thus, using this type of task would increase the generalizability of the results. This added feature would also allow researchers to investigate how productivity would be effected by (a) having different employees engaged in different tasks and (b) rotating work tasks between the team members.

Having people working on different tasks in such a setting also creates interdependencies. Production and packaging personnel must coordinate their efforts and someone must identify which are the high-priority orders. If inspection of the chains and packaging is done by group personnel, this adds another level of required interdependency. Researchers could observe how the group members facilitate each other's work, how they relate to each other during conditions of high versus low demand, and how problems in one part of the team affect the other members of the team.

In addition to allowing the use of more realistic experimental tasks, ProMES allows the researcher to manipulate important group variables that have not often been studied in the past. For example, ProMES makes it possible to determine the impact of changing priorities on the group's productivity. Most employees would tell you that the priorities within their work group change quite rapidly. Although this is probably more common in organizations with a "fire-fighting" mentality, it is fairly common in most organizations. While it is assumed that the shifting of resources and energies required by priority changes would impact productivity, it has been very difficult in the past to actually measure this. ProMES provides the methodology necessary to doing so.

In the example used above, priorities could be addressed by switching the team from a quantity focus to a quality focus. This would be done by changing the overall slope of the quantity and quality contingencies, reporting this to the group, and using the revised contingencies for calculation of feedback data. This change in priorities would require that the team relate to each other and to their assigned tasks in a very different manner. Researchers could track the impact of these changes on behavior.

Also, the effect that providing more complete feedback has on motivation could be determined. Feedback has been shown to have a positive effect on productivity (Ilgen, Fisher, & Taylor, 1979; Pritchard, Montagno, & Moore, 1978). ProMES provides feedback on output of specific indicators (indicator data), evaluative data on how well this level of output meets expectations (effectiveness score for indicators), and overall effectiveness. In addition, it has a way of identifying the priorities that should be used to increase productivity (cf. Pritchard et al., 1989; Pritchard, 1990a). This allows for study of many different feedback questions such as the effects of evaluative versus non-evaluative feedback, the effects of part versus total feedback, and the effects of giving priority information.

Finally, having a system like ProMES allows for the investigation of other interventions. Manipulations like goal setting and incentives can more easily be done in a complex task under ProMES. If the task has multiple indicators, like in the laboratory example above, to do goal setting one must set goals on each indicator. Setting so many goals is cumbersome and hard to interpret. Also with incentives, a single index is very handy for the awarding of incentives. The productivity effects of other interventions like gainsharing, quality circles, and changing the work environment are much easier to assess with a single index of productivity.

Conclusions

This chapter has focused on the important topic of group productivity. Continually improving productivity is important in assuring the future of our economy, the stability of each individual industry and firm, and a sense of well-being for our citizens. We have reviewed some of the most important problems with this research area, and have suggested methods for addressing these problems.

First, we suggested that future productivity research must define productivity as efficiency and/or effectiveness ratios. Secondly, we suggested that future research must be designed to assess more complex, interdependent group settings. Because this is the state of the actual work world, research must do a better job of capturing these complexities. Without this kind of research, the field will be limited in its generalizability.

We suggested the methodology provided by ProMES as one solution to these problems. In addition to addressing the conceptual and design issues, ProMES has been demonstrated to be effective at both measuring and improving productivity. Thus, it may be a valuable resource to other researchers and practitioners.

References

Annett, J. (1969). *Feedback and human behavior.* Baltimore, MD: Penguin.

Balk, W. L. (1975, March-April). Technological trends in productivity measurement. *Public Personnel Management,* pp. 128-133.

Campbell, J. P. (1977). On the nature of organizational effectiveness. In P. S. Goodman, J. M. Pennings, & Associates (Eds.), *New perspectives on organizational effectiveness* (pp. 13-55). San Francisco: Jossey-Bass.

Craig, C. E., & Harris, R. C. (1973). Total productivity measurement at the firm level. *Sloan Management Review, 14*(3), 13-28.

Dockstader, S. L., Nebeker, D. M., & Shumate, E. C. (1977). *The effects of feedback and an implied standard on work performance* (NPRDC TR 77-45), San Diego, CA: Navy Personnel Research and Development Center.

Duerr, E. C. (1974). The effect of misdirected incentives on employee behavior. *Personnel Journal, 53,* 890-893.

Feather, N. T. (1968). Change in confidence following success or failure as a predictor of subsequent performance. *Journal of Personality and Social Psychology, 9,* 38-46.

Felix, G. H., & Riggs, J. L. (1983). Productivity measurement by objectives. In W. B. Werther, Jr., W. A. Ruch, & L. McClure (Eds.), *Productivity through people* (pp. 349-356). St. Paul, MN: West.

Fleishman, E. A. (1982). Introduction. In M. D. Dunnette & E. A. Fleishman (Eds.), *Human performance and productivity: I. Human capability assessment* (pp. xv-xix). Hillsdale, NJ: Lawrence Erlbaum.

Ghiselli, E. E., Campbell, J. P., & Zedeck, S. (1981). *Measurement theory for the behavioral sciences.* San Francisco: Freeman.

Guzzo, R. A. (1988). Productivity research: Reviewing psychological and economic perspectives. In J. P. Campbell & R. J. Campbell (Eds.), *Productivity in organizations,* (pp. 63-81). San Francisco: Jossey-Bass.

Guzzo, R. A., Jette, R. D., & Katzell, R. A. (1985). The effects of psychologically based intervention programs on worker productivity: A meta-analysis. *Personnel Psychology, 38,* 275-291.

Hammond, K. R., & Summers, D. A. (1972). Cognitive control. *Psychological Review, 79,* 58-67.

Ilgen, D. R., Fisher, C. D., & Taylor, M. S. (1979). Consequences of individual feedback on behavior in organizations. *Journal of Applied Psychology, 64,* 349-371.

Ilgen, D. R., & Hamstra, B. W. (1972). Performance satisfaction as a function of the difference between expected and reported performance at five levels of reported performance. *Organizational Behavior and Human Performance, 7,* 359-370.

Ilgen, D. R., & Klein, H. J. (1988). Individual motivation and performance: Cognitive influences on effort and choice. In J. P. Campbell & R. J. Campbell (Eds.), *Productivity in organizations* (pp. 143-176). San Francisco: Jossey-Bass.

Ingham, A. G., Levinger, G., Graves, J., & Peckham, V. (1972). The Ringlemann effect: Studies of group sizes and group performance. *Journal of Experimental Social Psychology, 10,* 371-384.

Ivancevich, J. M., Donnelly, J. N., & Lyon, J. L. (1970). A study of the impact of management by objectives on perceived need satisfaction. *Personnel Psychology, 23,* 139-151.

Katzell, R. A., & Guzzo, R. A. (1983). Psychological approaches to productivity improvement. *American Psychologist, 38*(4), 468-472.

Kendrick, J. W. (1984). *Improving company productivity.* Baltimore: Johns Hopkins University Press.

Kerr, N. L. (1983). Motivation losses in small groups: A social dilemma analysis. *Journal of Personality and Social Psychology, 45*(4), 819-828.

Kerr, N. L., & Bruun, S. E. (1983). Dispensability of member effort and group motivation losses: Free-rider effects. *Journal of Personality and Social Psychology, 44*(1), 78-94.

Kopelman, R. E. (1986). *Managing productivity in organizations: A practical, people-oriented perspective.* New York: McGraw-Hill.

Latané, B., Williams, K., & Harkins, S. (1979). Many hands make light the work: The causes and consequences of social loafing. *Journal of Personality and Social Psychology, 37*(6), 822-832.

Latham, G. P., & Yukl, G. A. (1975). A review of research on the application of goal setting in organizations. *Academy of Management Journal, 18,* 824-845.

Locke, E. A., Shaw, K. N., Saari, L. M., & Latham, G. P. (1981). Goal setting and task performance: 1969-1980. *Psychological Bulletin, 90*(1), 125-152.

Mahoney, T. A. (1988). Productivity defined: The relativity of efficiency, effectiveness and change. In J. P. Campbell & R. J. Campbell (Eds.), *Productivity in organizations* (pp. 13-38). San Francisco: Jossey-Bass.

Mali, P. (1978). *Improving total productivity.* New York: John Wiley.

Muckler, F. A. (1982). Evaluating productivity. In M. D. Dunnette & E. A. Fleishman (Eds.), *Human performance and productivity: I. Human capability assessment* (pp. 13-47). Hillsdale, NJ: Lawrence Erlbaum.

Nadler, D. A. (1979). The effects of feedback on task group behavior: A review of the experimental research. *Organizational Behavior and Human Performance, 23,* 309-338.

Nunnally, J. C. (1978). *Psychometric theory* (2nd ed.). New York: McGraw-Hill.

Naylor, J. C., Pritchard, R. D., & Ilgen, D. R. (1980). *A theory of behavior in organizations.* New York: Academic Press.

Pritchard, R. D. (1990a). *Measuring and improving organizational productivity: A practical guide.* New York: Praeger.

Pritchard, R. D. (1990b). Organizational productivity. In M. D. Dunnette (Ed.), *The handbook of industrial/organizational psychology* (Vol. 4, 2nd ed.). Palo Alto, CA: Consulting Psychologists Press.

Pritchard, R. D., Jones, S. D., Roth, P. L., Stuebing, K. K., & Ekeberg, S. E. (1987). The feedback, goal setting, and incentives effects on organizational productivity. *Air Force Human Resources Laboratory Technical Report* (AFHRL-TR-87-3). Brooks AFB, TX: Occupation and Manpower Division, Air Force Human Resources Laboratory.

Pritchard, R. D., Jones, S. D., Roth, P. L., Stuebing, K. K., & Ekeberg, S. E. (1988). The effects of feedback, goal setting, and incentives on organizational productivity. *Journal of Applied Psychology Monograph Series, 73*(2), 337-358.

Pritchard, R. D., Jones, S. D., Roth, P. L., Stuebing, K. K., & Ekeberg, S. E. (1989). The evaluation of an integrated approach to measuring organizational productivity. *Personnel Psychology, 42*(1), 69-115.

Pritchard, R. D., & Montagno, R. V. (1978). The effects of specific vs. non-specific, and absolute vs. comparative feedback on performance and satisfaction. *Air Force Human Resources Laboratory Technical Report* (AFHRL-TR-78-12). Brooks AFB, TX: Occupation and Manpower Division, Air Force Human Resources Laboratory.

Pritchard, R. D., Montagno, R. V., & Moore, J. R. (1978). *Enhancing productivity through feedback and job design.* Air Force Human Resources Laboratory Technical Report (AFHRL-TR-78-44, AD-A061703). Brooks, AFB, TX: Occupation and Manpower Research Division, Air Force Human Resources Laboratory.

Riggs, J. L., & Felix, G. H. (1983). *Productivity by objectives.* Englewood Cliffs, NJ: Prentice-Hall.

Rizzo, J. R., House, R. J., & Lirtzman, S. I. (1970). Role conflict and ambiguity in complex organizations. *Administrative Science Quarterly, 15,* 150-163.

Rowe, D. L. (1981, November). How Westinghouse measures white-collar productivity. *Management Review,* pp. 42-47.

Schmidt, F. L., & Kaplan, L. B. (1971). Composite vs. multiple criteria: A review and resolution of the controversy. *Personnel Psychology, 24,* 419-439.

Seashore, S. E. (1972). *The measurement of organizational effectiveness.* Paper presented at the University of Minnesota, Minneapolis.

Simpson, W. E. (1972). Latency of locating lights and sounds. *Journal of Experimental Psychology, 93,* 169-175.

Steiner, I. D. (1972). *Group process and productivity.* New York: Academic Press.

Thorndike, R. L. (1982). *Applied psychometrics.* Dallas: Houghton Mifflin.

Tubbs, M. E. (1986). Goal setting: A meta-analytic examination of the empirical evidence. *Journal of Applied Psychology, 71,* 474-483.

Tuttle, T. C. (1981). *Productivity measurement methods: Classification, critique, and implications for the Air Force.* Air Force Human Resources Laboratory Report (AFHRL-TR-81-9, AD-A105 627). Brooks AFB, TX: Manpower and Personnel Division, Air Force Human Resources Laboratory.

Tuttle, T. C. (1983). Organizational productivity: A challenge for psychologists. *American Psychologist, 38,* 479-486.

Tuttle, T. C., & Weaver, C. N. (1986). *Methodology for generating efficiency and effectiveness measures (MGEEM): A guide for commanders, managers, and supervisors.* Air Force Human Resources Laboratory (Technical Paper 86-26). Brooks AFB, TX: Manpower and Personnel Division, Air Force Human Resources Laboratory.

Tuttle, T. C., Wilkinson, R. E., & Matthews, M. D. (1985). *Field test of the methodology for generating efficiency and effectiveness measures.* Air Force Human Resources Technical Report (AFHRL-TR-84-54, AD-A158 183). Brooks AFB, TX: Manpower and Personnel Division, Air Force Human Resources Laboratory.

Wiggins, J. S. (1980). *Personality and prediction: Principles of personality assessment.* Reading, MA: Addison-Wesley.

Williams, K., Harkins, S., & Latané, B. (1981). Identifiability as a deterrent to social loafing: Two cheering experiments. *Journal of Personality and Social Psychology, 40*(2), 303-311.

Woodman, R. W., & Sherwood, J. J. (1980). The role of team development in organizational effectiveness: A critical review. *Psychological Bulletin, 88,* 166-186.

Worchel, S., Hart, D., & Butemeyer, J. (1989). *Is social loafing a group phenomenon? The effect of member interdependence on work tasks.* Manuscript submitted for publication.

Zaccaro, S. J. (1984). Social loafing: The role of task attractiveness. *Personality and Social Psychology Bulletin, 10*(1), 99-106.

11 Familiarity and Work Group Outcomes

Paul S. Goodman
Samir Shah

This chapter examines the effect of familiarity on work group outcomes. Familiarity refers to the specific knowledge a group member holds about the unique configuration of work in a particular group. Outcomes refer to indicators of group effectiveness such as performance or satisfaction. A basic argument in this chapter is that low levels of familiarity reduce group effectiveness.

Some examples might be a way to sharpen the concept of familiarity. Several weeks ago when one of the authors was returning from a ski trip in Utah, there was a layover in Chicago and a change of planes was necessary to continue the trip to Pittsburgh. Subsequently, the connecting flight to Pittsburgh was cancelled because of mechanical failure. We were told to go to a different gate (and plane), but this flight was delayed because of mechanical problems. Once we were airborne, the captain provided the following explanation for the delay: The motor controlling the flaps was operating erratically, which would cause the plane to roll. Although this mechanical problem would not prevent a safe flight to Pittsburgh, it did represent a source of discomfort for the passengers. The captain added this key point: He had flown this plane with the bad flap earlier in the day; he was *familiar* with its unique problem and believed he could compensate and fly the plane to Pittsburgh without further mechanical work. (However, maintenance overruled him and delayed the flight until the flap problem was resolved.) Specific knowledge held by the captain and crew about the unique configuration of the plane (versus knowledge about how to fly a DC-9) can affect crew performance.

We have done a lot of research on coal mining crews. We selected this type of work group because in coal mining groups are highly interdependent, work in relative isolation from others, and there is a clearly definable group output. The coal mining environment is very dynamic. Changes in the equipment and conditions are persistent. From our observations of this work, it would appear that the knowledge of the specific conditions, equipment, and the people you coordinate with, should impact on group outcomes. In one crew we observed, there was a unique problem with the continuous mining equipment, it always tended to drift to the left. In another crew the roof was very fragile over a specific period of time. When we observed people doing the same job in different crews, we found they had developed unique work routines. Familiarity refers to the specific knowledge a group member holds about these unique configurations of work in a specific group setting. This specific knowledge (versus general knowledge about coal mining) should affect group outcomes.

The overall goal of this chapter is to delineate the concept of familiarity and argue that it is a neglected but important concept for group functioning. We approach this goal by: (a) conceptualizing familiarity in a work group context; (b) presenting the results from two studies designed to operationalize familiarity; (c) showing the links between familiarity and related concepts in the literature; (d) expanding the conceptualization of familiarity; and (e) discussing some practical implications.

Conceptualizing Familiarity

The Domains of Familiarity

We initially defined familiarity in terms of specific knowledge relevant to performing work tied to a specific setting. Prior to and during the transition to work, people acquire general knowledge specific to a role such as training to become a secretary, doctor, or manager. Familiarity goes beyond such general knowledge and refers to a specific body of knowledge unique to a particular work setting.

Our initial conceptualization of the domains of familiarity was derived from a view of technology composed of a system of machines, materials, environment, people, and jobs (Goodman, 1986). Familiarity refers to the knowledge of these components in a specific setting. Although a pilot may have the general body of knowledge needed to pilot a DC-9, each DC-9 has a unique configuration of machinery, people, jobs, and so forth that should affect effective crew performance. A coal miner might be certified to operate a continuous mining machine, but each new area to be mined poses a different configuration of machinery, environmental conditions, and people. Knowledge about mining habits and coordination practices unique to members of a particular crew should impact group performance.

Since our interest is in work groups, there are other relevant knowledge domains that are critical for group functioning (cf. Levine & Moreland, 1989). All groups have structural properties which would include the goals, strategy, culture, and norms. Culture includes the unique configurations of values, customs, rituals, and language of the group. Norms are more specific pro- or prescriptions about behavior. Groups represent complex social relationships. Another sub-domain of familiarity includes the knowledge to understand and interpret these relationships. The relationships may be internal or external to the group. External relationships may be within or outside of the organization. Table 11.1 presents a summary of domains of familiarity in a workgroup context.

Dimensional Aspects of Familiarity

In Table 11.1 we identified domains of familiarity. In this section we examine some of the dimensional differences between high and low familiarity. What do we mean by variation in familiarity? If we hypothesize that groups higher in familiarity perform better than groups lower in familiarity, we need to present some underlying theoretical rationale.

The literature on the nature of expertise (Chi, Glaser, & Farr, 1988) provides the direction for this analysis. We use this analysis because it is interesting and based to some extent on work-related tasks such as medical diagnosis, taxi cab driving, and programming. We acknowledge that being familiar in a task is not equivalent to being an expert in a task. Someone familiar with a job is not necessarily an expert, although expertise in an area generally includes familiarity. Also, the time frame to develop expertise is longer than the period to develop familiarity. However, the literature about expertise may provide some broader insights into what might underlie the familiarity construct. This

Table 11.1
Domains of Familiarity

Machinery
Environmental Conditions
Material
Jobs
People
Group Properties
   Goals, Mission, Strategy
   Culture
   Norms
Group Relationships
   Internal
   External

literature directs us away from simply thinking about familiarity (versus unfamiliarity) in terms of the *amount* of knowledge held about a particular work setting.

Chi, Glaser, and Farr (1988, pp. xvii-xx), in a review of this research, summarize some of the following findings about experts' performance. Some examples include:

1. Experts excel mainly in their own domains (cf. Rogers & Slobada, 1983).
2. Experts perceive large, meaningful patterns in their domain (Chase & Simon, 1973).
3. Experts see and represent a problem in their domain at a deeper (more principled) level than novices; novices tend to represent a problem at a superficial level (Weiser & Shertz, 1983).
4. Experts have strong self-monitoring skills.

Chi et al. (1988) try to explain the rationale for each of these findings. For example, the superior monitoring skills of experts are attributed to their greater domain knowledge and their different representations of that knowledge. The intriguing aspect of these selected findings is that they might inform us on how familiarity works.

Table 11.2 presents some dimensions that may be used to characterize differences in familiarity (cf. Chi et al., 1988). First, and most obvious, is that familiar workers have a larger body of knowledge. In our discussion, knowledge would be in terms of the domains in Table 11.1. Second, familiar workers may be better able to organize their knowledge

Table 11.2
Dimensions to Characterize Differences in Familiarity

Dimensions of Familiarity	Low Familiarity	High Familiarity
Knowledge base	Small	Large
Organization of knowledge domain	Less meaningful patterns	Very meaningful patterns
Representation of problems	Less time understanding a problem and representing it at a superficial level	More time on understanding the problem and representing it at a deeper level
Self-monitoring	Less aware of making errors and when to check	More aware of making errors and when to check
Type of response	Less automated responses	More automated reponses
Search	On most events	On special events

base into meaningful patterns. So the issue is not simply that workers have more knowledge, but workers higher in familiarity may organize knowledge differently.

Third, the familiar worker may represent problems differently. In their review on the nature of expertise, Chi et al. (1988) suggest that experts might spend more time on understanding the problem prior to generating solutions and that experts represent the problem in a deeper, more principle-based way. The ability to organize a large amount of information in a more meaningful way and to represent problems in a deeper, more principle-based way may account for differences between groups with higher and lower familiarity. In the mining example, crews high in familiarity may interpret and represent problems about environmental conditions differently, which might enhance crew performance.

Fourth, the familiar worker may be more aware when errors are made and when to check for errors. Here we assume that greater levels of knowledge and different ways to represent that knowledge lead familiar workers to be more aware of when problems might occur and when to check for problems. This ability to sense errors and to check for errors may have implications for the quality of work performance between groups high and low in familiarity. It may also be related to other group outcomes, such as accidents.

Fifth, as a function of practice, the familiar worker may have developed more automated responses to work stimuli, that is, the worker may approach the job in a manner similar to driving behavior, some of which is not based on conscious processing. The familiar worker should perform activities and transactions more quickly and effortlessly. One implication of this automated processing is that it may be associated with higher levels of group productivity.

And sixth, a corollary of more automated processing is that when faced with more recurrent stimuli, less search activity is undertaken by the most familiar worker. In addition, when search activities are initiated, the most familiar worker is probably more likely to be aware of rich sources of information (Louis, 1980).

There are a number of implications of specifying the properties of familiarity. The dimensions in Table 11.2 move us away from thinking of familiarity solely in terms of amount of knowledge. They present a conceptual representation of familiarity and a set of possible hypotheses, that is, each of these dimensions provides a possible contrast between high- and low-familiarity workers. Lastly, it points to what one might change to reduce the effects of unfamiliarity. For example, if unfamiliar workers jump more quickly to solve rather than understand a problem, then some mechanism to redirect the focus of their attention might seem appropriate.

Two Examples of Familiarity Studies

Two studies of underground coal mining crews are presented to illustrate the effect of familiarity on group outcomes. We selected these studies because they were specifically designed to examine the impact of familiarity on group outcomes. We selected mining crews because they are formal, interdependent work groups that generate a group-level product (tons of coal per shift) in an organizational context.

Study 1

This study examines the effects of familiarity on accidents in coal mines (Goodman & Garber, 1988). Our basic hypothesis is that lack of familiarity leads to more dangerous conditions that would contribute to higher rates of accidents.

Three types of people in coal mining can experience unfamiliarity. First, because the physical characteristics of a mine section change, a worker absent on the previous day returning to the mine will be less familiar with the work place, and thus—other things being equal—will have a higher probability of having an accident (Goodman & Garber, 1988, p. 82). Second, miners typically work in the same job in the same section, day in and day out, and another miner is generally assigned as a replacement while a miner is absent. The reassigned miner would be less familiar with the work setting, and—other things being equal—more likely to have an accident. Third, in a typical crew configuration, most mining activities require coordination between pairs of individuals who work closely together: the miner operator and the miner helper, the roof bolter and the bolter helper, and the two shuttle car operators. We focus here on these dyads because they are the fundamental unit of work, and consider explicitly that the worker adjacent to the replacement may also be placed in a more dangerous situation because of lack of familiarity with the replacement's mining practices and resulting difficulties in coordinating activities with this individual. This adjacent worker or partner of a replacement is presumed to have a higher probability of having an accident.

The data set for this analysis was generated from crews in five different mines (see Goodman & Garber, 1988, for more detail). The unit of analysis is the dyad, and there are three dyads in each crew: mine operator and helper, the two bolters, and the two car operators. The coder would identify a dyad in a crew for a particular day, determine in which category the dyad members should be assigned, and whether either individual had an accident. There are 10 coding categories (see Table 11.3). This coding was done for all dyads in the crew over approximately a one-year period, for all crews in the mine, and in five different mines.

Table 11.3 presents regression results for accident rates as a function of mine and familiarity categories. The coefficient of a mine dummy represents the expected difference in accident rates between that mine and the omitted mine, Mine 5. With regard to the main hypothesis, category A, the highest familiarity dyad (two regular employees, neither absent), has a considerably lower accident rate (0.511 accidents per 200 miner days) than category F, the lowest familiarity dyad (1.24 accidents per 200 miner days). The difference of 0.7 in the accident rate between the two categories is considerable, especially if that difference is compared to the average accident rate of one accident for every 200 miner days, across all categories. The accident rate for the two regular non-absent miners (category A) is somewhat less than that for the category of two regular miners who were absent the previous day (category C).

Table 11.3
Weighted Least Squares Regression Results: Accident Rates as a Function of Mines and Familiarity Categories

Independent Variable	Regression Coefficient	t(40) Ratio
Constant	.813	2.25
Mine 1	−.920	−4.91
Mine 2	−.639	−2.89
Mine 3	−.545	−2.27
Mine 4	−.138	−0.64
Category A: Two regulars, neither absent previous day	0.511	1.45
Category B: Two regulars, one absent previous day	0.909	1.80
Category C: Two regulars, both absent previous day	0.618	1.60
Category D: Two replacements, neither absent previous day	0.488	1.21
Category E: Two replacements, one absent previous day	1.000	1.40
Category F: Two replacements, both absent previous day	1.240	2.60
Category G: One regular, one replacement, neither absent previous day	0.745	2.03
Category H: Regular absent previous day, replacement present previous day	0.644	0.84
Category I: Regular present previous day, replacement absent previous day	1.910	2.98
Category J: One regular, one replacement, both absent previous day	0.584	1.42

Two replacements without absences (category D) have considerably lower accident rates than two replacements with absences. Two regular miners who were absent the previous day (category C) have lower accident rates than two replacements who were absent the previous day (category F). The basic conclusion is that familiarity makes a difference in accident rates, particularly in the extreme categories.

Study 2

This study (Goodman & Leyden, in press) examines the effects of familiarity on group productivity. The basic hypothesis is that crews whose members are familiar with their jobs, sections, and other crew members will be more productive than crews with lower levels of familiarity.

Familiarity in this study is divided into three categories: job, section, and crew. In any mining crew there are three separate jobs—the miner operator, the bolter, and the car operator. Each of these three jobs is unique, requiring a specific set of skills. Unfamiliarity occurs when a person who regularly performs one job fills in on another job. If a person is less familiar with the bolting job, we assume that, given the hazardous and dynamic nature of the environment, there will be less productivity from that individual. The section is the specific work area in a mine. It represents both the dynamic characteristics of the environment and the idiosyncratic nature of the machinery. Knowledge of the environment and unique properties of the machinery is critical for effective mining. For example, unfamiliarity with roof conditions of the mine should lead to lower productivity. The third dimension is the crew. Mining is a highly interdependent activity. Because each crew is likely to develop unique performance strategies among members in order to facilitate the interdependent task activities, unfamiliarity within a particular crew should make coordination of activities more difficult and, in turn, reduce productivity. Since mining is a multiple shift operation, different crews will work in the same section.

The measurement of familiarity in this study is fairly complicated (Goodman & Leyden, in press). The procedure differed from the prior study because we were interested in productivity at the crew level of analysis.

The essence of the measurement strategy is as follows. There are nine possible matches:

- Section-Job-Crew Match
- Section-Job Match
- Section-Crew Match
- Job-Crew Match
- Section Match
- Job Match
- Crew Match
- No Match (but working in mine)
- Other Match (no match and no record of working)

For each worker we count the number of times over a fixed prior period (three weeks) that the worker was in a similar situation. By "similar situation" we mean that the worker's section-job-crew today matches his section-job-crew yesterday. For example, if a worker worked in section A, job B, and crew C today and worked in the same section, job, and crew yesterday, this would get coded as a section-job-crew match. If a worker worked in the same job but in a different crew and section yesterday, this would get coded as a job match. The same analysis would be done for this employee comparing today with each day in the prior three work weeks, the shift cycle in this company. This same analysis would then be done for all crew members. That is, for each worker we would generate matches by comparing a given day with the past three weeks of work. So for each day we can aggregate the individual matches and get a measure of crew familiarity, indicated by distribution of responses across all nine match categories available. If the group members had been working in the same section, jobs, and crew for the three-week period, we would see value only in the section-job-crew category. We would calculate these matches daily for each individual, and then aggregate to the crew level for all nine match variables.

A full description of the analysis strategy is beyond the scope of this chapter (see Goodman & Leyden, in press), but conceptually the strategy is quite important. The unit of analysis is the crew or group. We begin with a baseline model that says that variation between crews can be explained by a labor variable (number of crew members), a technology variable (the quality of the equipment in the crew), and the environmental conditions. Then, we ask if the measures of familiarity add to this baseline model.

Table 11.4 presents data for one mine. Because the table appears complicated we should comment on the major results. First, we have argued (Goodman, 1986) that models of group performance incorporating the critical variables such as labor (measured by the number of people in different job categories per day), technology (primarily measured in terms of machine down time in minutes per shift), and environmental factors (measured by a dummy variable reflecting bad conditions) do seem to affect productivity as measured by tons per shift. The coefficient (.42) on mine delay, for example, suggests that close to a half a ton is lost per minute of down time on the continuous mine machine. These contextual variables, including the control variables, constitute the baseline model and were estimated in a separate equation.

Second, in Table 11.4 we include both the baseline variables and the familiarity variables. Familiarity measures have significant effects and the introduction of the familiarity measures increased the R^2 by 2.6.

Table 11.4
Production Function with Mine 1 Familiarity Variables

Variable	Regression Coefficient	t-Statistic
Labor Variables		
Prime crew	3.17	1.9
General inside laborers	5.16	4.8
Technology Variables		
Number of cars	17.13	9.8
Miner delay	−0.42	41.2
Car delay	−0.09	11.9
Direct bolter delay	−0.46	17.1
Indirect bolter delay	−0.02	2.0
Other activity delay	−0.41	20.2
Managerial delay	−0.51	12.8
Inside equipment delay	−0.38	23.7
Outside equipment delay	−0.36	13.9
Miner move delay	−0.36	10.7
Environmental Variables		
Physical Condition Dummy	−18.65	3.1
Control Variables		
Shift2 dummy	3.10	1.8
Shift3 dummy	4.29	2.5
Accident dummy	−7.91	1.9
Constant	201.90	18.8
Familiarity Variables		
S-MATCH	−34.99	0.4
J-MATCH	−35.51	2.8
C-MATCH	−54.75	2.9
SJ-MATCH	−40.98	1.1
SC-MATCH	−16.72	1.4
JC-MATCH	−31.93	7.1
SJC-MATCH		
NO-MATCH	−17.45	1.0
OTHER-MATCH	−25.10	5.5
R-square statistic	0.58615	
F-statistic	15.21 (sig 0.0000+)	
Mumber of Observations	1931	

The purpose of presenting these two studies is to show that familiarity can impact group outcomes. In both studies there are detailed data sets, measures, and analytic procedures that can isolate the effects of familiarity and other variables. We cite these two studies because they were specifically designed to capture familiarity. We have not found similar studies, at least at this level of detailed measures and analysis.

Although there is some evidence in these studies to support the impact of familiarity, a number of issues remain. First, a reading of Tables 11.3 and 11.4 shows that the different measures of familiarity perform differently. For example, the nine match variables (Table 11.4) were not all significant. Speculation on these specific results is outside the scope of this chapter. However, it illustrates that while familiarity may have an impact we need to learn more specifically how it operates. The second issue is that we need to tie familiarity into a broader literature. That is, we need to find other studies that may support or inform us about familiarity, even if they are in a different form than the studies cited above.

Familiarity and Related Concepts

There are other research areas that seem similar to familiarity. It is a useful exercise to acknowledge these areas for two reasons: First, it would indicate the potential generalizability of the familiarity concept; and second, some further insights about familiarity can be provided.

1. *Group Longevity and Performance.* This literature is similar to our concept of familiarity. It basically asks how length of experience, typically measured in years, relates to organizational performance. In Katz's (1982) study of research and development project groups, groups with lower longevity exhibited lower performance. A study on the productivity of software development teams (Banker, Datar, & Kemerer, 1987) indicates that the greater the percentages of novices in the teams, the lower the team productivity. In our terminology, lower longevity within the group means less familiarity and lower performance. (This longevity measure is a much grosser representation of familiarity than our more specific measures, which collected daily information on specific jobs.)

2. *Seniority, Job Experience, and Performance.* These studies also focus on the relationship between longevity and performance, but the unit of analysis is the individual instead of the group. Again, our interest is to illustrate this literature, not review it. A number of studies (Gordon,

Cofer, & McCullough, 1986; Gordon & Fitzgibbons, 1982) report no relationship between seniority and job performance in a new job (via promotion). This is not too surprising because seniority is a very imprecise measure of experience (i.e., it includes a variety of different experiences). These two studies also report that inter-job similarity is necessary for seniority to have an impact on performance and trainability. This seems closer to our concept of familiarity. People who move across similar jobs should have greater levels of familiarity with work and perform better. Schmidt, Hunter, and Outerbridge (1986) examined the impact of job experience and ability on different performance measures. They report that length of job experience directly affects job knowledge (a possible indicator of familiarity) which, in turn, affects supervisor ratings and work sample measures of job performance. Job experience directly affects work sample performance measures. General mental ability is related to both performance measures. The most important lesson from this study is that the researchers try to develop a causal model of direct and indirect relationships between experience and outcomes.

3. *Managerial Succession.* This literature examines the effect of organizational replacement on organizational performance. Research on this topic has focused on sports teams and work organizations. Although there is much debate on the effect of managerial replacement, there is some evidence that (a) a replacement with a good prior record and good experience can enhance organizational performance (Pfeffer & Davis-Blake, 1986) and (b) a replacement can reduce performance (Allen, Panian, & Lotz, 1979). In the latter context, mid-season succession of a manager seems to be more disruptive than end-of-season succession, and outside succession appears to be more disruptive than inside succession. These findings parallel our findings on familiarity. Succession between seasons permits a manager to become more familiar with the team players, strategy, and environment, which should create less disruptive effects. The inside successor should be more familiar with team personnel, strategies, and environment than outside successors.

4. *Newcomer Studies.* A number of recent studies have examined the role of the newcomer in the organization. Work by Louis (1980) has focused on developing a process representation of newcomer experience. The model includes processes by which the newcomer identifies similarities, differences, and discrepancies (or surprises) in the new environment, and engages in sense-making activities to attribute meaning

to the setting. Levine and Moreland (1989) have developed a model to explain how newcomers become full group members. The model traces the individual through five phases of group membership—investigation, socialization, maintenance, resocialization, and remembrance.

This research is important because it attempts to trace the process newcomers go through as they enter a new work environment. Although we have been able to demonstrate that familiarity has an effect on group outcomes, we know little about how someone unfamiliar with a new work setting becomes more familiar with that setting. In the next section we explore, in more detail, the processes underlying the concept of familiarity.

What have we learned? Although these concepts are fairly gross measures of experience, the research on group longevity and job longevity parallels our findings on familiarity. Findings about interjob similarity and the selected findings about managerial succession also speak to the generalizability of the familiarity concept. Research on newcomers contributes to our understanding of familiarity in a different way. This literature highlights the process that forms familiarity and the ways familiarity may influence work outcomes. The research on expertise cited earlier provides a potential conceptual framework for understanding the possible differences between high and low familiarity for either individuals or groups.

Conceptual Issues

In this section we will expand on the concept of familiarity. The following questions will be addressed: (1) What are the conditions in which familiarity will make a difference to work outcomes? (2) What are some of the processes by which an unfamiliar setting is transformed into a familiar one?

Factors Conditioning the Importance of Familiarity

In our discussion thus far, we have provided a conceptualization of familiarity and some direct and indirect evidence supporting its role in affecting group performance. However, we also know that group context plays a critical role in understanding group performance (McGrath, 1986).

Familiarity plays different roles in different work group contexts. Therefore, it is useful to know when familiarity will be an important predictor of work group behavior. It is also useful to know which group contexts are likely to create highest unfamiliarity for a newcomer. Three structural dimensions of work seem particularly important: its discretionary nature, its complexity, and its uncertainty. We have defined familiarity in terms of the specific knowledge one holds of multiple domains of work. In addition, we have argued that the domains (e.g., machinery, jobs, people) will be uniquely configured in each work setting and that there are many alternative configurations that can lead to the same outcomes. The task is to develop knowledge about the unique configurations.

In a setting where there is a high amount of discretion about the design and redesign of work, the configurations of work can be constantly changing. This should lead to a high degree of unfamiliarity for regular group members and replacements. If there is little discretion in design, there will be less uniqueness across groups with similar technology, and less effect of familiarity.

A second dimension deals with the complexity of work or the number of knowledge domains relevant for completing work. Earlier we referred to machinery, people, and environment as possible knowledge domains. We also expect groups to vary in the importance of the domains. There are many group tasks where machinery, materials, and environment may be irrelevant for group functioning. There are other groups where these domains are important. Groups also vary on the complexity of internal and external relationships. We believe that, as you increase the number of domains and the differentiation within domains, the complexities of the possible configurations greatly increase and so do the requirements for familiarity. As complexity increases, familiarity plays a greater role in group functioning and outcomes.

The third dimension concerns uncertainty in the group's environment. Some groups face frequent and unpredictable external shocks from their environment (e.g., a roof fall in a mining section). These shocks or surprises create changes in the configurations of work and create unfamiliarity. Other groups operate in a fairly certain or stable environment where unfamiliarity is not introduced. Both discretion and this uncertainty dimension introduce changes and unfamiliarity in the configurations of work; the former is primarily internal and planned, whereas the latter is more external to the group and stochastic in nature.

Table 11.5 provides a categorization of eight group types where familiarity will be differentially important. In groups with high discretion, complexity, and uncertainty, familiarity will play an important role in group functioning. Several things will happen in this type of group.

Table 11.5
Factors Conditioning Familiarity by Type of Group

Factors	Type of Group
High Complexity High Discretion High Uncertainty	Maintenance Teams—Autonomous
High Complexity High Discretion Low Uncertainty	A Surgery Team
High Complexity Low Discretion High Uncertainty	Rafting Team
High Complexity Low Discretion Low Uncertainty	Assembly Work Team—Traditional
Low Complexity High Discretion High Uncertainty	Autonomous Mining Crew
Low Complexity High Discretion Low Uncertainty	Restaurant Team
Low Complexity Low Discretion High Uncertainty	Volleyball Team
Low Complexity Low Discretion Low Uncertainty	Fast-Food Restaurant Team

The process of moving from unfamiliarity to familiarity will be more difficult and take a longer period of time. Inherently more unfamiliarity will be experienced in these groups. Lastly, unfamiliarity will have a greater effect on group outcomes. In groups with the opposite characteristics, we expect levels of familiarity not to be associated with group outcomes. The basic assumption underlying Table 11.5 is that contextual factors make a difference on the inherent amount of unfamiliarity in a group, the relative difficulty in becoming more familiar, and on the impact of familiarity on group outcomes.

Critical Processes

An important issue concerns how one moves from unfamiliarity to familiarity. What are some of the critical processes or mechanisms that explain movement to greater familiarity?

We start this exploration by assuming that individuals have cognitive maps (Goodman, 1968) to represent the group and the larger organization. The map is a mechanism that helps the individual select, retain, and provide meaning to information in the environment. The map is organized in terms of regions or domains that parallel some of the areas mentioned in Table 11.1.

In an unfamiliar situation the individual is confronted with states of ambiguity and anxiety. The ambiguity is generated because the individual's map is likely to be undifferentiated. It is unlikely that the individual will be able to identify appropriate cues and deliver the appropriate responses (Louis, 1980). Problems in interpreting cues are paramount. Regions in the map will be unstable and constantly changing. Actions can generate both positive and negative outcomes. The metaphor is of a person entering a dark room looking for the light and, when finding the light, looking for others in order to develop a single and stable picture of the room (Argyris, 1952). Associated with the ambiguity are feelings of anxiety. The anxiety level can be functional if it motivates the individual to "make sense" of the new environment.

The degree of ambiguity and anxiety experienced in the unfamiliar setting is conditioned by two factors. First, the individual's prior experience will make a difference. To the extent to which the individual has worked in the work-group setting, in a similar group, or interacted with group members prior to entry into the work group (cf. Levine & Moreland, 1989), levels of ambiguity and anxiety will be lower. Second, the structural properties of the group will make a difference. To the extent to which one enters a group high in discretion, complexity, and uncertainty, the levels of ambiguity and anxiety will be higher (see Table 11.5). In this type of work-group setting, unfamiliarity is an inherent characteristic.

Given that an unfamiliar situation will evoke some level of ambiguity and anxiety, we need to identify the processes that will move someone from an unfamiliar to a familiar state. Below, four processes are proposed.

Socialization by Others. This refers to the process whereby individuals acquire skill, knowledge, attitudes, and evaluative orientations through interacting with others. It is clear there are many possible agents of socializations (e.g., peers, supervisor) and forms or mechanisms of socialization. Following some of the work of Van Maanen and Schein (1979), we have conceptualized mechanisms of socialization into formal-informal and structured-less structured. Formal mechanisms are initiated by the firm, focus on groups of individuals, and occur prior to entering an unfamiliar setting. Informal mechanisms are initiated by and for the individual. In structured mechanisms, the socialization mechanisms are planned, in a sequence, and occur in a fixed time. Table 11.6 illustrates the different classes of socialization.

Formal structured training would occur prior to entering an unfamiliar situation. This form of training typically is targeted to multiple individuals and focuses on general learning versus learning about specific configurations of work. Working off-line in a simulated work setting would be a way to learn some unique characteristics of work in a sheltered environment (Cell 2). Goodman and Miller (1990) have argued that this form of socialization may be useful in understanding functioning of complex technology. The issue will be the extent to which the simulated work setting matches the actual work setting. In Cell 3, the worker is in a unique work setting but paired with a coach. In this "apprenticeship" environment, the trainer in a systematic way imparts knowledge to increase the new worker's familiarity with the machinery, people, and programs. In Cell 4, informal interactions with others provide knowledge about the unique aspects of work.

All four of these mechanisms can contribute to acquiring knowledge about the domains specified in Table 11.1. However, given our conceptualization of familiarity in terms of knowledge of the unique configurations of work, we would hypothesize that Cells 3 and 4 would be more powerful mechanisms to moving one from unfamiliarity to familiarity.

Practice and Knowledge of Results. The acquisition of knowledge about the unique configuration of work can come simply through practice. The individual, through trial and error, initiates action and receives feedback. The feedback provides a means to reinforce or to correct the initiated action. Current research on expertise attests to the importance of practice over a long time (Anderson, 1985). In our context, the worker has general knowledge about how to perform the general task. Through trial and error, unique properties of the work setting are identified, interpreted, and stored. The individual can initiate trial-and-error experiments about the task-related domains or about unique group properties.

Table 11.6
Forms of Socialization

	Formal	*Informal*
Structured	1 Classroom training	3 Working with resident expert
Less structured	2 Working off-lines self-paced	4 Observing others; talking with co-workers

Observation. Individuals can learn about the unique aspect of a work setting by observing others' behaviors, outcomes, or behavior outcome events (Goodman & Moore, 1976). We introduce observation (and practice) to indicate that there are important ways to acquire information independent of socialization attempts by others. We also think that observation may be used more to learn about group properties (e.g., norms) and less frequently for acquiring task-related knowledge. Practice is probably more important for gaining task-related knowledge.

Sense Making. This is a process that generates meaning for cues in the work environment (cf. Louis, 1980; Weick, 1979). It is a process generated by discrepancies between expectation and experiences. Its function is to resolve the discrepancies by "making sense" or attributing new interpretations. Sense making appears in the three processes discussed above. Our focal individual comes to the work setting with a map colored by prior experiences. Discrepancies evoked by socialization attempts of others, practice, or observation of others requires the initiation of some sense-making process. How this process unfolds depends on prior experiences with similar situations, personal dispositions, local interpretations schemes, and other interpretations (Louis, 1980, p. 242). The sense-making process is important because it focuses on how people develop social constructions in their environment. The three processes outlined above are the main contributors to the movement toward familiarity. Sense making affects the three processes by creating attributed meaning to discrepant stimuli in the environment. One should also note that sense making varies in terms of level of familiarity. Familiar workers will have an easier time attributing meaning to discrepant stimuli because they have seen similar stimuli in the past or know where to search.

These four processes are not presented in the form of a completed process model. Rather, we see them as conceptual tools for tracing the movement from unfamiliarity to familiarity. In our analysis we have tried to indicate how the processes differ and how they may be functional for different domains of familiarity at different time periods.

Practical Implications

Although our primary interest is in better understanding the concept of familiarity, the concept may have some practical implications. If we can assume that familiarity makes a difference in work-related outcomes, then there are a variety of possible strategies for dealing with familiarity. First, organizational policies can be designed to limit the *level* of job movement in groups. If there is a lot of movement in and out of software development teams, and this adversely affects productivity, then one might require members to stay in a group for a certain period of time before they can leave. (We are not arguing for no circulation of members.)

Second, given that there will always be temporary (via absenteeism) or permanent changes (via turnover), there are many possible staffing policies for the replacement pool. For example, in the earlier mining study, if the replacement pool had been specialized by job or crew, the levels of unfamiliarity would have been reduced. Training strategies should also impact on levels of familiarity. If our delineation of domains of familiarity is correct, it would indicate possible training areas, that is, training could be organized around unique aspects of machinery, people, and group programs. In our discussion of learning mechanisms we indicate that coaching or apprenticeship may be a more useful strategy in providing knowledge about unique configurations of work. It would seem reasonable to compare this mechanism with others in affecting levels of familiarity. In our discussion of the potential differences between high and low familiarity (Table 11.2), we identified some possible learning objectives. If, for example, high-familiarity workers do a better job in self-monitoring than low-familiarity workers, one might design training to enhance capabilities in self-monitoring.

Similarly, training could be organized around the other differences suggested in Table 11.2

Discussion

One goal of this chapter is to introduce the concept of familiarity as a relevant variable in understanding work group outcomes. We have demonstrated that familiarity does affect work group outcomes (e.g., accidents and productivity). In addition, we have shown that familiarity relates to a variety of different literatures.

We have tried to extend our own thinking on familiarity by identifying the domains of familiarity. In our discussion on the dimensions or properties of familiarity, we generated a set of hypotheses about why high- and low-familiarity workers may be different. This is a key part of our conceptualization because it prepares explanations for why familiarity should affect group outcomes. The stage is set for a lot of interesting research in this area.

The contextual arguement is important in understanding the role of familiarity. In Table 11.5 we proposed a set of structural dimensions that should moderate the impact of familiarity on work group outcomes. In groups high in discretion, complexity, and uncertainty, familiarity should be an important predictor of group performance. In future work one needs to explore not only the impact of contextual factors but also how they interact with the dimensional structure (Table 11.2) of familiarity. For example, we hypothesized that familiar workers engage in more self-monitoring activities, but we do not know whether self-monitoring affects group performance differently in the different contexts identified in Table 11.5.

It is also important to take a developmental orientation to familiarity. How do workers become more familiar? What are the critical mechanisms? In this chapter we have identified four processes. The interesting question will be to examine how these processes affect the acquisition of familiarity with specific domains (Table 11.1). For example, what are the roles of practice and observation in acquiring familiarity with machinery, people, jobs, and norms? At an even more micro level, we could examine how these processes relate to the dimensional structure of familiarity (Table 11.2). For example, will practice or observation of others have a greater impact on how groups develop deeper representations of problems or better self-monitoring activities? These and many other questions attest to the role the concept of familiarity may have on stimulating exciting new research opportunities on groups in organizations.

References

Allen, M. P., Panian, S. K., & Lotz, R. E. (1979). Managerial succession and organizational performance: A recalcitrant problem revisited, *Administrative Science Quarterly, 24,* 167-180.

Anderson, J. R. (1985). *Cognitive psychology and its implications.* New York: Freeman.

Argyris, C. (1952). *An introduction to field theory and interaction theory.* New Haven, CT: Yale University, Labor and Management Center.

Banker, R. D., Datar, S. M., & Kemerer, C. F. (1987, Dec. 6-9). Factors affecting software maintenance productivity: An exploratory study. *Proceedings of the Eighth International Conference on Information Systems* (pp. 835-836). Pittsburgh, PA.

Chase, W. G., & Simon, H. A. (1973). Perception in chess. *Cognitive Psychology, 4,* 55-81.

Chi, M.T.H., Glaser, R., & Farr, M. J. (1988). *The nature of expertise.* Hillsdale, NJ: Lawrence Erlbaum.

Goodman, P. S. (1986). *Designing effective work groups.* San Francisco: Jossey-Bass.

Goodman, P. S. (1968). The measurement of an individual's organization map. *Administrative Science Quarterly, 13*(2), 246-265.

Goodman, P. S., & Garber, S. (1988). Absenteeism and accidents in a dangerous environment: Empirical analysis of underground coal mines. *Journal of Applied Psychology, 73*(81), 81-86.

Goodman, P. S., & Leyden, D. P. (in press). *Familiarity and group productivity. Journal of Applied Psychology.*

Goodman, P. S., & Miller, S. (1990, Spring). Designing effective training through the technological life cycle. *National Productivity Review,* pp. 169-178.

Goodman, P. S., & Moore, B. (1976). Factors affecting the acquisition of beliefs about a new reward system. *Human Relations, 29*(6), 571-588.

Gordon, M. E., Cofer, J. L., & McCullough, P. M. (1986). Relationships among seniority, past performance, interjob similarity, and trainability. *Journal of Applied Psychology, 71*(3), 518-521.

Gordon, M. E., & Fitzgibbons, W. J. (1982). Empirical test of the validity of seniority as a factor in staffing decisions. *Journal of Applied Psychology, 67*(3), 311-319.

Katz, R. (1982). The effects of group longevity on project communication and performance. *Administrative Science Quarterly, 27,* 81-104.

Levine, J. M., & Moreland, R. L. (1989, February). *Cognitive integration in work groups.* Paper presented at the Conference on Socially Shared Cognition, Learning Research and Development Center, University of Pittsburgh, Pittsburgh, PA.

Louis, M. (1980). Surprise and sense making: What newcomers experience in entering unfamiliar organizational settings. *Administrative Science Quarterly, 25,* 226-251.

McGrath, J. (1986). Studying groups at work: Ten critical needs for theory and practice. In P. S. Goodman (Ed.), *Designing effective work groups* (pp. 362-391). San Francisco: Jossey-Bass.

Pfeffer, J., & Davis-Blake, A. (1986). Administrative succession and organizational performance: How administrator experience mediates the succession effect. *Academy of Management Journal, 29,* 72-83.

Rogers, D. R., & Slobada, J. H. (1983). *Acquisition of symbolic skills.* New York: Plenum.

Schmidt, F. L., Hunter, J. E., & Outerbridge, A. N. (1986). Impact of job experience and ability on job knowledge, work sample performance, and supervisor ratings of job performance. *Journal of Applied Psychology, 71*(3), 432-439.

Van Maanen, J., & Schein, E. H. (1979). Toward a theory of organizational socialization. In B. M. Straw (Ed.), *Research in organizational behavior* (pp. 209-264). Greenwich, CT: JAI.

Weick, K. E. (1979). Cognitive processes in organizations. In B. M. Staw (Ed.), *Research in organizational behavior* 1, 41-72. Greenwich, CT: JAI.

Weiser, M., & Shertz, J. (1983). Programming problem representation in novice and expert programmers. *Instructional Journal of Man-Machine Studies. 14,* 391-396.

Index

About the Contributors

Hermann Brandstätter, born in 1930 in Grünburg, Austria, studied psychology and philosophy at the Universities of Innsbruck and Munich, held positions at the Universities of Munich and Augsburg, Germany, and is presently Head of the Department of Social and Economic Psychology at the Johannes Kepler University of Linz, Austria. His research interests have been primarily in the fields of personnel selection, group decision making, emotional experience in everyday life situations, and economic psychology.

Dawna Coutant-Sassic is a graduate student in the social psychology program at Texas A&M University. She received her bachelor's degree from Davidson College in Davidson, North Carolina. Areas of interest for Coutant-Sassic include minority influence, norm development, the balance of intergroup power, and the application of these ideas in political psychology.

Paul S. Goodman, Ph.D., is a Professor of Industrial Administration and Psychology at the Graduate School of Industrial Administration, Carnegie Mellon University. Previously he was on the faculty of the Graduate School of Business at the University of Chicago and was a visiting professor at Cornell University. Goodman's main professional interests are in research on work groups, organizational design and change, and impacts of new technology on effectiveness. His research has been published in many professional journals, including the *Journal of Applied Psychology, Organizational Behavior and Human Performance,* and *Human Relations.* Two recent books are *Designing Effective Work Groups* (1986, Jossey-Bass) and *Technology and Organizations* (1990, Jossey-Bass). He is currently Director of the Center for the

Management of Technology at Carnegie Mellon University. The center sponsors joint research with industry on the management of technology.

Michele Grossman graduated from Texas A&M University with a B.S. degree in psychology. Presently, she is a graduate student completing her master's degree in psychology at Texas A&M University. Research interests for Grossman include group decision making and problem solving, intergroup relations, political group development, gender stereotypes, and social marketing.

Katherine A. Hannula is a doctoral student in the Department of Psychology at Texas A&M University. Her primary research interests include stereotyping and prejudice, individual differences in racial attitudes, and resource allocation in groups.

Susan E. Jackson, Ph.D., is Associate Professor of Psychology at New York University. She received her Ph.D. and M.A. degrees in psychology from the University of California at Berkeley, and has previously held faculty positions in the Graduate School of Business Administration at New York University, the Graduate School of Business at the University of Michigan, and the Department of Psychology at the University of Maryland. Her research and publications have addressed a variety of topics, including: the organizational conditions that contribute to job stress and burnout among human service professionals; decision making processes in organizations; how organizational conditions influence the design of human resource management systems; and, most recently, the organizational consequences of work force diversity. A book on the latter topic is currently being prepared under the auspices of the Society for Industrial and Organizational Psychology. She is an active member of the Academy of Management and the Society for Industrial and Organizational Psychology. In addition, she currently serves on the editorial boards of the *Journal of Applied Psychology, Personnel Psychology,* and *Human Resource Planning.* She is Consulting Editor for the *Academy of Management Review.*

Norbert L. Kerr, Ph.D., obtained his M.A. and Ph.D. degrees in social psychology from the University of Illinois following undergraduate studies in physics at Washington University, St. Louis. He has held academic positions at the University of California, San Diego, and Michigan State University, where he is currently Professor of Psychology.

His primary research interests center on group processes, especially group decision making; motivation in task groups; jury decision making; and most recently, social dilemmas. He is co-editor (with Robert M. Bray) of *The Psychology of the Courtroom* (1982, Academic Press) and is co-author (with Robert S. Baron and Norman Miller) of a forthcoming text on small groups. From 1987 to 1990 he served as Associate Editor of the Interpersonal Relations and Group Processes section of the *Journal of Personality and Social Psychology*.

David Kipnis, Ph.D., is Professor of Psychology at Temple University. He is the author of numerous articles and two books, *The Powerholders* (1976, University of Chicago Press) and *Technology and Power* (1990, Springer-Verlag), that address his major scholarly interest: the control and use of social power.

John M. Levine received his Ph.D. in social psychology at the University of Wisconsin and is currently Professor of Psychology at the University of Pittsburgh. His research focuses on small group processes, including group socialization, the cognitive consequences of disagreement in groups, majority and minority influence, and decision making in hierarchical groups under stress. He is Associate Editor of the *Journal of Experimental Social Psychology*.

Lawrence A. Messé, Ph.D., is a social psychologist primarily interested in understanding the influence of personal variables (e.g., norms and roles, motives, cognitive styles, etc.) on interpersonal behaviors that are expressed in a variety of social settings. Within this framework, he has contributed to the empirical and theoretical literatures on such diverse topics as reward distribution behaviors in work contexts and person perception factors in parent-child encounters. Currently, he is continuing to investigate the implications of superior status for group productivity and outcomes. He is also co-authoring (with William D. Crano and Marilynn B. Brewer) a textbook on social psychology. For many years, he has been a Professor in the Department of Psychology at Michigan State University.

Richard L. Moreland received his Ph.D. in social psychology at the University of Michigan and is currently an Associate Professor of Psychology at the University of Pittsburgh. He is interested in many aspects of small groups, especially the changes that they undergo over time. This interest has led him to study such phenomena as the formation and termination of groups, group development, and the socialization of group members. A practical concern with improving the problem-solving abilities of groups, along with a theoretical awareness of the power of groups to define reality for their members, led to the present chapter on problem identification by groups.

Charlan Jeanne Nemeth, Ph.D., is Professor of Psychology at the University of California, Berkeley. She received her B.A. in Psychology and Mathematics from Washington University, her M.A. from the University of Wisconsin, and her Ph.D. from Cornell University. Her research interests have included how minority issues come to prevail, majority/minority interactions in jury deliberations, how decisions can be improved and how truths can be detected as a product of influence processes, and, most recently, the improvement of performance and decision making, enhancing creativity, and improving cognitive processes as a result of exposure to minority dissent.

Robert D. Pritchard received his Ph.D. in 1969 from the University of Minnesota in Organizational Psychology. He was Assistant and later Associate Professor of Psychology at Purdue University from 1969-1977. He was Professor of Psychology at the University of Houston from 1977-1988 where he also served as the Director of the Industrial and Organizational Psychology Program. He has been Professor of Psychology and Director of the Industrial and Organizational Psychology Program at Texas A&M University since 1988. He has received several research awards, is a Fellow in the American Psychological Association and in the American Psychological Society, has been chair of the Society of Organizational Behavior and president of the Houston Association of Industrial and Organizational Psychologists. He has been on the editorial boards of several professional journals and has served as the Acting Editor of *Organizational Behavior and Human Decision Processes*. He has also been on the Executive Committee of the Industrial and Organizational Psychology Division of the American Psychological Association, is a member of the Texas Commission on Incentives and Productivity, has been appointed to the Board of Directors of the International Foundation for Research in Performance Management Systems, and is part of a panel working on productivity issues for the National Research Council.

Nancy Rhodes received her B.A. from the University of Vermont. She is currently a Ph.D. candidate in the Department of Psychology at Texas A&M University. Her research interests include individual differences in persuasibility and sex differences in group interaction.

Charles D. Samuelson, Ph.D., is Assistant Professor of Psychology at Texas A&M University. His research interests include social dilemmas, group decision making, and energy conservation. His past research has investigated factors that influence preferences for structural solutions to social dilemmas. In his current work, he studies the sharing rules used by group members to allocate common resources. He has published research articles in a variety of journals in social and organizational psychology such as the *Journal of Personality and Social Psychology* and *Organizational Behavior and Human Decision Processes*. He received a B.S. degree from Tufts University and M.A. and Ph.D. degrees in social psychology from the University of California at Santa Barbara.

David N. Sattler received a Ph.D. in social psychology from Michigan State University. He is currently teaching at the University of California at San Diego. His research, which has appeared in the *Journal of Personality and Social Psychology,* explores the effects of individual, normative, and situational factors on behavior in groups. He is currently investigating behavior in social dilemmas—situations where individual and collective interests are in conflict—and the social psychological consequences of resource scarcity.

John E. Sawyer, Ph.D. (1987) is an Assistant Professor of Industrial and Organizational Psychology at Texas A&M University. His research interests include the effects of uncertainty on individual and group behavior in organizations. He has published multiple articles on social judgment theory applications to organizational behavior in *Organizational Behavior and Human Decision Processes*. Additional manuscripts investigating role ambiguity, task clarity, and performance feedback are forthcoming. Dr. Sawyer received his B.A. degree from California State University, Long Beach, and his master's and doctoral degrees from the University of Illinois-Urbana.

Samir Shah is a doctoral student at Carnegie Mellon University's Graduate School of Industrial Administration. He received his master's degree in chemical engineering from the Indian Institute of Technology.

His research interests include looking at the impact of computer mediated communications on organizational behavior.

Jeffry A. Simpson received his Ph.D. from the University of Minnesota in 1986, specializing in social/personality psychology. He currently is Assistant Professor of Psychology at Texas A&M University. His areas of research interest include interpersonal relations, personality and social behavior, and evolutionary psychology. He has authored several empirical articles focusing on the relation between personality and processes underlying the initiation and dissolution of romantic dyads.

Garold Stasser, Ph.D., is a Professor of Psychology at Miami University (Ohio). His major scholarly interests include group decision making, information exchange and idea generation during group discussion, and computer simulation of social interaction.

Klemens Waldhör received a master's degree in computer science at the University of Linz in 1984. He received his doctoral degree in computer science with interdisciplinary work using computer simulation in group decision making at the University of Linz in 1987. From 1981 through 1986 he was employed as an assistant in the Department of Psychology, working on a project in group decision making as well as in the development of software environments that support the design and control of psychological experiments. In 1986 he joined the group "man-computer-interaction" at TA Triumph-Adler AG, Germany. His research activities included knowledge based software architectures, user interface management systems, and all aspects of knowledge representation, especially explanation systems. Currently he is working on multilingual lexica and their applications in handwriting recognition in the context of ESPRIT Project MULTILEX.

Margaret D. Watson holds a B.S. in psychology from Oklahoma State University and an M.Ed. in counseling psychology from the University of Houston. She is currently a doctoral candidate in the Department of Psychology at Texas A&M University. She has worked extensively as a management consultant and trainer and is interested in utilizing new techniques to improve organizational productivity and effectiveness.

Wendy Wood is an Associate Professor in Social Psychology at Texas A&M University. Her research interests include sex differences in social behavior as well as individual differences in influenceability. Her work on sex differences has examined sex stereotypes, sex differences in interaction and group performance, and most recently women's styles of influence in task groups. In the area of influence, her work focuses on the effects of topic-relevant knowledge and of general personality dispositions on susceptibility to influence appeals. Currently, she is contemplating with relief and some regret the final months of her term on the editorial board of *Personality and Social Psychology Bulletin*.

Stephen Worchel received a B.A. degree at the University of Texas and a Ph.D. degree at Duke University. He held faculty positions at the University of North Carolina and University of Virginia before becoming department head at Texas A&M University in 1983. Worchel's research interests are in the areas of conflict and conflict resolution, group dynamics, political psychology, and environmental influences on behavior. He has conducted much of his research in cross-cultural settings, collecting data in Thailand, Poland, Israel, Greece, and the People's Republic of China. Worchel received a senior Fulbright Research Fellowship in 1980 for work in Athens, Greece, and was a visiting scholar at Fudan University, Shanghai, PRC, in 1990. He is presently studying group development and attempting to show how developmental phases of groups affect interpersonal dynamics. He is also involved in research examining the conditions that lead to a rise in nationalism and to an individual concern with tracing one's roots.